T0270706

Embedded Software System Testing

This book introduces embedded software engineering and management methods, proposing the relevant testing theory and techniques that promise the final realization of automated testing of embedded systems.

The quality and reliability of embedded systems have become a great concern, faced with the rising demands for the complexity and scale of system hardware and software. The authors propose and expound on the testing theory and techniques of embedded software systems and relevant environment construction technologies, providing effective solutions for the automated testing of embedded systems. Through analyzing typical testing examples of the complex embedded software systems, the authors verify the effectiveness of the theories, technologies, and methods proposed in the book.

In combining the fundamental theory and technology and practical solutions, this book will appeal to researchers and students studying computer science, software engineering, and embedded systems, as well as professionals and practitioners engaged in the development, verification, and maintenance of embedded systems in the military and civilian fields.

Embedded Software System Testing
Automatic Testing Solution Based on Formal Method

Yongfeng Yin and Bo Jiang

CRC Press
Taylor & Francis Group
Boca Raton London New York

CRC Press is an imprint of the
Taylor & Francis Group, an **informa** business

First edition published in English 2024
by CRC Press
6000 Broken Sound Parkway NW, Suite 300, Boca Raton, FL 33487-2742

and by CRC Press
2 Park Square, Milton Park, Abingdon, Oxon, OX14 4RN

CRC Press is an imprint of Taylor & Francis Group, LLC

© 2024 Yongfeng Yin, Bo Jiang

Translated by Qingran Su, Ruinan Qiu, Yang Guo, Yi Song, Rui Yin

English Version by permission of Beijing Huazhang Graphics&Information Co. Ltd. (China Machine Press)

ISBN: 978-1-032-48818-9 (hbk)
ISBN: 978-1-032-48819-6 (pbk)
ISBN: 978-1-003-39092-3 (ebk)

DOI: 10.1201/9781003390923

Typeset in Minion
by codeMantra

Contents

List of Figures

List of Tables

Preface

WITH THE CONTINUOUS DEVELOPMENT of computer technology, human beings have entered the digital age, in which especially embedded systems have become a necessity for everyone's life. Research has shown that people's requirements for the complexity and scale of the system software and hardware have exceeded the current design, implementation, testing and maintenance capabilities, resulting in the system often being faulty, so the quality and reliability of embedded systems have gradually become a concern. Based on the authors' experience in embedded software system testing for many years, this book introduces the embedded software engineering and management methods from the composition, classification, and characteristics of embedded systems and expounds the embedded software system testing theory and test environment construction technology, which provides an effective solution for the automatic testing of embedded systems.

Authors

Yongfeng Yin is a Professor and Vice President at the School of Software, Beihang University, China. From 2015 to 2016, he was a visiting scholar at Colorado State University, USA. His research interests include critical software, software reliability, and embedded software testing.

Bo Jiang is an Associate Professor at the School of Computer Science and Engineering, Beihang University, China. His research interests include software testing, blockchain security, and operating system.

List of Abbreviations

ADS2	avionics development system-2
ATLAS	abbreviated test language for all systems
ATS	automated test system
CADC	central air data computer
CCS	communication system calculus
CNI	communication navigation and identification
CSP	communication sequences process
CTL	computation tree logic
DCMP	display control and management processor
DTE	data transfer equipment
EFSM	extend finite state machine
ESSTE	embedded software simulation testing environment
FCS	flight control software
FSM	finite state machine
I/GNS	inertial/GPS navigation system
ICD	interface control document
MC	mission computer
OCL	object constraint language
RT-EFSM	real-time extend finite state machine
RT-ESSTE	real-time embedded software simulation testing environment
RT-ESSTVMS	real-time embedded software simulation testing virtual machine specification
RT-ESTDEE	real-time embedded software testing description execution engine
RT-ESTDL	real-time embedded software testing description language
RTRSM	real-time requirements specification model
SCS	safety-critical software

SUT	software under test
timeCTEC	time-constrained transition equivalence class
TPS	test program set
TTCN-3	testing and test control notation 3
UIO	unique input/output sequences
UML	unified modeling language
US$_{ex}$	extended unique sequences
VDM	vienna development method

Introduction

W ITH THE CONTINUOUS DEVELOPMENT of computer technology, humans have entered the digital age. Embedded software has been widely used in high-tech research and application fields, especially in aviation, aerospace, medical, transportation, and modern weapon equipment development. In view of the importance and particularity of embedded software, its failure often leads to serious consequences. Therefore, the quality and reliability of embedded software are paid increased attention, and effective embedded software system testing is one of the most important means to ensure software quality.

The authors of this book have nearly 20 years of practical experience in embedded software system testing engineering, trying to cross the traditional entry-level and basic-level system testing technology and provide a systematic solution for frontline employees engaged in embedded software system testing from formal testing theory to automatic test description method and automatic simulation test environment construction. Finally, the effectiveness of the theory, technology, and method involved in this book is further verified by explaining the typical complex embedded software system testing engineering examples.

Chapter 1 introduces the basic concepts of embedded systems and software. Chapter 2 discusses embedded software engineering and related knowledge of quality and reliability. Chapter 3 introduces the theory framework and technology of embedded software system testing based on the formal method. Chapter 4 discusses the automatic test description method of real-time embedded software, mainly from the design and operation mechanism of real-time embedded software test description language. Chapter 5 focuses on the testing technology of intelligent terminal application (embedded) software systems. Starting from the foundation of Android system, it discusses the test case generation, regression test, and stress test. Chapter 6 expounds on the construction technology of embedded software system testing environment, puts forward the design

DOI: 10.1201/9781003390923-1   1 idea of real-time embedded software simulation testing virtual machine specification, and discusses the architecture design of real-time embedded software simulation testing environment, the design and implementation of test execution engine and efficiency analysis. Chapter 7 gives an example of typical avionics-embedded software system testing.

The readers of this book are mainly undergraduates and postgraduates majoring in computer, software engineering, embedded systems, and related majors in colleges and universities. It can also provide reference for professional and technical personnel in the field of military or civil embedded system development, verification, and maintenance.

This book is edited by Yongfeng Yin. Yongfeng Yin authored Chapters 2–4, 6, 7, and Bo Jiang authored Chapters 1 and 5. In addition, graduate students Qingran Su, Xuefeng Wang and Jiakang Liu have done a lot of work in the text collation and appendix preparation, and I would like to express my sincere thanks.

I particularly thank Professor Bin Liu of Beihang University and Feng Wang of Researcher of Military Academy for reading this book and giving a lot of valuable opinions and suggestions. I also thank many colleagues of the Aviation Industry Computer Software Reliability Management and Evaluation Center of Beihang for their help.

From the perspective of methodology, the theory and technology of embedded software system testing are in the process of continuous development. Readers are urged to criticize and correct any errors they discover to help us continuously improve and perfect the book.

Yongfeng Yin

CHAPTER 1

Embedded System and Software

E MBEDDED SYSTEM IS AN application-centered and computer-based special computer system that can adapt to the requirements of different applications on functions, reliability, cost, volume, and power consumption, and it integrates configurable and scalable software and hardware. Embeddedness, specificity, and computer system are the three basic core elements of an embedded system. This chapter summarizes the embedded system and software, so that readers will have a more comprehensive understanding of it.

1.1 OVERVIEW OF EMBEDDED SYSTEM

1.1.1 Embedded Systems and Real-Time Systems

As one of the greatest inventions of human society in the 20th century, the emergence of computers has gradually brought mankind into the digital age. At the same time, the arrival of the post-PC era makes people increasingly exposed to a new concept: embedded products. An increasing number of complex hardware and software systems are embedded in medical, automotive, industrial control, transportation, communications, aviation, aerospace and modern weapons and equipment, such as NASA's airborne systems with nearly 500,000 lines of code, excluding 350,000 lines for ground control and processing. In American telecommunications, the total number of source codes of supporting software exceeds 100 million lines. Table 1.1 shows the application of software in aircraft systems.

DOI: 10.1201/9781003390923-2   3

TABLE 1.1   Application of Software in Aircraft Systems

Years	Aircraft Type	The Proportion of Aircraft Systems Functions Realized by Software (%)
1960	F-4/F-100	8
1964	A-7	10
1970	F-111	20
1975	F-15	35
1982	F-16/F-16A	45
1990	B-2	65
2000	F-22	80
2006	F-35	85

In 1990, IEEE (Institute of Electrical and Electronics Engineers) gave the definition of embedded system: An embedded computer system is part of a larger system and performs some of the requirements of that system; for example, a computer system used in an aircraft rapid transit system. Usually, devices used to control, monitor, or assist machines and devices are called embedded systems. Embedded systems generally include a series of hardware and software facilities, and embedded software is the software part of embedded systems such as spacecraft control system, aircraft avionics system, mobile phones based on Android, IOS and other systems, set-top boxes, automotive electronics systems, and communication systems routers. In addition, in a broad sense, the control system composed of MCU (STM32), SOC, and other hardware is also called embedded system. The above embedded software often has real-time characteristics, so it is also called real-time embedded system.

Usually, real-time systems are dedicated computer systems that must perform calculations and I/O operations within time constraints specified by the external environment. POSIX Standard 1003.1 defines the real-time system as "the operating system has the ability to provide services to meet the requirements within a limited response time range". In real-time computing, the external environment can be seen as a set of constraints – generally considered time constraints (also known as time limits). The existence of time limit is the most essential difference between real-time calculation and non-real-time calculation. The difference between a real-time system and a non-real-time system is that a real-time system must provide some mechanism to ensure that the time limit will not be destroyed. For non-real-time systems, the correctness of the system only depends on the correct execution of the instructions, which is manifested in whether the instructions are carried out in the logical order of the instructions and is not related to when the instructions begin to execute and when they are completed. For example, a program for calculating the square root of double-precision floating-point number can be run on Pentium III microcomputer at 500 MHz or 8086 microcomputer at 4.77 MHz. The difference between the two is only the speed of calculation, without affecting the correctness of the calculation results. The three indicators commonly used to measure real-time systems are as follows:

- Response time: The time when the computer system identifies external events respond.

- Survival time: The effective waiting time of the data. The data is valid in this period.

- Throughput: The total number of times the system can handle within a given time.

For the real-time system, the correctness of the system is not only related to the correctness of the calculation results, but also more importantly, the calculation must be completed within the specified time; otherwise, the system will make mistakes or fail.

1. **Hard real-time systems and soft real-time systems**

   According to the characteristics of real-time systems, they can be divided into "soft real-time systems" and "hard real-time systems".

The characteristics of the "hard" real-time system are as follows:

- There can be no delay in any case.

- If the delay occurs, the output result is invalid.

- When the deadline cannot be met, the system will lead to catastrophic failure.

- When the deadline cannot be met, the system will cause huge economic losses.

- The system response time is usually in the order of milliseconds or microseconds.

   For example, the flight control system and the nuclear reactor control system are typical "hard" real-time systems.

The characteristics of "soft" real-time system are as follows:

- The delay of output results will increase the cost.

- Delay will lead to the decline of system performance.

- The system response time is usually in the order of milliseconds or seconds.

    For example, online live broadcasting system is a typical "soft" real-time system.

2. **Single machine real-time system and distributed real-time system**

    According to the distribution characteristics of real-time system operating environment, real-time systems can be divided into single machine real-time systems and distributed real-time systems.

    (1) Single machine real-time system.

    In a single machine real-time system, all tasks run on the same computer and are only scheduled by the same operating system. The biggest advantage of a single machine real-time system is that its software and hardware structure is simple and easy to develop.

    (2) Distributed real-time system.

    In the distributed real-time system, multiple tasks are distributed on multiple computers, and the tasks on different nodes communicate through the Internet. These tasks work together to form a real-time system. The architecture of distributed real-time system is shown in Figure 1.1.

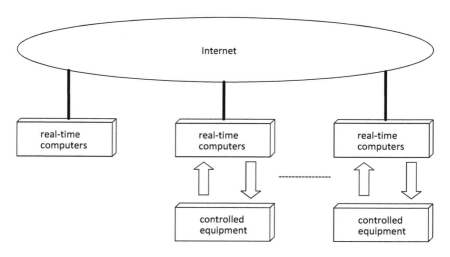

FIGURE 1.1 Architecture of distributed real-time system.

In the distributed real-time system, some node computers are connected with the controlled equipment (generating or receiving data and receiving real-time control). It is not only necessary to complete some real-time computing tasks but also need to control the peripheral equipment in real time. In addition, there are other node computers that are not connected to any controlled equipment. They only complete real-time computing tasks.

Based on the above classification, the real-time embedded system has the following characteristics in addition to the characteristics of general application software:

- Embeddedness

  Most real-time systems are special and complex, which need high fault tolerance, and are typically "embedded" into a larger system, that is, embedded software. A typical embedded system structure is given in Figure 1.2.

- Interaction with external environment

  A typical real-time system often interacts with external devices, which may control a certain device or process. The real-time system collects data from the outside through sensors and controls the external equipment by outputting excitation signals.

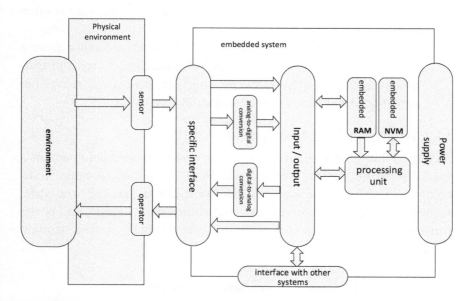

FIGURE 1.2   Typical embedded system structure.

- Real-time constraints

  Real-time systems often have strong time constraints, requiring that the event processing must be completed within the specified time. If it is delayed, it will often cause disastrous consequences.

- Real-time control

  Real-time software often involves real-time control. It determines how to control external cross-linked devices through the collected data. Real-time software is not all real-time components, but it also has no real-time parts, such as post analysis and processing of data.

- Reactive systems

  Many real-time systems are reactive systems,[50] which are event-driven and need to respond to external incentives. In general, the response of real-time system to external excitation mostly depends on the state, that is, the response output of the system depends not only on the current excitation but also on the previous system excitation.

- Concurrent processing

  A remarkable feature of most real-time systems is the existence of concurrent processing, and many external events need to be processed at the same time. Usually, the arrival of external events is unpredictable. It should be noted that the input load of the real-time system changes significantly with time, and this load is often unpredictable.

  To sum up, in this book, there will be no difference among real-time system (software), embedded system (software), and real-time embedded system (software), which are collectively referred to as real-time embedded system (software).

1.1.2 Features of Embedded Systems

As a special kind of computer application system, embedded system is a special computer system with application as the center, computer technology as the basis, software and hardware can be tailored, and strict requirements for function, real-time, reliability, cost, volume, and power consumption. Compared with the traditional computer system, its main features are as follows:

1. **Embedded systems are generally specialized.**

   In general, embedded system is not a general-purpose system, but it is user- and application-oriented. In general, it will be combined with users and applications. It appears as a special system or module. Its design, development, and tailoring of operating system are aimed at meeting the requirements of specific fields and applications so as to ensure minimum redundancy, maximum efficiency, and balanced power consumption, and strive to obtain the best performance, such as flight control system specially used for aircraft control, and control system of nuclear power plant or electric equipment.

2. **The software and hardware of the embedded system can be tailored.**

   As a special computer system, the main highlight of embedded system is that embedded system can select the required contents of software and hardware according to the actual needs, which has great flexibility and selectivity.

3. **The embedded system is compact, and the kernel is small.**

   Considering the strict constraints of cost, resources, and space, embedded systems often require to use as few resources as possible on the premise of meeting the system requirements, and generally support an open and scalable architecture. As a result, the kernel of embedded operating system (EOS) is much smaller than that of general operating system. For example, the kernel of OSE distributed system of ENEA company can reach 5K, and it can achieve high performance while greatly saving storage and running space.

4. **Embedded systems generally require high real-time performance.**

   In general, embedded systems have real-time requirements because most embedded system application scenarios are harsh and have strict requirements on time, volume, and power consumption. The poor real-time performance of the system will lead to serious or even disastrous consequences, such as nuclear power plant control, spacecraft orbit entry, flight control, aeroengine control, and radar target acquisition and recognition.

5. **The embedded processor is restricted by the application requirements**

   The hardware and software of embedded system must be designed efficiently, tailored and redundant, and strive to achieve higher performance and efficiency on the same processor so as to be more competitive in specific applications. Compared with the general-purpose processor, the biggest difference of the embedded processor is that it uses most of its work in the system designed for a specific user group and usually has the characteristics of low power consumption, small volume, and high integration. It can integrate many tasks into the chip, which is conducive to the miniaturization of the embedded system design, greatly enhanced mobility and closer connection with the network.

In general, embedded microprocessors have the following four characteristics:

- Using scalable architecture, the embedded microprocessor with the highest performance can be developed most quickly.

- It has strong support for real-time multitasking, can complete multitasking, and has short interrupt response time so as to minimize the execution time of internal code and real-time kernel.

- It has strong storage area protection functions because the software structure of embedded systems has been modularized. To avoid the wrong cross action between software modules, it is necessary to design a powerful storage area protection function, which is also conducive to software fault diagnosis.

- Embedded microprocessors must have low power consumption, especially for battery-powered embedded systems in portable wireless and mobile computing and communication devices. The power consumption is only milliwatt or even micro watt.

6. **Embedded system software shall be solid and reliable.**

   Embedded system software is the key and core element to realize the function of embedded system. To improve the software execution speed and system reliability, embedded software is generally solidified in the memory chip or single chip microcomputer itself, rather than stored in the carrier such as disk. Therefore, software coding requires high quality, reliability, security, and real time.

7. **Embedded system needs special development tools and environment.**

   Embedded systems are widely used, but they have more requirements for cost, volume, and power consumption to be more skillfully embedded in applications. The embedded system itself does not have the ability of independent development. After the system is developed and solidified to a specific hardware (target machine), users generally cannot modify it. Embedded system development is often simulated on the general computer (host computer), debugged with debugging and simulation tools, and finally downloaded and solidified through the linker.

1.1.3 Composition of Embedded Systems

With the continuous development of technology, embedded systems have become the product of the combination of advanced computer technology, semiconductor technology, and electronic technology. This determines that it must be a technology-intensive, capital-intensive, highly decentralized, and innovative knowledge integration system. The general composition of embedded system is given in Figure 1.3.

As can be seen from Figure 1.3, the embedded system can be divided into hardware and software:

- Similar to the ordinary PC system, the hardware part of the embedded system usually includes high-performance microprocessor, I/O interface, power management, memory, and peripheral circuits, but it is still very different from the general PC system because the embedded system is restricted by the application requirements in terms of power consumption, volume, cost, reliability, speed, processing capacity, and electromagnetic compatibility.

- The software part is the core of the function realization of embedded system, which usually includes device driver, EOS, embedded application program, and so on. The emergence of PC makes desktop software develop rapidly, and the vigorous development of

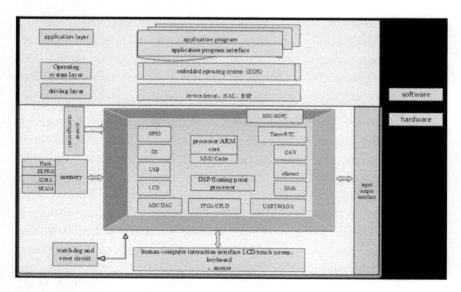

FIGURE 1.3   Composition of embedded system.

embedded software industry also provides infinite driving force for system application. A wide variety of embedded products with complex and changeable application scenarios provide more and more convenience for human beings. Now people's daily life cannot be separated from embedded products.

In fact, not all embedded systems contain the above components. When designing embedded systems, system designers will properly optimize and combine the design according to system capability, application scenario, power consumption, volume, real time, and other factors so as to achieve the best performance and efficiency.

1. **Hardware layer**

The hardware layer provides the operation platform of embedded system, mainly including high-performance microprocessor, I/O interface, timer, power management, memory, and peripheral circuits. The main instructions are as follows:

- Embedded microprocessor: As the core of embedded system hardware layer, embedded processor undertakes the important task of control system, which makes the host device intelligent, flexible design and easy to operate. To complete these tasks reasonably and efficiently, the general embedded processor should have the following characteristics: strong real-time multi-task support ability, memory protection function, scalable microprocessor structure, strong interrupt processing ability, and low power consumption. At present, the mainstream embedded microprocessors include arm, MIPs, DSP, PowerPC, and x86.

- Memory: Embedded systems need memory to store and execute code. The memory of embedded system includes cache, main memory, and external memory. Cache is a memory array with small capacity and high speed. The main goal of its design is to reduce the memory access bottleneck caused by memory (such as main memory and auxiliary memory) to the microprocessor core so as to make the processing speed faster and more real time. The main memory is located inside the microprocessor and is used to store the program and data of the system and users. Its on-chip memory has small capacity and fast speed. External memory is used to store a large amount of program codes or information. It has a large capacity, but the reading speed is much slower than that of memory. It is used to save user information for a long time.

- General equipment interface and I/O interface: The interaction between the embedded system and the outside world requires a certain form of general equipment interface, such as A/D, D/A, and I/O. The peripherals realize the input/output function of the microprocessor by connecting with other devices or sensors outside the chip. Each peripheral usually has only a single function. It can be outside the chip or built into the chip. There are many kinds of peripherals, from a simple serial communication device to a very complex 802.11 wireless device.

2. **Driver layer**

The driver layer is an indispensable and important part of the embedded system. The use of any external device needs the support of the corresponding driver layer program. It provides the device operation interface for the upper software. The upper software does not need to pay attention to the specific internal operation of the device, but only needs to call the interface provided by the driver layer program. The driver layer program generally includes hardware abstraction layer Hal, board-level support package BSP, and device driver. The implementation functions of board-level support package BSP generally include the following two aspects:

- When the system starts, complete the initialization of the hardware. For example, set system memory, registers and device interrupts, that is, determine which functions BSP should implement according to the CPU type selected for embedded development, hardware, and initialization of EOS.

- Provide drivers with access to hardware. The driver often accesses the device register and operates on the device register. If the whole system is uniformly addressed, the developer can directly access the device register with the function of C language in the driver. However, if the system is addressed separately, C language cannot directly access the registers in the device, and only the functions written in assembly language can access the registers of peripheral devices. BSP is a function package that provides upper-layer drivers with access to hardware device registers.

3. **EOS layer**

EOS layer is a kind of system software with a wide range of uses. It is mainly responsible for the allocation and scheduling of all software and hardware resources of the embedded system, and controlling and coordinating concurrent activities. It must reflect the characteristics of its system and be able to achieve the required functions of the system by loading and unloading some modules.

Compared with the general operating system, EOS not only has the most basic functions of the general operating system, such as task scheduling, synchronization mechanism, interrupt processing, and file processing, but also has the following characteristics:

- Strong real-time performance: EOS has strong real-time performance and can be used for various equipment control.

- Loadability: Open and scalable architecture.

- Unified interface: Provides drive interfaces for various devices.

- It provides powerful network functions, supports MIL-STD-1553B, ARINC429/629, TCP/IP protocol and other protocols, provides TCP/UDP/IP/PPP protocol support and unified MAC access layer interface, and reserves interfaces for various mobile computing devices.

- Strong stability, weak interaction: Once the embedded system starts running, it does not need too much user intervention, which requires that the EOS responsible for system management has strong stability. The user interface of EOS generally does not provide operation commands. It provides services to user programs through system call commands.

- Solidification code: In the embedded system, the EOS and application software are solidified in the ROM of the embedded system computer. Auxiliary memory is rarely used in embedded systems.

- It can provide simple and friendly graphical user interface (GUI) and graphical interface, which is easy to learn and use.

- Better hardware adaptability, that is, good portability.

At present, there are more than 40 kinds of EOSs commonly used for embedded system development in the world. The mainstream EOS in the market include VxWorks, Palm OS, WindowsCE, PSOs, QNX, µC/OS-II, and Symbian and embedded Linux.

4. **Application layer**

As the top layer of the embedded system, the application layer is mainly composed of multiple relatively independent application tasks, which interact directly with the end user. It is generally customized and developed according to the specific needs of the user. Each application task completes specific functions, such as I/O task, calculation task, communication task, and UI interaction. The EOS uniformly schedules the operation of each task.

The application layer involves user experience, which is directly related to whether the user needs are accurately realized. Therefore, the design quality of the application layer directly determines the success or failure of the whole embedded product. Therefore, the quality and reliability of the software application layer software have high requirements.

1.1.4 Application Fields of Embedded Systems

Different from general-purpose computer systems such as PC, embedded systems usually perform predefined tasks with specific requirements. Because the embedded system is only for some special tasks, designers can optimize it and reduce the size and cost. Therefore, the embedded system is usually suitable for mass production and reducing the single cost, and the profit is greatly increased with the increase of the number of products sold. With the upgrading of equipment manufacturing industry and the rapid development and promotion of aerospace, industry 4.0, medical electronics, smart home, logistics management, and power control, embedded system has gradually become a standard product in many industries by using its own technical characteristics. Because embedded systems have the remarkable characteristics of high security, controllability, programmability, low cost, and small volume, it has a very broad application prospect in industrial manufacturing and daily life. The following selects typical application fields for description.

1. **Smart city field**

With the increasing development and popularization of Internet of things technology, embedded systems have been widely used, which has injected innovative elements into the intelligent network of smart city. The smart city first needs to realize the perception of the Internet of things and cloud computing services that turn massive information into smart action. Internet of things technology supports remote automatic meter reading, safety, fire prevention, and anti-theft system of water, electricity, and gas meters. The embedded special control chip will replace the traditional manual inspection and achieve higher, more accurate, and safer performance. Taking the smart home control system as an example, it can intelligently control the household appliances and lighting in the residence, realize family safety prevention, and provide residents with a warm, comfortable, safe, energy-saving, advanced, and noble home environment in combination with other systems, so that residents can fully enjoy the convenience and wonderful life brought by modern technology.

2. **Weapons and equipment field**

   Embedded computer systems have been widely used in military and civil mechatronic products and industrial automation control systems. Embedded system is mainly used for various signal processing and control. It is used for various military electronic equipment of the land, sea, and air forces such as various military weapon control, tanks, ships, and bombers, military communication equipment such as radar and electronic countermeasure, and various special equipment for field command and operation.

   Typical applications of "embedded" systems in the military field include flight control systems and engine control systems of various aircraft and weapon systems, weapon test data acquisition and real-time processing systems, and military handheld intelligent devices (military PDA products). The wide application of the above embedded systems plays an important role in improving the information level, quality, and reliability of weapons and equipment.

3. **Intelligent transportation field**

   Intelligent transportation system (ITS) is not only an important part of smart city but also suitable for the development trend of the world. ITS is mainly composed of subsystems such as traffic information collection, traffic condition monitoring, traffic control, information release, and communication. All kinds of information are the basis of ITS operation, and the embedded traffic management system plays a vital role in ITS just like the nervous system in the human body. The embedded system is applied in speed radar (returning digital speed value), transport fleet remote control command system, vehicle navigation system, etc. in these application systems, and the traffic data can be obtained, stored, managed, transmitted, analyzed, and displayed so as to provide traffic managers or decision makers with decision-making and research on the current situation of traffic conditions.

ITS has strict requirements for products, and various advantages of embedded system products can meet the requirements very well. The application of embedded integrated intelligent products in the field of intelligent transportation has been recognized by a more number of people. Embedded system technology has been widely used in vehicle navigation, flow control, information monitoring, and vehicle service. Mobile positioning terminals embedded with GPS and GSM modules have been successfully used in various transportation industries.

4. **Intelligent medical treatment**

Embedded systems have been widely used in the medical field. The use of embedded systems and Internet of things technology can realize the interaction between patients and medical personnel, medical institutions, and medical equipment and gradually achieve the purpose of timely and accurate communication. Embedded technology will become the core of intelligent medical treatment in the future. Its essence is to comprehensively apply sensor technology, RFID technology, wireless communication technology, data processing technology, network technology, video detection and identification technology and GPS technology to the whole medical management system for information exchange and communication so as to realize intelligent identification, positioning and tracking.

In the near future, the medical industry will integrate more high technologies such as artificial intelligence and sensing technology so as to make medical services intelligent in real sense and promote the prosperity and development of medical undertakings. In the near future, smart medicine will enter the lives of ordinary people.

5. **Environmental engineering field**

With the increasing impact of human life on the environment, our environment has been disturbed by many factors such as climate warming, industrial pollution, and agricultural pollution. Under the traditional manual detection, it is impossible to realize the real-time monitoring and management of large-scale environment. The embedded system has many applications in environmental engineering, such as real-time monitoring of hydrological data, flood control system and water and soil quality, earthquake monitoring, and real-time meteorological information. The water source and air pollution monitoring will be realized by using the latest technology. In many areas with bad environment and complex ground conditions, the embedded system will realize unmanned monitoring which can greatly improve the efficiency and effectiveness of environmental monitoring.

6. **Robot field**

The development of robot technology and embedded system has been closely linked. The earliest robot technology was the numerical control technology proposed by MIT in the 1950s. At that time, it was far from reaching the chip level, just a simple NAND gate logic circuit. Since then, due to the slow development of processor and intelligent control theory, robot technology has not been fully developed from the 1950s to the early 1970s.

Recently, due to the high development of embedded processors, robots have shown a new development trend from hardware to software. The development of embedded chip will make the robot have more obvious advantages in miniaturization and intelligence. At the same time, it will greatly reduce the cost of the robot and make it more widely used in industrial and service fields.

7. **Intelligent vehicle field**

Intelligent vehicle is a comprehensive intelligent system integrating environmental perception, planning and decision-making, multi-level auxiliary driving and other functions. It is a typical high-tech complex with the centralized use of computers, sensing, information fusion, communication, artificial intelligence, and automatic control.

In recent years, the frequent occurrence of traffic accidents has made the intelligent vehicle operating system a new market demand. Through advanced electronic technology, drivers can drive more safely. The embedded system will be applied to the intelligent temperature control of automobile, automobile MCU system, on-board entertainment system, intelligent navigation, intelligent driving, and automobile radar management so as to effectively improve the intelligent level and safety of automobile.

8. Industrial automation field

As a national strategy, industry 4.0 has been gradually promoted. It is a general trend to apply automation technology to realize industrial production and management in the future, and embedded systems are one of the key technologies. Various intelligent measuring instruments, numerical control devices, programmable controllers, control machines, distributed control systems, fieldbus instruments and control systems, industrial robots, mechatronics mechanical equipment, automotive electronic equipment, etc. are needed in industrial automation. They will widely adopt microprocessor/controller chip level, standard bus template level, and system-embedded system.

1.2 OVERVIEW OF EMBEDDED SOFTWARE

1.2.1 Embedded Software Classification

As the soul of embedded system, embedded software refers to the software collection used to control and manage system functions in embedded system. In general, there are two classification methods for embedded software, as shown in Figure 1.4.

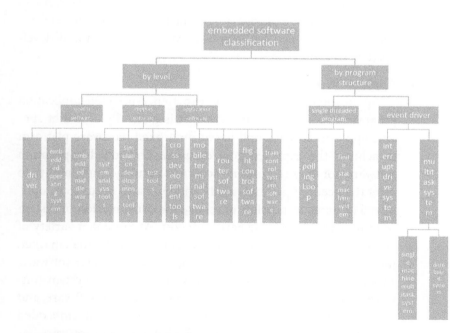

FIGURE 1.4   Embedded software classification.

1. **Divide according to the software level.**

According to the level of software in embedded system, embedded software is divided into system software, support software and application software. The specific description is as follows:

1. System software

System software refers to the software used to control and manage computer system resources in the embedded system, and mainly refers to the EOS. The mainstream EOSs include Windows CE, Palm OS, Linux, VxWorks, PSOs, QNX, OS-9, and LynxOS. The EOS in China started late. Such products in China are mainly Linux operating systems based on independent copyright, and among them, ZHONGSOFT Linux, Hongqi Linux, and Dongfang Linux are the representatives.

2. Support software

Support software refers to the software tool set used to assist software development, including embedded database, system analysis tools, system simulation tools, cross development tools, and software testing tools. At present, the mainstream embedded mobile database systems include Sybase and Oracle. China's embedded mobile database system started relatively late. At present, it is represented by open-base Mini researched and developed by Neusoft group.

3. Application software

Application software is a user experience-oriented application program in an embedded system. It is generally aimed at specific application fields and based on a fixed hardware platform to achieve the expected goal of users. Embedded application software not only requires its accuracy, security, and stability to meet the needs of practical application but also needs to be optimized as much as possible to reduce the consumption of system resources and reduce the hardware cost. At present, a variety of embedded application software have appeared in China's market, including all kinds of mobile terminal software, router software, switch software, flight control software, navigation system software, train control system software, browser, email software, and word processing software. Application software in embedded systems are the most active force. Each application software has a specific application background. Although it is small in scale, it is highly professional. Therefore, embedded application software is not subject to the monopoly of foreign products like operating systems and support software. It is the advantageous field of embedded software in China.

2. **Divide according to the software structure.**

According to the structure of embedded software, embedded software can be divided into single thread program and event driver.

1. Single thread program

Single thread program is the simplest embedded software. It does not need multitask scheduling or interrupt service program. It has no main control program and can be further divided into a circular polling system and finite state machine system. The advantages of single thread program are simple structure, high execution efficiency, and convenient program maintenance. The disadvantages are poor fault tolerance. Once a software fault occurs, the system cannot recover and carry out fault tolerance processing, resulting in poor software security. It is generally suitable for simple applications with low requirements for real time and security.

2. Event-driven program

Event-driven program is an embedded application more complex than single thread program. It can solve the problem of software security and fault tolerance. It can be generally divided into an interrupt driver system and multitask system, while multitask system can be divided into single machine multitask system and distributed system.

• The interrupt-driven program considers the interrupt priority to solve the problem of program fault tolerance. When multiple interrupt service requests occur at the same time, and each interrupt priority or handler error needs to be considered, the main control program will process each interrupt request in real time according to the established strategy to meet the needs of system design.

• Multitasking systems are often developed based on EOSs, which means that in a multitasking environment, a running program can obtain processor time only when other programs are approved. Each application (task) must collaboratively give up control of the processor so that other applications can run. At present, the mainstream EOSs support cooperative multitasking and preemptive multitasking. If necessary, the EOS can interrupt the currently running task to run another task. Through the above operations, task switching, scheduling, communication, synchronization, mutual exclusion, and complex clock management can be realized so as to greatly improve the fault tolerance and security of the embedded system, and enable users to obtain the best use experience and complete the established tasks or functions.

• With the increasingly complex requirements of embedded systems, the requirements for embedded software are becoming higher and higher, and the application scenario and architecture of software are becoming increasingly complex. At present, more and more embedded systems adopt distributed architecture to solve key problems such as multi-user concurrency, parallel processing, node load balancing, and distributed fault tolerance through distributed computing.

1.2.2 Embedded Operating Systems

1. **Development of EOS**

As a special kind of embedded software, EOS is widely used and has a special mission. Other applications are based on EOSs. EOS is the first program to execute after system reset. It is mainly responsible for the allocation and scheduling of all software and hardware resources in the system, and controlling and coordinating concurrent activities. It encapsulates CPU clock, interrupt, timer memory, and I/O and provides users with a standard AP interface. In addition, it must reflect the characteristics of its system and be able to achieve the required functions of the system by loading and unloading some modules.

The early embedded system had single function and simple control, so it did not need the EOS. However, with the increasingly complex function and structure of the embedded system and the higher requirements for reliability, security, volume, and power consumption, the EOS gradually appeared. Through the EOS, the tasks complete the switching and management, synchronization, mutual exclusion.

The organic integration of interrupt management greatly improves the performance and efficiency of embedded system.

Embedded systems originated in the 1960s. The control of electronic mechanical telephone exchange in communication system was called "stored program control system" at that time, and the real development of embedded computer was after the advent of microprocessor. In November 1971, Intel successfully integrated arithmetic unit and controller circuit for the first time, and launched the world's first microprocessor Intel 4004 (size 3 mm)×4 mm, with 16 pins in the outer layer and 2300 transistors in the inner layer, using a 10-micron process). Since then, various manufacturers have successively launched many 8-bit and 16-bit microprocessors, including Intel 8080/8085 and 8086, Motorola 6800 and 68000, and ZILOG Z80 and z8000. The system with these microprocessors as the core is widely used in weapons and equipment, instruments, medical equipment, robots, household consumer electronics, and other fields. With the wide application of microprocessors, a broad embedded application market has gradually formed. Computer manufacturers begin to provide users with OEM products in the form of plug-ins, and then users choose a set of suitable CPU board, memory board, and various I/O plug-in boards according to their own needs so as to form a special embedded computer system, and embed it into its own system equipment.

First, to be flexible and compatible, a series and modular single board computer has emerged. Popular single board computers include ISBC series of Intel company and MCB of ZILOG company. Later, people can design a special embedded computer without selecting chips. Instead, they can build a special computer system as long as they select each functional module. Users and developers hope to buy the most suitable OEM products from different manufacturers and insert them into the purchased or self-made chassis to form a new system. In this way, they hope that the plug-ins are compatible with each other, which leads to the birth of industrial control microcomputer system bus. In 1976, Intel introduced multibus, and in 1983, it was expanded to multibus II with a bandwidth of 40MB/s. The simple STD bus designed by Prolog in 1978 is widely used in small embedded systems.

The 1980s can be said to be the era of the rise of many heroes. Embedded industrial products based on single chip microcomputer and DSP have gradually become the protagonist of embedded control in various fields. With the improvement of microelectronic technology, integrated circuit manufacturers began to integrate the microprocessor, I/O interface, A/D, D/A conversion, serial interface, ram, ROM, and other components required in embedded applications into one VLSI so as to manufacture the micro controller for I/O design, which is commonly known as single chip microcomputer. It has become a rising star of embedded computer system, and the subsequent DSP products have further improved the technical level of embedded computer system and quickly penetrated into various fields such as national defense and military, consumer electronics, medical electronics, intelligent control, communication electronics, instruments and meters, transportation, and so on.

In the 1990s, driven by the huge demand for distributed control, flexible manufacturing, digital communication and information appliances, embedded systems further accelerated their development. DSP products for real-time signal processing algorithms are developing toward high speed, high precision, and low power consumption. The third-generation DSP chip TMS320C30 launched by Texas Instruments guides the development of microcontrollers to 32-bit high-speed intelligence. In terms of application, handheld computer, handheld PC, and set-top box technology are relatively mature and develop rapidly. In particular, there were few brands of handheld computers in the U.S. market in 1997. At the end of 1998, all kinds of handheld computers sprung up one after another. In addition, Nokia launched smart phones, Siemens launched set-top boxes, Wyse launched smart terminals, and national semiconductor (incorporated into Texas Instruments) launched webpad. The small computer loaded on the car can not only control various equipment in the car (such as audio) but also connect with GPS to automatically control the car.

In the 21st century, mankind has really entered the era of networking. It is bound to be an important direction for the development of embedded systems to apply embedded computer systems to all kinds of networks. The function, interface, and scalability of EOSs are becoming increasingly powerful, which can well adapt to the current networked operation scenario. With the development and popularization of new technologies such as cloud computing, big data, and artificial intelligence, EOS will obtain greater and wider applications and developments in the future. As an essential component in the future embedded system, the development trend of EOS mainly includes:

- Customization: the EOS will provide a simplified system call interface for specific applications and specifically support one or a class of embedded applications. EOS will have scalable and reducible system architecture, and provide multi-level system architecture. The EOS will include various plug-and-play device driver interfaces.

- Networking: facing the network and specific applications, the EOS is required to be equipped with a standard network communication interface. The development of EOS will be easier and easier to transplant and network. The EOS will have network access function, provide TCP/UDP/IP/PPP protocol support and unified MAC access layer interface, and reserve interfaces for various mobile computing devices.

- Energy saving: the EOS continues to adopt micro kernel technology to realize small size, micro power consumption, and low cost to support small electronic devices. At the same time, it improves the reliability and maintainability of products. The EOS will form the minimum kernel processing set, reduce the system overhead, improve the operation efficiency, and can be used for various non-computer devices.

- Intellectualization: through the close combination with artificial intelligence technology, the EOS will provide a sophisticated, easy to operate, simple interface and personalized multimedia human-computer interaction interface to meet the increasing user needs and improve the user experience.

- Security: the EOS should be able to provide a security mechanism, and the reliability of the source code is getting higher and higher.

- Standardization: with the wide application and development of EOS and the increasing opportunities for information and resource sharing, it is necessary to establish corresponding standards to standardize its application, which should be easy to cut and scale so as to better adapt to different application scenarios and user needs.

2. Introduction of typical EOS

Combined with the current development status of embedded system and mainstream application market, the following describes the typical EOS. Limited to space, only the main operating system information is given. Readers who are interested can consult relevant online or offline resources.

1. VxWorks

VxWorks operating system is an embedded real-time operating system (RTOS) designed and developed by American WinDriver company in 1983. It is a key part of tornado embedded development environment. Tornado is a set of RTOS development environment launched by WinDriver company, which is similar to Microsoft Visual C, but provides richer debugging and simulation environments and tools. Good sustainable development ability, high-performance kernel, and friendly user development environment make VxWorks gradually occupy a place in the field of embedded RTOS. At present, VxWorks has been widely used in data network, remote communication, medical equipment, transportation, aviation, and other fields.

The features of VxWorks are as follows:

- It has a tailorable microkernel structure.

- Efficient task management.

- Strong debugging ability.

- The software can be simulated and debugged through the software debug function.

- Flexible inter task communication.

- Microsecond interrupt processing.

- Rich function library.

- Support POSIX 1003 1B real-time extension standard.

- Support multiple physical media.

- Standard and complete TCP/IP network protocol support, etc.

2. Windows CE

Windows CE is an open and scalable 32-bit EOS developed by Microsoft. It is an electronic device operating system based on handheld computers. Windows CE has good compatibility with windows series, which is undoubtedly a major advantage of Windows CE promotion.

The graphical user interface (GUI) of Windows CE is excellent where C in CE represents compact, consumer, connectivity, and companion and E stands for electronics. Different from Windows 95/98 and Windows NT, Windows CE is a new EOS with all source codes developed by Microsoft. Although its operating interface comes from Windows 95/98, Windows CE is a new information equipment platform redeveloped based on Win32 API. Windows CE is modular, structured, based on Win32 Application Program Interface, and processor independent. Windows CE not only inherits the traditional windows graphical interface but can also use the programming tools on Windows 95/98 (such as Visual Basic and Visual C++), use the same functions and use the same interface grid on Windows CE platform, so that most application software can continue to be used on Windows CE platform with simple modification and transplantation.

The design goals of Windows CE are modularity and scalability, good real-time performance, strong communication ability, and support a variety of CPUs. Its design can meet the needs of a variety of equipment, including industrial controllers, communication hubs, and enterprise equipment such as sales terminals, as well as consumer products such as cameras, telephones, and home entertainment equipment. A typical embedded system based on Windows CE is usually designed for a specific purpose and works without being online. It requires that the operating system used is small and has a built-in response to interrupts.

Features of Windows CE are as follows:

- It has flexible power management functions, including instant sleep/wake-up mode.

- Object store technology is used, including file system (FS), registry, and database. It also has many high-performance and efficient operating system features, including on-demand

page change, shared storage, cross processing synchronization, and support for large capacity heap.

– Good communication skills. It widely supports various communication hardware, direct local area connection and dial-
up connection, provides connection with PC, intranet, and
Internet, and provides the best integration and communication with Windows 9x/NT.

– Nested interrupts are supported. Allow higher priority interrupts to be responded to first, rather than waiting for lower
level ISR to complete. This makes the operating system have
the real-time performance required by the EOS.

– Better thread responsiveness. The upper limit of response time
for high-level IST (interrupt service thread) is more stringent.
The improvement in thread response ability helps developers
master the specific time of thread conversion and helps them
create new embedded applications through enhanced monitoring ability and hardware control ability.

– 256 priorities. It can make developers have more flexibility
in controlling the timing arrangement of embedded systems.

– Windows CE API is a subset of Win32 API and supports
nearly 1500 Win32 APIs. With these APIs, you can write
any complex application. Of course, in Windows CE system,
the API provided can also be determined according to the
requirements of specific applications.

3. Embedded Linux

Linux originated from a hobbyist named Linus Torvalds in
Finland, and now it is one of the most popular open-source operating systems. Linux has developed into a powerful and well-
designed operating system in just 10 years since its advent in 1991.
With the progress of network technology, Linux OS has become a
strong opponent of Microsoft's DOS and Windows 95/98. Linux
system can not only run on PC platform but also shine in embedded system. With the rapid development of various embedded
Linux OS, it has gradually formed a platform that can be compared with VxWorks, Windows CE μC/OS-II and other EOS.
Linux has become an ideal choice for embedded operation. Its

biggest feature is that its source code is open and follows the General Public License (GPL) protocol. In recent years, Linux has been a research hotspot in the field of embedded development. According to the prediction of International Data Group (IDG), Embedded Linux will account for more than 50% of the share of EOSs in the future. According to preliminary statistics, about 45% of the embedded systems under development have selected Linux as the EOS, which shows the vitality of Linux and the recognition of many developers. The main reasons are as follows:

– Because its source code is open, developers can modify it at will to meet their own application needs and ensure that error detection and correction are easy and timely through corresponding test auxiliary tools. GPL compliance eliminates the need to pay a license fee for each embedded application. In addition, the Linux development community has a large number of application software to choose from and use. Most of these software comply with GPL, are open-source and free, and can be applied to their own systems after a little modification. A large number of free, excellent, and open-source development tools and a large group of developers have brought infinite vitality to Linux development.

– As long as you understand UNIX/Linux and C language and master the principles and methods of embedded development, you can start developing your own embedded system applications. With the popularity of Linux in China, there are more and more such talents, so the cost of software development and maintenance is low.

– Linux kernel is lean and requires less resources, so it is very suitable for embedded system development. In addition, Linux supports a large number of hardware. There is no essential difference between embedded Linux and ordinary Linux. Almost all the hardware used on PC supports embedded Linux, and the driver source code of various hardware can be easily obtained, which brings great convenience for users to write their own proprietary hardware drivers.

One disadvantage of running Linux on embedded system is that the Linux system needs to add real-time software modules to provide real-time performance, and the kernel space of these modules is the part of the operating system to realize scheduling strategy, hardware interrupt exception and execution program. Because these real-time software modules run in kernel space, code errors may destroy the operating system and affect the reliability of the whole system, which will be a serious weakness for real-time applications.

Hongqi embedded Linux developed by Zhongke Hongqi Software Technology Co., Ltd. is becoming one of the first choices of many embedded equipment manufacturers in China. Hongqi company has successively launched embedded Linux systems for PDA, set-top box, thin client, and switch and put them into practical application.

Taking Hongqi embedded Linux as an example, the characteristics of embedded Linux are as follows:

- It provides compact kernel, high performance, stability, and multitasking.

- It is applicable to different CPUs and supports a variety of architectures, such as x86, arm, MIPs, alpha, and SPARC.

- It can provide perfect embedded GUI and embedded X-Windows.

- It provides embedded browser, mail program, MP3 player, MPEG player, notepad, and other applications.

- It provides complete development tools and SDK and provide the development version on PC.

- Users can customize and provide graphical customization and configuration tools.

- The driver set of commonly used embedded chips supports a large number of peripheral hardware devices with rich drivers.

- For embedded storage solutions, it provides real-time version and perfect embedded solutions.

- It provides perfect Chinese support, strong technical support, and complete documents.

- It provides open-source, rich software resources, extensive support from software developers, low price, flexible structure, and wide application.

4. μC/OS-II

μC/OS-II is developed on the basis of μC/OS, and it is a compact and preemptive multitasking real-time kernel written in C language. μC/OS-II can manage 64 real-time tasks and provide functions such as task scheduling and management, memory management, synchronization and communication between tasks, time management, and interrupt service. It has the characteristics of high execution efficiency, small space, excellent real-time performance, and strong scalability. Therefore, it also occupies a large market share in the field of embedded development.

In terms of FS support, μC/OS-II is a small and medium-sized embedded systems. Even if it contains all functions, the compiled kernel is less than 10 KB, so the system itself does not provide support for FSs. However, μC/OS-II has good scalability. You can also add FS-related content if necessary.

In terms of hardware support, μC/OS-II can support most popular CPUs because the kernel of μC/OS-II is very small, the minimum code after cutting can reach 2KB, and the minimum data RAM space required is 4KB. The migration of μC/OS-II is relatively simple. You only need to modify the code related to the processor.

The main features of μC/OS-II are as follows:

- Open-source code: after expansion, it is easy to transplant the operating system to different hardware platforms.

- Portability: most of the source code is written in C language, which is easy to transplant to other microprocessors.

- Curable.

- Tailoring, selectively using the required system services to reduce the required storage space.

- Preemptive, completely preemptive real-time kernel, that is, the task with the highest priority under the condition of running readiness.

- Multi-task: 64 tasks can be managed, the priority of tasks must be different, and the time slice rotation scheduling method is not supported.

- Determinacy: the execution time of function call and service has its determinacy, which does not depend on the number of tasks.

- Practicability and reliability: the example of successful application of the real-time kernel is the best evidence of its practicability and reliability.

- Because μC/OS-II is only a real-time kernel, which means that unlike other real-time existence systems, it only provides users with some API function interfaces, and there is still a lot of work to be completed by users themselves.

  In conclusion, μC/OS-II is an EOS kernel with simple structure, complete functions, and strong real-time performance. It is very suitable for CPUs without MMU function. It requires very little kernel code space and data storage space, has good real-time performance and good scalability, and is suitable to be transplanted to various CPU platforms because the source code is open-source and the online development community and forum have a lot of materials and application examples.

5. Palm OS

   Palm is a product of 3Com company, and its operating system is Palm OS. Palm OS is a 32-bit EOS. Palm provides serial communication interface and infrared transmission interface, which can easily communicate and transmit data with other external devices. With an open OS application program interface, developers can develop their own applications as needed. Palm OS is an open system with strong technology. Now there are about thousands of applications specially written for Palm OS. From the perspective of program content, Palm OS covers everything from personal management and games to industry solutions. With the support of rich software, the functions of Palm OS–based handheld computers have been continuously expanded.

   Palm OS is a set of OS specially developed for handheld computers. When writing programs, Palm OS fully considers the relatively small memory of handheld computers, so it only occupies a little memory. Since the space occupied by applications written based on Palm OS is also very small (usually only tens of KB), Palm OS–based handheld computers (although only a few MB of RAM) can run many applications.

Because Palm products are characterized by simple use and light body, the main features of Palm OS are as follows:

– Energy-saving function of operating system. The power supply required by the handheld computer is as small as possible. Therefore, in the Palm OS application, if there is no event running, the system equipment will enter the state of doze. If the application is not active for a period of time, the system automatically enters the sleep state.

– Reasonable memory management. Palm's memory is all read-write fast RAM. Dynamic RAM is similar to RAM on PC. It provides temporary storage space for global variables and other data that do not need to be permanently saved. Storage RAM is similar to the hard disk on a PC and can permanently save applications and data.

– Palm OS data is stored in a database format. A database consists of a set of records and some database header information. To ensure program processing speed and memory space, when processing data, Palm OS does not copy the data from storage heap to dynamic heap for processing, but directly processes it in storage heap. To avoid calling the memory address incorrectly, Palm OS stipulates that all this must be implemented by calling the API in its memory manager.

The combination of Palm OS and HotSync software can synchronize the information on the handheld computer and PC and expand the functions of desktop to the handheld computer. Palm has a wide range of applications, such as contact and worksheet management, email and Internet communication, and salesperson and group automation. Palm is also rich in peripheral hardware, including digital camera, GPS receiver, modem, GSM wireless phone, digital audio playback equipment, portable keyboard, voice recorder, bar code scanning, wireless paging receiver, and detector. The application of palm combined with GPS can not only be used for navigation and positioning but also be combined with GPS for climate monitoring, place name survey, etc.

6. μClinux

μClinux is an excellent embedded Linux version. Its full name is micro control Linux, which literally refers to micro control Linux. Compared with standard Linux, the kernel of μClinux is very small, but it still inherits the main characteristics of Linux operating system, including good stability and portability, powerful network functions, excellent FS support, rich standard APIs, and TCP/IP network protocol. Because there is no MMU memory management unit, its multitasking implementation requires some skills.

μClinux inherits the multi-task implementation mode of standard Linux in structure. It is divided into real-time process and ordinary process. It adopts first come first service and time slice rotation scheduling, respectively. It is improved only for the characteristics of medium and low-grade embedded CPU, does not support kernel preemption, and has general real-time performance. In addition, μClinux has complex structure, relatively difficult transplantation, large kernel, and poor real-time performance. If the developed embedded products pay attention to file system and network application, μClinux is a good choice.

In conclusion, μClinux's biggest feature is that it is designed for a processor without MMU, which is suitable for STM32F103 without MMU function. However, transplanting this system requires at least 512KB RAM space and 1MB ROM/flash space, while stmf103 has 256K flash and needs external memory, which increases the cost of hardware design.

7. eCos

eCos, that is, embedded Configurable operating system. It is an open-source, configurable, and portable RTOS for deep embedded applications. Its main characteristics are as follows:

– eCos is characterized by flexible configuration and modular design. The core part is composed of small components, including kernel, C language library, and bottom running package.

– Each component of eCos can provide a large number of configuration options (real-time kernel can also be used as optional configuration). It can be easily configured by using the configuration tools provided by eCos, and eCos can meet different embedded application requirements through different configurations.

- The configurability of eCos operating system is very powerful. Users can join the required FS by themselves. eCos operating system also supports most of the popular embedded CPUs. eCos operating system can be transplanted between 16 bit, 32-bit, and 64-bit architectures.

- Because the kernel of eCos is very small, the minimum code can be 10 KB after cutting, and the minimum data RAM space required is 10 KB.

- In terms of system transplantation, the portability of eCos operating system is very good, which is better than μC/OS-II and μClinux is easy.

In conclusion, eCos is characterized by flexible configuration and supports the migration of CPU without MMU. It is open source and has good portability. It is also more suitable for transplantation to the CPU of STM32 platform. However, The application of eCOS is not yet as widespread as μC/OS-II and and there is limited literature available. eCos is suitable for some commercial or industrial cost-sensitive embedded systems, such as some applications in the field of consumer electronics.

8. FreeRTOS

FreeRTOS is a mini RTOS kernel. As a lightweight operating system, its functions include task management, time management, semaphore, message queue, memory management, recording function, software timer, and collaboration, which can basically meet the needs of small systems.

The main features of FreeRTOS are as follows:

- Since RTOS needs to occupy certain system resources (especially ram resources), only a few RTOSs such as μC/OS-II, embOS, salvo, and FreeRTOS can run on a small RAM single chip microcomputer.

- Compared with commercial operating systems such as μC/OS-II and embOS, FreeRTOS operating system is a completely free operating system. It has the characteristics of open source, portability, reduction, and flexible scheduling strategy. It can be easily transplanted to various single chip computers.

- FreeRTOS kernel supports priority scheduling algorithm. Each task can be given a certain priority according to i importance. The CPU always lets the task in ready state and with the highest priority run first.

- FreeRTOS kernel also supports rotation scheduling algorithm. The system allows different tasks to use the same priority. When there is no higher priority task ready, tasks with the same priority share CPU usage time.

   Compared with common μC/OS-II and other EOSs, FreeRTOS operating system has both advantages and disadvantages. The main shortcomings of FreeRTOS are as follows:

- In terms of system service function, FreeRTOS only provides the implementation of message queue and semaphore, and cannot send messages to message queue in the order of last in first out.

- FreeRTOS is only an operating system kernel, which needs to expand the third-party GUI, TCP/IP protocol stack, and file system to realize a more complex system.

9. mbed OS

   As an open-source EOS, arm company provides mbed OS to all manufacturers for free. Mbed provides a relatively more systematic and comprehensive intelligent hardware development environment.

   - Main functions of mbed OS: provides a general operating system basis for developing Internet of things devices to solve the fragmentation of embedded design; supports all important open standards for connectivity and device management to achieve future oriented design; enables secure and scalable edge devices to support new processing capabilities and functions; and solves complex energy consumption problems through automatic power management.

   - The main features of mbed OS: fast development speed, powerful function, and high security. It is designed for mass production. It can be developed offline or edited on the web page.

X

TX is an embedded RTOS of the arm company. It is written tandard C structure and compiled with RealView compiler. t only a real-time kernel but also has rich middle tier com-. It is not only free but also the code is open.

- Main functions: start and stop tasks (processes). In addition, it also supports process communication, such as task synchronization, management of shared resources (peripherals or memory), and message transmission between tasks. Developers can use basic functions to start the real-time runner, start and end tasks, and transfer control between tasks (round robin scheduling).

- Main features: support time slice, preemptive, and cooperative scheduling. There is no limit to the number of tasks, and each task has a priority of 254; unlimited number of semaphores, mutually exclusive semaphores, message mailbox, and soft timer; and support multithreading and thread safe operation. Using the MDK dialog–based configuration wizard, you can easily complete the MDK configuration.

11. QNX

QNX, born in 1980, is a commercial UNIX like embedded RTOS conforming to POSIX specification.

- Main functions of QNX: supports the simultaneous scheduling and execution of multiple tasks on the same computer; multiple users can also share a computer. These users can submit tasks to the system through multiple terminals and interact with QNX.

- Main features: the core only provides four services: process scheduling, inter process communication, underlying network communication, and interrupt processing. Its processes run in an independent address space. All other OS services are implemented as collaborative user processes, so the QNX core is very small (qnx4. X is about 12KB) and runs very fast.

12. NuttX

NuttX is an embedded RTOS. The first version was released by Gregory Nutt under a loose BSD license in 2007.

- Main functions: it can be built as an open and flat embedded RTOS, or a micro kernel with system call interface can be built separately. It can be easily extended to a new processor architecture, SoC architecture or board-level architecture; real time, deterministic and support priority inheritance; BSD socket interface; extension of priority management; optional tasks (processes) with address environment, etc.

- Main features: flexible configuration and modular design. The core part is composed of small components, including kernel, C language library, and bottom running package. Each component can provide a large number of configuration options (real-time kernel can also be used as optional configuration). It can be easily configured by using the configuration tools provided by eCos, and eCos can meet different embedded application requirements through different configurations.

13. SylixOS

The EOS SylixOS was born in 2006. It is an open-source cross platform large-scale RTOS. After more than ten years of continuous development, SylixOS has become one of the most comprehensive domestic operating systems. Its main features are as follows:

- SylixOS is a RTOS whose kernel is completely written by Chinese people. The relevant kernel code is open source, and the source code autonomy rate is scanned in the Ministry of Industry and Information Technology. The kernel code autonomy rate is 100%, and the autonomy rate of all codes is 89.1%.

- The open-source community has rich free software, which is very convenient for transplantation.

- The interface is compatible with POSIX standard. At present, there are many product and project application cases, involving aerospace, military defense, rail transit, smart grid, industrial automation, and many other fields.

1.3 SUMMARY

In this chapter, we systematically introduce the characteristics and composition of embedded system and real-time system, give the classification of embedded software, sort out the development process of EOS and typical EOS, and provide necessary background and technical description for readers to establish the basic concepts of embedded system and embedded software.

CHAPTER 2

Embedded Software Engineering and Quality Characteristics

S OFTWARE ENGINEERING IS AN engineering methodology that guides the development and maintenance of computer software. It is a discipline that studies the construction and maintenance of effective, practical, and high-quality software with engineering methods. This chapter will use limited space to introduce the embedded software engineering process and management technology, and finally give the quality characteristics of embedded software.

2.1 EMBEDDED SOFTWARE ENGINEERING

IEEE has the following definitions in the glossary of software engineering terms:

Software engineering is: (ADS2) Applying engineering methods to software processes, that is, applying systematic, strictly constrained, and quantifiable methods to software development, operation, and maintenance; RT-LAB/ATB:RT-LAB research on the method described in (ADS2). The software engineering aims to develop software products with applicability, effectiveness, modifiability, reliability, understandability, maintainability, reusability, portability, traceability, interoperability, and meeting user needs under the premise of given cost and schedule. Pursuing these goals will help improve the quality and development efficiency of software

DOI: 10.1201/9781003390923-3

products and reduce the difficulty of maintenance. Software engineering involves programming languages, databases, software development tools, system platforms, standards, design patterns, etc.

With the continuous development of computer technology, software development has experienced the evolution process of program design stage, software design stage, and software engineering stage.

1. **Program design stage**

    The program design stage appeared from 1946 to 1955. The characteristics of this stage are: there is no concept of software; the program design is mainly developed around hardware, with small scale and simple tools, and there is no clear division of labor (developers and users); program design pursues space saving and programming skills; there is almost no documentation (except the program list); and the program mainly served for scientific computing at that time.

2. **Software design stage**

    The software design stage appeared from 1956 to 1970. The characteristics of this stage are: the hardware environment is relatively stable, and the development organization form of "software workshop" appears. The product software (which can be purchased on the shelf) was widely used, and the concept of software was gradually established. With the development of computer technology and the increasing popularity of computer applications, the scale of software is becoming larger and larger, high-level programming languages are emerging in endlessly, the application field is constantly expanding, developers and users have a clear division of labor, and the demand for software in the society is surging. However, it should be pointed out that there is no major breakthrough in software development technology, the quality of software products is not high, and the production efficiency is low, which leads to the "software crisis".

3. **Software engineering stage**

    The emergence of the "software crisis" forced the computer industry to study and change the technical means and management methods of software development. Since the 1970s, software development has entered the stage of software engineering, from which software has entered the era of software engineering. The specific of this stage is that the hardware has developed in four directions: giant, miniaturization, networking, and intelligence. Database technology has been mature and widely used. The third- and fourth-generation design languages have emerged in succession.

4. **Prospect of future software engineering**

With the continuous development of computer science and software engineering technology, software engineering itself is also evolving and progressing. The prospects of software engineering in the future are as follows:

- Traditional software engineering technologies, such as domain-based architecture (DSSA) and model-driven development (MDD), will be further valued and popularized and gradually play a powerful role.

- With the continuous popularization of middleware technologies such as COM, DCOM, and CORBA, distributed application software can easily realize resource sharing among different software technologies. Distributed software engineering technology has made great progress and gradually become a new trend in the software development industry.

- With the continuous development of new technologies such as cloud computing and big data, the current computer capacity has gradually tended to server-side and cloud side. Practical middleware technology and fast computer computing processing capacity are not only the only way to develop large-scale software but also one of the main trends of new technology development.

- With the development of Internet technology, cross network platforms and cross system fields are re-integrated under the unification of standard interface protocols. In the process of new software development, the integration of unified basic platform and protocol framework plays a vital role in software development.

- With the accelerating trend of globalization, the traditional software development and management methods are no longer suitable. Open-software computing will become the inevitable trend of software engineering development under the background of accelerated globalization and cooperation.

Embedded software has also gone through the above evolution process. With the continuous development of computer technology and software technology, embedded software development has become a complex system engineering, which must comply with the requirements of system engineering and software engineering. Embedded software engineering, especially in aviation, aerospace, electronics, nuclear industry, transportation, energy, and other fields, has made great progress and gradually produced a series of standards and specifications to guide the development, application, and maintenance of embedded software.

2.1.1 Embedded Software Development Model

The standard GJB2786A-2009 gives the general requirements for software development stipulates the activities and requirements of the software development process. The comparison between software development process and hardware development process is shown in Figure 2.1.

The first stage of system development is the system requirements analysis and system design stage, which mainly demonstrates the feasibility of the overall scheme of the system according to the requirements of the client. After the overall scheme of the system is basically determined, the functions of the system should be decomposed to determine which functions of the system are realized by hardware and which functions are realized by software, and the development task books should be issued to the hardware development department and the software development department, respectively. After the review and approval of the development mission statement, the hardware and software can be developed in parallel. Specific instructions are as follows:

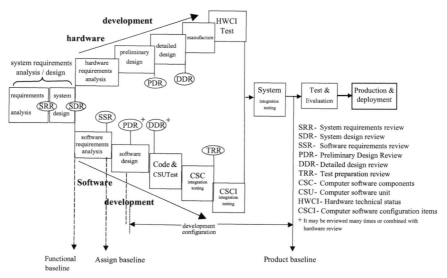

FIGURE 2.1   System development process and software development process.

- The uplink in Figure 2.1 is the development process of hardware: it consists of hardware requirements analysis, preliminary design, detailed design, manufacturing, and hardware configuration item test.

- The downlink of Figure 2.1 is the software development process: it consists of requirements analysis, software design, coding and unit testing, software integration and testing, software configuration item integration and testing, etc.

According to the idea of software engineering, from the development process of software and hardware, the difference between software development and hardware development is that the software development process often requires a long test stage (accounting for about 40% of its development cycle). The reason is that software is the logical product of human brain thinking, not a physical product. The hidden defects in software cannot be detected directly with various instruments and equipment like hardware. Therefore, we must eliminate the defects in the software step by step through different testing means in each stage and in different ways (such as static and dynamic testing and black-box and white-box testing).

When the software and hardware have completed their respective configuration item tests, the software and hardware will be integrated together for system integration and testing. After the system testing is completed, it can enter the test and evaluation stage (generally referred to as the design finalization stage). After the design finalization, it can enter the production and deployment.

The above-mentioned process is the development process of the software, which is the main component of the software lifetime. However, as a software, the lifetime must include the use and maintenance stage after deployment, until the final abandonment after the system completes its mission.

In general, each stage of embedded software lifetime includes:

- system analysis and software definition stage;

- software requirements analysis stage;

- software design stage (including outline design and detailed design);

- software implementation stage (including coding and software unit testing);

- software testing stage (including software integration test, configuration item test and system test);

- software acceptance and delivery stage;

- software use and maintenance stage.

2.1.2 System Analysis and Software Definition Phase

In the system analysis and software definition stage, the embedded system is comprehensively analyzed to clarify the parts related to software development in the embedded system. After the system assigns tasks to the computer system, the computer system first analyzes and determines the requirements of its superior system, then designs the system architecture, reasonably assigns the system requirements to software, hardware, and possible manual operations, defines each software development project, and writes the system requirements for software into a software development task book.

The main work and fv in Table 2.1.

2.1.3 Software Requirements Analysis Phase

The task of the software requirements analysis stage is to determine all the requirements of the developed software, such as function, performance, interface, security, resource environment, etc., based on the completion of the system analysis and software definition stage; plan software development, quality assurance and configuration management; and prepare software requirements specifications, software development plans, quality assurance plans, configuration management plans, system testing plans, and other important documents.

The main problem of embedded software requirement analysis is what the system (or user) wants the software to do. Software requirements specification is the most important technical document in software development. It is the basis of the whole software development work. The software development plan is a comprehensive management plan that runs through the whole software development process and is the basis of the whole project development management.

The main work and process control in this stage are shown in Table 2.2.

2.1.4 Software Design Phase

This stage is the core of software engineering. Its main task is to establish the overall structure of the software and the relationship between functional modules according to the software requirements specification, define the interface of each functional module, design the global database/data structure, specify the design limitations, and write the software design description. This stage mainly includes two steps, namely, outline design and detailed design.

TABLE 2.1   System Analysis and Software Definition Stage Work

Development Stage	Entry Conditions	Main Work	Method Tools	Stage Products	Completion Flag	Main Control Means
System analysis and software definition stage	The system has completed the function allocation of the computer system	1. System analysis. 2. System design. 3. Define each software development project. 4. Determine the critical level of the software and whether it needs to be independently tested by a third party. 5. Prepare the software development task statement (which specifies various technical and management requirements, and special attention should be paid to specifying the acceptance method). 6. Review. 7. Sign the software development assignment.	The method of system engineering is used for system analysis and design. In the task decomposition, we can adopt the structured idea, from top to bottom, and gradually refine. During system analysis and design, some graphic tools can be used to carry out work, usually the following graphic tools. 1. System flow chart, showing the operation control and data flow of the system. 2. System resource diagram, showing the configuration of data units and processing units suitable for solving a problem or a group of problems. 3. Data flow chart, indicating the data path to solve a problem. 4. Function diagram, which represents the hierarchical relationship of modules of a system and further describes the input processing output diagram (IPO) of module information. 5. Structure diagram (SC).	1. Specification of system requirements; 2. System design description; 3. The software development task statement is included in the controlled library after review, and thus forms the initial baseline of software configuration management - functional baseline.	1. Complete all stage products. 2. The system requirements and system design have passed relevant reviews and come into force after approval. 3. The software development task statement has been reviewed and signed into effect, and the software function baseline has been established.	1. Analysis 2. Review 3. Standardization

TABLE 2.2 Work in Software Requirements Analysis Stage

Development Stage	Entry Conditions	Main Work	Method Tools	Stage Products	Completion Flag	Main Control Means
Software requirements analysis stage	1. The software development assignment was formally reviewed and signed. 2. The development project team has been established. 3. The functional baseline has been established.	1. Determine the software operating environment. 2. Determine the requirements for software functions, performance, interfaces, security, resources and environment, and prepare software requirements specifications. 3. Identify key software components. 4. Determine the development plan and complete the software scale estimation, resource plan, schedule, etc. 5. Make software system testing plan. 6. Review.	The following methods can be adopted for software requirements analysis: 1. Use structured methods for requirements analysis. The logical model of the system is described by data flow diagram, the control flow of the system is described by control flow diagram, the control is described by state transition diagram, and the data flow in the data flow diagram is described by data dictionary. 2. Use object-oriented method to analyze requirements. Establish the functional model of software problem domain. A set of data flow diagrams are used to describe the dependencies between problem domain data and related data processing functions. Describe the external interface of software configuration items, and describe each class and object responsible for the external interface.	1. Software requirements specification. 2. Software development plan, quality assurance plan, configuration management plan (can be merged). 3. Software system testing plan.	1.Complete all phase products (software requirements specification, development plan, system testing plan). 2.The software requirements specification passed the review and became effective upon approval. 3. Software allocation baseline establishment.	1. Analysis 2. Review 3. Specifications 4. Configuration management

1. Outline design

In the software design stage, it is necessary to map the determined software requirements into the corresponding software architecture, and each component of the architecture should be a module with clear functions.

The goal of outline design is to provide the architecture of embedded software and lay the foundation for the next detailed design.

2. Detailed design

The detailed design is to describe each module in the software architecture, including the algorithm and detailed design and clarify the interface information of each module on the basis of the outline design. At the same time, it is necessary to design the software unit test scheme to facilitate the unit test in the subsequent software implementation stage.

The main work and process control in this stage are shown in Table 2.3.

2.1.5 Software Implementation Phase

In the software implementation stage, there are two tasks: coding and unit testing.

- Use the specified programming language to code all software units, compile and debug the compiled code until the compilation passes without errors.

- Unit test the coded modules to verify the design and implementation of all software units. The content includes the interface of the test module, local data structure, important execution path, error handling, boundary conditions, and so on.

The main work and process control in this stage are shown in Table 2.4.

2.1.6 Software Testing Phase

In modern software engineering theory, software testing is an important means to ensure software quality and reliability. As an important software system, embedded software has the characteristics of embeddedness, real-time, special development tools, limited memory, and a wide variety of interfaces, which determines that the testing of embedded software has its particularity.

TABLE 2.3 Work in Software Design Stage

Development Stage		Entry Conditions	Main Work	Method Tools	Stage Products	Completion Flag	Main Control Means
Software design stage	Outline design stage	1. The software requirements specification has been formally reviewed and signed. 2. The software development plan is approved and takes effect. 3. The dispatch baseline has been established.	1. Establish software architecture. Realize the transformation from logical model to physical model, allocate various functions to various software components (functional modules), and define the input and output of various software components. 2. Clarify the design criteria and guide the software design. 3. Complete the realization of non-functional requirements, including performance, interface, operation, resources, verification, security, portability, reliability, maintainability, and other requirements. 4. Determine the software integration test plan. 5. Prepare outline design description and review.	The following methods can be adopted: 1. Function decomposition method decomposes the software into hierarchical structure. A top-down approach must be adopted, starting from the top-level software components, to decompose the software layer by layer into a hierarchical structure system composed of several software components. 2. Data flow oriented structured design method, etc.	1. Software outline design description (including external interface design). 2. Software integration test plan.	1. Complete all phase products (software requirements specification, development plan, system testing plan). 2. The software requirements specification is reviewed and approved to take effect. 3. Software allocation baseline establishment.	1. Review 2. Specifications 3. Configuration management

(Continued)

TABLE 2.3 (Continued) Work in Software Design Stage

Development Stage	Entry Conditions	Main Work	Method Tools	Stage Products	Completion Flag	Main Control Means
Detailed design	The software outline design passed the review and was included in the controlled library.	1. Refine the software components step by step until several software units (programmable modules) are formed. 2. Complete the software unit process description, and determine the module algorithm and data structure. 3. Determine the interface information between units. 4. Prepare detailed design description and review. 5. Determine the software unit test plan.	Commonly used tools: 1. Graphic tools: logical construction is represented by specific graphics. 2. List tool: use tables to represent the details of the process. 3. Language tools: use class language (pseudo code) to represent process details.	Detailed software design description.	1. Complete the detailed design description of the software and pass the review. 2. The detailed design description of the software is included in the controlled library.	

On the basis of unit testing completed in the implementation stage of embedded software, generally, the subsequent software testing should include integration testing, configuration item testing and system testing. The brief description is as follows:

1. **Integration testing**

   There are generally two integration methods for embedded software integration testing: one is integration testing on the host computer, and the other is integration testing on the target computer.

2. **Configuration item testing**

   Software configuration item test is to comprehensively verify all functions, performance, interfaces, security, recoverability, strength, allowance, and other requirements defined in the software requirements specification on the basis of integration testing, and test whether the whole software configuration item meets the requirements.

3. **System testing**

   Embedded systems often contain multiple software configuration items. In this case, whether the embedded software can correctly connect with other software and hardware in the system, and whether it has correctly completed the functions and performance assigned by the superior system, must be confirmed by system testing.

   The purpose of embedded software system testing is to verify whether the software can be correctly connected with the system in the real system working environment or simulation testing environment, and to confirm whether the software is consistent with the software function, performance and interface requirements proposed in the software development specification.

   For real-time embedded software, system testing is one of the most important testing methods because all the above tests cannot test the timing errors and software and hardware interface errors hidden in real-time software. Therefore, the software for system testing must run on the target machine and adopt the real i/o interface.

   The main work and process control in this stage are shown in Table 2.5.

2.1.7 Software Acceptance and Delivery

After the embedded software products are developed and tested, the software should be accepted and delivered. Software acceptance is an activity

TABLE 2.4 Work in Software Implementation Stage

Development Stage	Entry Conditions	Main Work	Method Tools	Stage Products	Completion Flag	Main Control Means
Software implementation stage	1. The software detailed design review is passed and signed. 2. The detailed design description of the software has been included in the controlled library. 3. Software unit (module) documents are available.	1. Program coding, including comments on the source code. 2. Compile and debug to ensure that the software unit code passes compilation or assembly without errors. 3. Static analysis, using static analysis tools. 4. Code review: read and review the compiled source code item by item according to the code review list. 5. Unit test, according to the plan, design and compile the pile module and drive module required for unit test, and prepare the necessary test data. 6. Review, review the source code and unit test work.	The following methods can be adopted for software requirements analysis: 1. Structured programming method, object-oriented programming method, etc. 2. Static analysis technology, including control flow analysis, data flow analysis, interface analysis, expression analysis. 3. Code review: according to the code review sheet, review the reviewed program code one by one according to the detailed software design specification document so as to ensure the consistency between the code and the design and ensure the correctness of the code. 4. Unit testing, static and dynamic testing of software units, statistical coverage.	1. Software source code. 2. Test data, including test cases, test data, test results / records, etc. 3. Unit test AIDS, drivers, pile modules, etc. should also be carefully stored for review and regression testing, Software requirements specification.	1. Software units are compiled or assembled without errors. 2. Complete code static analysis and code review. 3. Complete the unit test. 4. Through the software implementation stage review. 5. Controlled libraries of all software units.	1. Analysis 2. Review 3. Specifications 4. Configuration management

TABLE 2.5 Software Testing Phase Work

Development Stage		Entry Conditions	Main Work	Method and Tools	Stage Products	Completion Flag	Main Control Means
Software testing phase	Integration testing	1. The integrated software unit can be compiled or assembled without errors. 2. The integrated software unit passes the unit test. 3. Integration test environment and tools are available. 4. The integrated software unit has been placed under configuration management.	1. Implement the software integration test plan. 2. Verify the correctness of the control path of the software, the integrity of the internal data of the software and the external interface, function, performance, accuracy, error identification and recovery of software components. 3. Prepare software integration test report. 4. Review.	There are two integration testing strategies: 1. In the non-incremental mode, each software unit is tested first, and then assembled at one time, and then the whole program is tested. This method is fast and takes less machine time, which is conducive to parallel development, but it is easy to cause confusion. 2. Incremental method, gradually combine the next software unit or component to be assembled with the tested software components.	1. Software integration test description. 2. Software integration test report, including all test records and results. 3. All software problem reports and software modification reports. 4. All modified software source codes consistent with the software modification report.	1. Complete all tests specified in the software integration test instructions. 2. All software problems were handled as required. 3. The software documents that have passed the regression test are included in the controlled library. 4. Pass the software integration test phase review.	1. Review 2. Specification 3. Testing techniques and tools 4. Configuration management

(Continued)

TABLE 2.5 (Continued) Software Testing Phase Work

Development Stage	Entry Conditions	Main Work	Method and Tools	Stage Products	Completion Flag	Main Control Means
Configuration item testing	1. Complete the software integration test and pass the review. 2. The configuration item test environment and tools are available. 3. Software configuration items have been placed under configuration management.	1. Execute the software configuration item test plan. 2. Verify all functions, performance, interfaces, safety, recoverability, strength, allowance, and other requirements defined in the software requirements specification, and test whether the entire software configuration item meets the requirements. 3. Prepare software configuration item test report. 4. Review.	1. Test case design based on requirements. Design test cases according to the software requirements specification, including normal range test cases and abnormal range test cases. 2. For software with high reliability and safety requirements, to further ensure the high quality of the software, after the software developer has completed all software testing, it is also necessary to authorize an authoritative professional technical institution that is relatively independent of the software development client and the developer to conduct independent third-party software configuration item testing on the software.	1. Software configuration item test description. 2. Software configuration item test report, including all test records and results. 3. All software problem reports and software modification reports. 4. All modified software source codes consistent with the software modification report.	1. Complete all tests specified in the software configuration item test instructions. 2. All software problems were handled as required. 3. The software documents that have passed the regression test are included in the controlled library. 4. Pass the software configuration item test phase review.	1. Review 2. Specification 3. Testing techniques and tools 4. Configuration management

(Continued)

TABLE 2.5 (*Continued*)   Software Testing Phase Work

Development Stage	Entry Conditions	Main Work	Method and Tools	Stage Products	Completion Flag	Main Control Means
System testing	1. Complete the software configuration item test and pass the review. 2. System testing environment and tools are available. 3. All software configuration items have been placed under configuration management.	1. Establish a real System testing environment or simulation test environment, and the hardware environment and interface of software operation should adopt real components. 2. Design and implement test cases according to the requirements of system testing. 3. Analyze test data, complete problem analysis and report. 4. Carry out regression test. 5. Prepare System testing report. 6. Review, review the system testing work.	1. The focus of system testing is whether the timing of embedded system is correct and whether the interface with related systems is coordinated. 2. The boundaries of all input / output information should be examined. 3. Combine the software with its embedded system for strength test. 4. The system shall be tested in closed loop and non-intrusive real time.	1. Software system testing instructions. 2. Software system testing report, including all test records and results. 3. All software problem reports and software modification reports. 4. All modified software source codes consistent with the software modification report.	1. Complete all tests specified in the software system testing instructions. 2. All software problems were handled as required. 3. The software documents that have passed the regression test are included in the controlled library. 4. Pass the software system testing phase review.	1. Review 2. Specification 3. Testing techniques and tools 4. Configuration management

that the development task entrusting party authorizes its representative to carry out. Through this activity, the task entrusting party verifies that the software meets the requirements according to the contract or task statement, and accepts the ownership or use right of some or all software products according to the contract or task statement.

Delivery is the process that the developer of the development task hands over the software products that have passed the acceptance to the entrusting party. Each software product should be accepted and delivered after all development activities are completed.

1. **Premise of software acceptance**

    The software project submitted for acceptance must meet the following conditions:

    1. The software passes the software configuration item test (for embedded software, it should pass the software system testing);

    2. Complete various documents specified in the assignment (contract, the same below);

    3. Software products have been placed under configuration management;

    4. Meet other acceptance conditions specified in the assignment.

2. **Software acceptance basis**

    The basis for software acceptance is the standards and specifications specified in the software development assignment, the relevant technical documents referenced in the assignment or the appendix, the assignment, or the model system.

3. **Software acceptance process**

    The software acceptance and delivery must be carried out according to the regulations, and the formal procedures must be performed according to the following work steps:

    1. Apply for software acceptance;

    2. Formulate software acceptance plan;

    3. Establish a software Acceptance Committee;

    4. Conduct software acceptance test;

    5. Conduct software acceptance review;

6. Form software acceptance report;

7. Handover of software products.

4. **Software product delivery**

When necessary, the developer shall further supplement and improve the software products according to the opinions of the Acceptance Committee. After these follow-up works are completed and approved by the Acceptance Committee or its designated personnel, the software products shall be delivered.

Under the approval and supervision of the Acceptance Committee, the product items in the software product handover project list are verified item by item and handed over to the entrusting party. After the handover, both the entrusting party and the developer shall sign and seal on the software product handover project list as the receiving unit and the handover unit respectively, indicating that the software product delivery is completed.

5. **Software continuous assurance**

After the delivery of the software, the continuous guarantee work shall be jointly undertaken by the software developer and the entrusting party. The responsibilities of both parties are as follows:

1. Responsibilities of the developer

   1. The installation and inspection of the software shall be completed under the guaranteed environment specified in the assignment.

   2. The code provided shall support the regeneration and transplantation under the guaranteed environment specified in the assignment.

   3. Provide the client with training and other services required to ensure the normal operation of the software in accordance with the provisions of the assignment;

   4. It should help users solve technical problems encountered in the use of the software according to the provisions of the assignment.

2. Responsibilities of the entrusting party (or end user)

   1. Establish an appropriate use organization, allocate appropriate personnel, and clarify the responsibilities of various personnel;

2. Organize necessary training to equip relevant personnel with necessary knowledge and skills;

3. Provide the necessary environment and resources for the normal operation and maintenance of the software;

4. Establish reasonable and effective software use procedures and management methods;

5. Collect and record relevant data in the use of software, especially failure data.

2.1.8 Software Use and Maintenance Phase

Software maintenance refers to the modification activities carried out after the delivery of software products to correct faults, improve performance and other attributes, or adapt the products to the changed environment. Software maintenance is generally divided into three types: perfect maintenance, adaptive maintenance, and corrective maintenance. Perfectness maintenance is to modify and expand to expand functions and improve performance to meet the changing needs of users. Adaptive maintenance is a modification made to adapt to changes in the software operating environment. For example, modifications required due to changes in hardware configuration and system software. Corrective maintenance is to maintain the operation of the system and correct the errors generated in the development process but not found during testing and acceptance.

In addition, someone also proposed the fourth kind of maintenance, namely preventive maintenance, which is a change to the software to further improve the maintainability and reliability of the software or to provide a better foundation.

The maintenance of software is not exactly the same as that of hardware. The maintenance of software means modification. It does not have the maintenance work of replacing spare parts like hardware.

1. **Software maintenance work content:**

   1. Corrective maintenance, including correcting design errors, program errors, data errors and document errors.

   2. Adaptive maintenance, including adapting to changes in rules or laws that affect the system; changes in hardware configuration, such as changes in model, terminal, external equipment, etc.; changes in data format or file structure; and the change of

software support environment, such as the change of operating system, compiler, or utility program.

3. Integrity maintenance, including expansion and enhancement functions such as expanding the scope of problem solving and algorithm optimization; improve performance, such as improving operation speed and saving storage space; and facilitate maintenance such as adding some notes to improve readability.

2. **Software maintenance organization:**

When carrying out software maintenance, a software maintenance organization must be established. The organization shall include:

1. Software maintenance management organization;

2. Software maintenance supervisor;

3. Software maintenance administrator;

4. Software maintenance team.

The main tasks of the software maintenance organization are to approve the maintenance application, formulate and implement the maintenance plan, control and manage the maintenance process, be responsible for the review of software maintenance, organize the acceptance of software maintenance, and ensure the completion of software maintenance tasks.

3. **Software maintenance process**

First understand the existing software, then modify the existing software, and finally review and accept the modified software. The following steps can be followed:

1. Collect software maintenance information;

2. Determine the type of software maintenance;

3. Application and approval of software maintenance;

4. Planning and implementation of software maintenance;

5. Software maintenance review and acceptance.

2.2 EMBEDDED SOFTWARE ENGINEERING MANAGEMENT

Software quality and reliability are directly related to the success or failure of system development. Therefore, how to ensure the quality of software products has always been a problem that the software engineering community has paid great attention to and committed to solving. In the face of the software crisis in the late 1960s, the international software community has jointly discussed the solution, and the only conclusion is to absorb the engineering experience of hardware for software development, that is, to implement software engineering. In the past few decades, the international software engineering community has been exploring and developing the implementation methods of software engineering. Now software engineering has become an independent discipline. Practice has fully shown that the implementation of software engineering is indeed the only effective way to ensure software quality and solve software crisis.

The core of implementing software engineering and ensuring software quality is to organize software development with software engineering methods. As we all know, product quality mainly depends on the quality of the product development process. The same is true of software products. The quality of software mainly depends on the development process of software. As software products are "the product of human brain logic", once formed, software products have the characteristics of "invariability" and "no physical loss" without artificial changes. Therefore, the quality of software products is mainly determined by the software development process.

Organizing software development with software engineering method includes two aspects: developing software with software engineering method, that is, engineering development of software; manage software development with software engineering method, that is, engineering management of software.

People usually say that the quality of software is designed (developed) and managed. To ensure the quality of embedded software, we must pay attention to the engineering development of software on the one hand, and the engineering management of software on the other hand, both of which are indispensable.

2.2.1 Software Engineering Management

The engineering management of software is extremely important. Summing up the experience and lessons of embedded system software development at home and abroad, we can think that management is still the key to determine software quality.

Software engineering management refers to a series of organization, planning, coordination, and supervision that must be carried out for a software engineering project to determine and meet the needs. Over the years, a large number of investigations have found that management is still the key to the success of software development projects.

As early as the mid-1970s, the U.S. Department of Defense organized forces to study the reasons for the failure of software projects and found that 70% of the failed software projects were caused by poor management. Therefore, it is believed that management affected the overall situation, and set off an upsurge of research on software management technology. Twenty years later, according to three classic research reports in the United States, this situation has not changed: software development is still difficult to predict, and only about 10% of projects can deliver software that meets the needs at the predetermined cost and schedule. Management is still the main factor for the success or failure of software projects. It is pointed out that rework in the development process is a sign of immature software process.

Software engineering management has the following characteristics:

- Without proper management, software development cannot be completed well, and there is no software engineering.

- The larger and more complex the software engineering project is, the larger the proportion of management workload in the whole software development workload is.

- The basic goal of management is to meet the predetermined requirements of the engineering project at the minimum cost, and the basic task is to ensure that the software requirements are properly determined and satisfactorily realized.

The key of software engineering management is:

- Control the whole process of software development;

- Comprehensive management of software quality;

- Establish a multi-level software development and management system.

2.2.2 Software Development Methodology

As far as the current embedded system software is concerned, the engineering development of software is mainly related to the methodology of software development.

Current software development methodologies mainly include:

1. **Structured approach**

   Structured methods include structured analysis, structured design, structured programming and structured testing.

   The structured method believes that the software system exists in a certain structural form and is composed of several subsystems. The software system can be decomposed from top to bottom to low-level modules according to certain criteria.

   At present, most embedded software still adopts structured development methods.

2. **Object-oriented method**

   The object-oriented method is to construct the model and organize the software system with the object as the center. This method believes that the objective world is composed of objects, and the interaction and connection between different objects constitute different systems. The method space of using computers to solve problems should be consistent with the problem space of the objective world.

   The object in the object-oriented method is a package composed of data and its operations. Objects are instances of classes. A class is a collection of objects with the same properties and services.

3. **Clean room method**

   The clean room method is a formal method of requirement analysis and design based on the structural analysis and design method. This method believes that the software programming team should strive to develop a system that is almost error free before entering the test.

4. **Formal method**

   The formal method is based on strict mathematical proof, which requires that the specification of software requirements should be described in formal language to ensure its correctness, and then through a series of transformations until an executable program is generated. The software development based on formal methods plays a positive role in the subsequent model-based software development.

5. **Model-based software development**

With the continuous evolution of software engineering technology, model-based systems engineering (MBSE) and software engineering (MBSwE) are gradually replacing the traditional software development methods, and are increasingly valued by the software development community. The model-based development combines the physical model of the system with the embedded software to ensure the coordinated work of all components of the system. Through the unified construction of professional models and integrated collaborative simulation, the technicians of all disciplines and links can more intuitively understand and express the embedded system, and improve the consistency and automation of development.

To sum up, in embedded software development, the choice of development methodology depends on the characteristics of the software project, the available support environment and technical support, as well as the technical level and experience of developers. Since the above software development methodology has professional technical explanations in many software engineering books, this book will not repeat it.

2.3 EMBEDDED SOFTWARE QUALITY FEATURES

Several concepts related to software quality are as follows:

- Software quality: software quality is the degree to which a software product meets the user's requirements.

- Software quality management: software quality management is a coordinated activity that commands and controls the organization in terms of software quality.

- Software quality control: software quality control is the measurement and monitoring of the process of developing available software products.

According to the above definition, software quality is the degree to which a set of inherent characteristics of a software product meet the user's use requirements. To make the quality of software products meet the requirements of users, software quality management must be implemented. The author discusses process control from the perspective of software quality management. It is to discuss the quality control of software lifetime process, especially the software development process. As long as these processes are properly controlled in terms of quality, the quality of the developed software products can meet the requirements of users.

According to modern software engineering thought, the core of software quality control also lies in process control. Software quality characteristics are a set of attributes that describe and evaluate the quality of software products. According to ISO/IEC 25051:2014 software engineering systems and software quality requirements and evaluation (SQuaRE) and GB/T 25000.51-2016 systems and software engineering systems and software quality requirements and evaluation, software quality can be defined as 8 characteristics and 39 sub-characteristics.

The eight quality characteristics of software are as follows:

- Functionality: when the software is used under specified conditions, the software product meets the specified requirements and implicit requirements.

- Performance efficiency: under specified conditions, the performance level and efficiency that software products can provide are related to the resources they use.

- Compatibility: the ability of software products to exchange information with other software products.

- Usability: when used under specified conditions, it is an attribute related to the effort required by users to use the software.

- Reliability: the ability of software to realize its specified functions under specified conditions and within a specified time interval.

- Information security: the ability of software products in terms of confidentiality, integrity and resistance to external intrusion and theft.

- Maintainability: the modularity level of software products and the ability to be modified, tested, and maintained.

- Portability: the ability of software products to move from one environment to another.

See Figure 2.2 for the relationship between the above 8 features and their derived 39 sub-features.

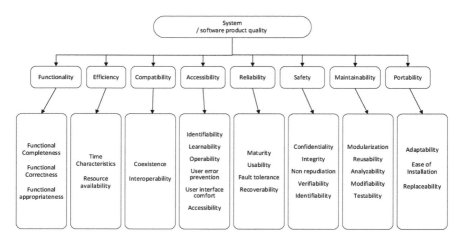

FIGURE 2.2   Quality characteristics and sub-characteristics of software.

2.4 SUMMARY

In this chapter, combined with software engineering technology, we give the development model of embedded software, describe each stage of embedded software development in detail, and describe the main work, methods and tools, stage products, completion marks and main control methods involved in each stage. In addition, combined with the current practical requirements of how to make software engineering management, the main methods and technologies of software engineering management are given. Finally, combined with the requirements of software quality control, the quality characteristics of embedded software are given.

Software engineering is an engineering methodology that guides the development and maintenance of computer software. It is a discipline that studies the construction and maintenance of effective, practical and high-quality software with engineering methods. This chapter uses limited space to introduce the embedded software engineering process and management technology, and finally gives the quality characteristics of embedded software.

CHAPTER 3

Embedded Software System Testing Techniques Based on Formal Methods

THE THEORY OF EMBEDDED software automation system testing based on formal methods is one of the most significant features of this book, which stems from the many advantages of formal methods. This chapter will start from formal testing methods, propose a real-time extended finite state machine model, and then explore embedded software system testing automation techniques based on this model.

3.1 OVERVIEW OF SOFTWARE FORMAL TESTING TECHNIQUES

3.1.1 Overview of Software Formal Testing

Formal methods originated from Dijkstra and Hoare's program verification. Formal methods have been studied for decades, but there is still no uniform definition of formal methods. The Encyclopedia of Software Engineering defines formal methods as "formal methods for developing computer systems are mathematically based techniques used to describe the properties of systems. Such formal methods provide a framework

DOI: 10.1201/9781003390923-4

TABLE 3.1   A Classification of Formal Methods

Serial Number	Classification	Method
1	Model-based approach	CTL model, Z-method VDM method, state machine model, UML
2	Algebraic-based approach	OBJ method, CLEAR method
3	Process algebra-based approach	CSP, CCS
4	Logic-based approach	temporal logic, propositional logic, higher-order logic
5	Network-based approach	Petri nets, predicate transformation nets

within which one can describe, develop, and systematically verify systems". Usually, any method that uses rigorous mathematical tools and has precise mathematical semantics can be called a formal method. One way of classifying formal methods is shown in Table 3.1.

Formal methods have been used for modeling and testing communication protocols and embedded software, and many research results have been achieved. They are also increasingly being used in safety-critical software verification. The European Space Agency and NASA highly recommend using formal methods for the development of safety-critical software. In practice, real-time embedded software is often safety-critical software. Formal methods in real-time embedded software system testing can eliminate ambiguity in testing, enhance the accuracy and consistency of testing, and improve the degree of test automation and test efficiency.

Domestic and international technology development and research show that the current research areas of software modeling and testing techniques based on formal methods are summarized in Figure 3.1.

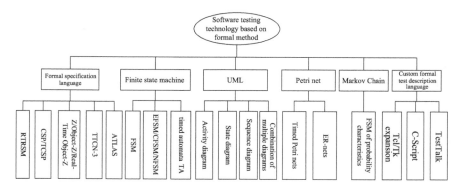

FIGURE 3.1   Software modeling and testing techniques based on formal methods.

3.1.2 Formal Statute-Based Language

The representative embedded software modeling and testing techniques based on formal specification languages are RTRSM, CSP, TCSP, Z language, TTCN-3 language, and ATLAS language. The modeling of real-time embedded software should support domain features such as event-driven, state transition description, complex dynamic interaction behavior, and strict time constraints.

Real-time Requirements Specification Model (RTRSM) is a visual modeling language aiming at the requirements specification for embedded software systems. It is based on an expanded Hierarchical Concurrent Finite State Machine (HCA) as its core, with templates that support synthesis as its basic component units. It can use transition validity and event reservation mechanisms to describe temporal constraints, with a strong ability to describe temporal conditions, which can naturally and directly support modeling of interaction behavior, executable and with good formal semantics. The RTRSM supports the decomposition of the system through templates in the form of tables, including interfaces and data definitions and formalized rule sets equivalent to state diagrams.

CSP (Communication Sequences Processes) is a formal language proposed by Hoare in 1978 to model systems with concurrent relationships. It is based on sequential communication and describes the behavior of processes mainly through the set of process events and the trajectory of processes. The relationship between processes can be described by concurrency, selection, recursion, etc. Based on the CSP, the time factor is added to form the TCSP (Timed CSP), a description language of the temporal communication sequence process. This language has an excellent formal basis, well-defined syntax-semantics, and a clear and concise representation of concurrent processes with time.

The Z language was developed by the Programming Research Group (PRG) at Oxford University in England. It is a language for writing specifications or a representation. IBM has used it to rewrite specifications for its User Information Control System (CICS) with great success, reducing software development costs by 9% and greatly influencing the Z language. Z is a formal specification language based on first-order predicate logic and set theory, with the advantages of precision, simplicity, and non-dualism. It is conducive to ensuring the correctness of programs, especially for developing high-security systems where field debugging is not possible. Another key feature is the ability to reason and prove Z specifications. It allows software developers or users to quickly identify inconsistencies in specifications and improve software development efficiency with the continuous

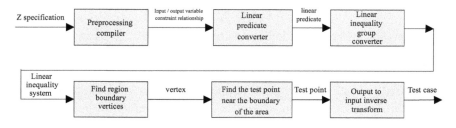

FIGURE 3.2   Automatic test case generation based on Z language.

development of technology by the emergence of some extensions of Z languages, such as Object-Z and Real-Time Object-Z. A technique for automatic generation of software test cases based on Z specification is shown in Figure 3.2. This is done by finding the linear predicates describing the input and output of the software through the analysis of the software Z specification. The above linear predicates are converted into a corresponding set of linear inequalities, and the corresponding region boundary vertices are obtained by solving the set of linear inequalities. The vertices near the region boundary are found, and the test cases are brought by inverting the input and output. In addition, there is also a method of software testing and metrics using Z specification. Still, this method requires testers with rich testing experience and a profound mathematical foundation to complete, and the efficiency of testing is relatively low because it is manual testing. Since the Z language is based on mathematical concepts and is abstract and concise, its formal specifications are too abstract and difficult to understand. At the same time, software developers and testers are used to non-formal methods and lack training in formal-based methods, and the Z language still lacks support from automation tools. The proof of correctness of formal specifications based on the Z language is time-consuming and laborious, thus limiting its engineering applications.

TTCN-3 (Testing and Test Control Notation 3) is a text-based test description language that has been improved and extended by TTCN (Tree and Tabular Combined Notation), unified the original confusing concepts and definitions simplified the representation. TTCN-3 applies to the description of various interactive systems and has been widely used in the fields of protocol testing, web service testing, and CORBA-based platform testing. The current test field exists to use a graphical representation of TTCN-3 and then convert the graph to a code description. The specific conversion rules are as follows: the graphics are represented by MSC (Message Sequence Chart), which can sufficiently express the communication behavior of the system and its cross-linked environment. TTCN-3 describes the complete test set through modules, and a module consists of a

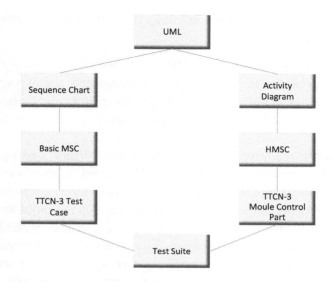

FIGURE 3.3   TTCN-3 test set building idea.

definition part and an operation part. The definition gives test components, test ports, data types, variables, constants, functions, and test cases. The control part defines some local definitions and calls test cases and controls their execution order. The basic MSC diagram can describe the test actions represented in the test cases while we can organize the test cases represented by the basic MSC at a higher level through HMSC (High-Level MSC) (Figure 3.3).

The ATLAS language is a UUT description language defined by the international test standards ABBET (Wide Area Test Environment) and SMART (Standard Modular Avionics Repair and Test). It uses a signal-oriented description of the process of interpreting the test requirements of a UUT for execution on a specific ATS.

There are two more mature versions of ATLAS, ARINCStd626 (led by ARINC and released in 1976) and IEEEStd716 (led by SCC20 (Standard Coordinating Committee 20) established by IEEE and released in 1985). With engineering applications, ATLAS gave an effective way to design ATS in a signal-oriented way and exposed many problems.

1. Too many changes in ATLAS versions and significant changes in different versions of the standard.

2. Content is nonsense and has too many keywords.

3. The long update cycle of the ATLAS language does not keep pace with changing requirements and new technological developments.

4. Expensive development tools, high training costs, and little support documentation.

5. With the continuous introduction of new technologies, the ATLAS system has become large and cluttered, with problems such as vague signal definitions, indistinguishable properties of similar signals, repeated definitions of the same term, and repetitive keyword definitions.

The problems mentioned above limited the further development of ATLAS. Recognizing this problem, SCC20 started to apply various new software technologies to the upgraded version of ATLAS to transform ATLAS, so ATLAS2000 was proposed. ATLAS2000 is a multi-level structured language whose foundation consists of a kernel and a proto-language for creating test application requirements. The modular structure of the ATLAS2000 language system enables the encapsulation of reusable test units. Such a structure allows the user to develop and describe complex test requirements based on the underlying units.

3.1.3 Based on Finite State Machine and Time Automation Models

A state machine is a formal method for describing the state and state transitions of a system. Usually, a state machine consists of states, transitions, events, activities, actions, etc. The behavior of an object can be precisely described using a state machine. The use of state machines is widespread in computer science, especially in the modeling and verification of communication protocols and embedded software.

Since real-time embedded software is state-based, the finite state machine (FSM) model describes the system's behavior in terms of trigger events and state transition. It is suitable for the formal description of the development and testing of real-time embedded software in general. In addition, numerous extension methods based on FSMs have emerged to enhance the description capability of FSMs, simplify the description, make the changes between states clear, and finally improve the description and analysis of local and even the whole model such as CFSM (Communicating FSM), EFSM (Extended FSM), CEFSM (Communicating EFSM), PFSM (Probability FSM), and so on. In addition, Timed Automata (TA), which is developed based on FSM, has also achieved more research results.

The finite state machine-based testing model assumes that the software is always in a certain state at a given moment. The current state determines the possible inputs to the software, and the current inputs determine the transition from that state to other states. The FSM model is particularly suitable for test methods expressing test data as a sequence of inputs and automatically generating test sequences using graph traversal algorithms.

FSMs can be represented as state transition diagrams or transition matrices, and test cases can be generated based on state coverage or transition coverage. FSM models have a mature theoretical foundation, can be designed, manipulated, and analyzed using formal languages and automata theory, and are suitable for describing reactive systems. Early classical software testing methods based on FSM include T method, U method, D method, and W method. With the continuous development of FSM technology, test methods based on extended FSMs gradually emerged, such as the EFSM-based test input data automatic selection method. It automatically selects the test data required for test input through interval reduction and segmented gradient optimal descent algorithms. As a result, it can replace the manual selection of test data work, improves test efficiency, and significantly reduces the cost of the software testing process. The extended finite state machine (EFSM) can portray the behavior of software systems more accurately than the FSM. Due to preconditions for transition in the EFSM, if we simply use the FSM-based testing method for the EFSM, the process will create many problems, such as the test sequence is not executable, uncertain, and other problems.

The Timed Automata (TA) is obtained by adding a clock constraint to the transition and an invariant constraint to the state based on the traditional FSM. The clock constraint added to the transition means that the transition is activated only when this constraint is satisfied, whereas the invariant constraint added to the state means that the system can stay in this state only when this invariant is satisfied. A real-time system testing method based on the extension of time automata is that the system model described by time-safe input/output automata is converted into a stable symbolic state transition graph without abstract time-delayed transition. Then a testing method based on the marked transition system is used to statically generate a sequence of transition actions that satisfy various structural coverage criteria. Finally, a procedure for constructing and executing test cases based on the transition action sequences is given, introducing a time-delay variable objective function and using a linear constraint solver to dynamically solve for the time-delay variables in the transition action sequences.

3.1.4 Based on the UML

The Unified Modeling Language (UML) is a general-purpose graphical modeling language for object-oriented development, which is widely used in software engineering and is gradually becoming an industry standard. UML supports the modeling of large, complex systems by capturing information about the system's static structure and dynamic behavior and is particularly suitable for real-time embedded systems. Many studies have combined formal semantics and graphical methods to obtain easy-to-use modeling methods with formal features using relevant elements of UML.

In the UML model-based testing of real-time embedded software systems, the use of UML for modeling real-time embedded systems mainly uses use case diagrams, state diagrams, activity diagrams, sequence diagrams, etc. Among them, state diagrams, activity diagrams, sequence diagrams, etc. can be used to describe the behavior of real-time embedded systems, and methods of modeling and testing using a variety of UML diagrams have emerged.

1. **UML state diagram-based testing method**

    UML statecharts EFSMs. It emphasizes modeling complex real-time systems, provides a framework for hierarchical statecharts, i.e., a single state can be decomposed into many lower-level states, and describe concurrency mechanisms. Therefore, it is increasingly used in the field of real-time embedded software testing. A representative UML state diagram-based automation tool, DAS-BOOTo, can automatically generate test stub modules and test scripts based on test guidelines. The system first exports the state diagram to an XML file from a UML model editing tool using the XMI tool. It then reads the state diagram model from the XML to generate the corresponding test case scripts and test stake modules. Still, the approach does not consider complex state model diagrams such as the hierarchical structure of the state diagram and concurrent states. In addition, combining formal methods to generate test cases using state diagrams has also been studied, such as Z language and Petri nets. In addition, there is also research on generating test cases for UML state diagrams containing concurrency. The core is to flatten state diagrams' hierarchical and concurrent structure and then generate test cases according to control flow and data flow, respectively. This approach provides a valuable idea for combining UML state diagram-based and EFSM testing methods.

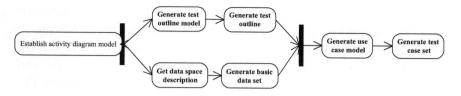

FIGURE 3.4   Test case generation process based on test outline.

2. **UML activity diagram-based testing method**

UML activity diagram is essentially an automaton that describes the sequence of activities that a system must perform to accomplish a specified function or task. As for complex real-time embedded software systems, various complex operational processes are undoubtedly crucial for testing. Therefore, activity diagrams become essential for real-time embedded software functional testing, especially for operational process-oriented testing. Figure 3.4 presents a test case generation technique through a UML activity diagram, which proposes a test outline concept. A test outline is composed of a collection of all test scenarios designed according to certain test criteria. A basic data set is generated after obtaining the input data space of various interaction operations with certain test criteria. Then a test case model is then constructed based on the test outline and the basic data set. The final set of test cases is designed and generated based on a certain optimization combination strategy.

In addition, there are also testing methods based on UML use case diagrams, sequential diagrams, and those based on a combination of multiple UML diagrams, which are not repeated here.

3.1.5 Based on the Petri Net Model

The Petri net model can better describe concurrent systems, representing the control flow with a set of states and transitions with tokens. Petri net is a mathematical and graphical tool for describing and analyzing systems. For information processing systems with concurrent, asynchronous, distributed, parallel, uncertainty, or randomness, it can be easily analyzed using this method to obtain information about the system structure and dynamic behavior and has been widely used in simulation modeling and testing of complex systems.

Petri net variants for real-time system modeling include timed Petri nets (TPNs) and ER nets. In these variants, location, token, transition, etc. can be associated with time constraints. TPN improves Petri nets by introducing the relative time factor of transition implementation in the variants, enabling them to be applied to the analysis of real-time systems. TPN can be analyzed for both system behavior and temporal attributes, where reachability and schedulability can be used as both system performance references. It is more effective to analyze the performance of complex systems with real-time concurrency. Typical representatives of timed Petri nets include Merlin's timed Petri nets, Coolahan's time-delay Petri nets, and advanced random Petri nets by Lin Chuang, a domestic scholar. The Merlin's timed Petri nets are most commonly used.

The testing method based on the Petri net model can describe the system behavior in a highly abstract way, shielding the system hardware implementation details, and is mainly used to verify the correctness, safety, and reliability of the system design. However, the problem with use case generation based on this model is that it can only generate the temporal information of event sequences but not the actual test input data (e.g., quantitative temporal information data).

3.1.6 Based on the Markov Chain Model

Markov chain model is a statistical model based on statistical theory, which can describe the use of software and has been widely used in modeling complex systems and statistical testing of software. Markov chain is a kind of FSM with probabilistic transition characteristics, which can automatically generate test cases according to the transition probability between states and analyze the test results.

The Markov chain model is mainly applicable to statistical testing. Many kinds of software, the average expected time of state and transition coverage can be obtained through simulation to measure the performance index and reliability index of software. Thus, facilitating the planning of testing time and cost for large-scale software systems in the early stage of development. A team in China uses controlled Markov chain theory to design and optimize software testing strategies. They proposed software testing cybernetic ideas, discussed adaptive software systems within the framework of the controlled Markov chain method, and compared it with random testing. They found that the adaptive testing method has greater superiority compared with the traditional random testing method.

3.1.7 Based on a Custom Formal Test Description Language

In addition to the research mentioned above on existing formal methods, numerous research results have been achieved in researching self-defined languages at home and abroad. Since the introduction of scripting technology is an essential support for test automation, most of these formal methods based on self-defined languages are dedicated scripting languages for specific test systems or tools. The typical test scripting techniques are summarized in Table 3.2.

The U.S. Jet Propulsion Laboratory uses extended Tcl/Tk as the test script language, through which most of the functions within the entire vehicle lifetime can be simulated. The test scripts are loaded through the upper graphical development environment, downloaded to the network nodes (subsystems). Each test script completes the simulation test of the corresponding functions on its respective node through the script interpreter. However, this environment has poor real-time performance, cannot control the time characteristics, can only perform functional simulation, and is a distributed system, a semi-automatic test environment. China's Huazhong University of Science and Technology has developed a simple network protocol design and test platform (SNPDTP) for the Internet. They have developed its test scripting language (C-Script), which uses a simplified C syntax and modifies some features, such as adding a time-driven mechanism and support for the description of network protocols. Since the system is developed for network protocol design and testing, it does not consider the real-time features and test feedback processing needed for embedded software and only simulates the implementation of

TABLE 3.2 Summary of Common Test Scripting Techniques

Script Type	Structured or Not	Script Intelligence	Script	Test Case Definition	Processing
Linear Script	Not	Constants	None	Script	Descriptive
Structured Scripts	Yes	Constants	if/loop statements	Script	Descriptive
Shared Scripts	Not or Yes	Constants and Variables	if/loop statements	Script	Descriptive
Data-Driven Scripts	Yes	Variables	if/loop statements Data Reading	Scripts and Data	Descriptive
Keyword Script	Yes	Variables and keywords	if/loop statements Data Reading Keyword explanation	Data	Descriptive

the network environment in a software way. Still, some of its design ideas can be learned. The language uses a separation of the components of the test description. It forms a test script in a programming language, which is then interpreted and executed by an interpreter to drive the test.

However, this method is only able to test for non-real-time software. It does not introduce the requirements for describing temporal characteristics (such as concurrency, synchronization, and priority) in real-time software testing, which is difficult for users to grasp quickly. Hence, the method is not suitable for the description of real-time embedded software testing.

3.2 EMBEDDED SOFTWARE FORMAL TESTING TECHNIQUES

3.2.1 Basic Concept

1. **State Machine**

    State machines are a formal method for describing system states and state transitions, a theoretical basis for computer science, and a powerful modeling approach. The use of state machines is widespread in computer science, especially in modeling and verification of communication protocols and real-time embedded software.

    In general, the behavior of a system can be categorized into three types.

    1. Simple behavior: The system always responds in the same way, independent of the system history for a given input.

    2. Continuous behavior: the system's current state is history-dependent and cannot identify a single state.

    3. State-based behavior: the current state of the system is history-dependent and can be clearly distinguished from other system states.

        Since real-time embedded software is mostly state-based and the FSM model describes the system's behavior in terms of triggering events and state transition, it is suitable for the formal description of the development and testing of real-time embedded software in general.

A traditional state machine is a diagram showing states and state transitions. A state machine consists of five parts: states, transitions, events, activities, and actions.

1. State: represents the condition of a model during its lifetime, such as satisfying certain conditions, performing certain operations, or waiting for certain events. The lifetime of a state is a finite period.

2. Transition: represents the link between two states, and events can trigger transitions between states.

3. Events: generated at a specific time, which can trigger state transitions, such as signals, creation and destruction of objects, timeouts, and changes in conditions.

4. Activity: a non-atomic execution performed in a state machine, consisting of a series of actions.

5. Action: An executable atomic computation that changes state or returns a value.

The behavior of an object can be precisely described using state machines: from the initial state of the object, it starts responding to events and executing some actions, these events cause state transitions, the object starts responding to states and executing actions again in the new state and so on until the end. In computer science, the use of state machines is widespread: in compilation technology, FSMs are usually used to describe the lexical analysis process; in the process scheduling of the operating system, the transformation relationship between various states of the process is usually described by state machines; in object-oriented analysis and design, the state of the object, the transition of the state, the event that triggers the state transition, and the object's response to the event can be described by state machines.

2. Finite State Machine

An FSM is a type of state machine, and a FSM model is a formal model. A FSM can be represented as a six-tuple $(S, S_0, \delta, \lambda, I, O)$.

S: the set of finite states.

S_0: the initial state of all states.

δ: state transition function.

λ: output function.

I: limited input character set.

O: Limited output character set.

According to the nature of FSM, it can be divided explicitly as follows.

- Complete FSM: for an FSM, if for each state and input, δ and λ are defined, then it is said to be a complete FSM; otherwise, it is called an incomplete FSM.

- Reset capacity FSM: for a FSM, an FSM has a reset function if there exists an input that, for any state, causes the FSM to transition to the initial state.

- Initially connected FSM: an FSM is said to be initially connected if it can reach every state from the initial state.

- Strongly connected FSM: An FSM is said to be strongly connected if for each pair of states (S_i, S_j) in the FSM, there exists a sequence of inputs that allows a transition from state S_i to state S_j.

    FSMs can be classified according to whether or not they use input signals.

    - Mealy machine: its output signal is related to the current state and all input signals, i.e., the output of a mealy-type FSM can be viewed as a function of the current state and all input signals.

    - Moore machine: its output signal is related to the current state only, i.e., the output of a Moore-type finite state can be regarded as a function of the current state.

        - FSMs can be divided according to whether the transition state and output are determined.

    - DFSM: for a given input and all states, the transition state and output are determined.

    - NFSM: for specific outputs and already existing states, the transition states and outputs are indeterminate.

There are three main representations of FSMs: graphical, tabular, and matrix methods, among which the graphical method is more commonly used.

The advantages of FSMs are that they are relatively simple, predictable, easy to implement, and easy to test. Disadvantages of FSMs: (1) When dealing with complex problems, there is a possibility of state space explosion; (2) In multi-FSM systems, the state of the system is the Cartesian product of all FSM states, and the number of states of the system has the problem of state combination complexity, and deadlock can occur; (3) FSMs can better describe the transition characteristics between states, but FSM cannot well describe the transformation between input and output characteristics (i.e., transformation characteristics of data); and (4) FSM only reflects the relationship between protocol events and protocol states and cannot express other protocol elements: protocol variables, protocol behaviors, predicates, etc.

3. Extended Finite State Machine

The main purpose of EFSMs is to enhance the description capability of FSMs, simplify the description, make the changes between states clear, and eventually improve the description and analysis capability of local and even the whole model. It can be used as a tool for later developers to describe and solve. There are four common types of EFSM models: NFSM (Non-deterministic FSM), CFSM (Communicating FSM), EFSM (Extended FSM), CEFSM (Communicating EFSM), and PFSM (Probability FSM), and the evolution of their model extensions is shown in Figure 3.5.

Among them, EFSM is a relatively more commonly used one in software testing. An EFSM is a six-tuple $<S, S_0, I, O, T, V>$.

S: the set of non-empty finite states.

S_0: the initial state of all states.

I: a non-empty set of input messages.

O: a non-empty set of output messages.

T: a non-empty state transition set with $t \in T$, and $t = \langle \text{Head}(t), I(t), P(t), \text{operation}/O(t), \text{Tail}(t) \rangle$, where $\text{Head}(t)$ is the departure state of transition t; $I(t)$ is the input message of EFSM contained in the input set I or is empty; $P(t)$ is the

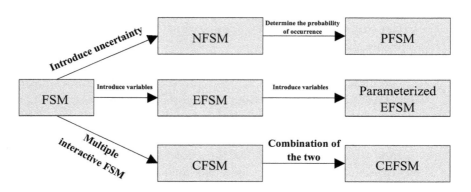

FIGURE 3.5   Several common FSM extension models.

precondition for the execution of transition t, which can be empty; operation is the operation performed during state transition, which generally consists of a series of variable assignment statements or output statements; $O(t)$ is the output of the message contained in the output set O, which can be empty; Tail(t) is the arrival state of transition t.

V: the set of variables, which can be expressed as $V = <\text{IV, CV, OV}>$, where IV represents the set of input variables, which the tester can control; OV represents the set of output variables; CV represents the set of environment variables, which can be local or global variables, and variables that are neither input nor output variables can be classified as environment variables. The tester does not control CV and OV, and their values are determined by the values are determined by the operation of state transition.

As seen from the definition of EFSM, it adds variables, operations, preconditions for transition, etc. to the FSM model. EFSM has a storage function, and it has a default reset (Reset) function for each state, i.e., $\delta(S_i, r) = S_0$. With the EFSM model, the behavior of software systems can be described more precisely, so it can be widely used in object-oriented software systems for the behavior of objects and the interaction between objects. EFSM overcomes the last two of the disadvantages mentioned above of FSM better. Still, the problems of consistency, reachability, and synchronization have not been solved, and it introduces a new problem – the uncertainty problem.

3.2.2 FSM-Based Software Testing Techniques

In 1956, Moore established a framework for finite state testing, defined the concepts of distinguishing and homing experiments, and gave algorithms for determining state equivalence and constructing homing sequences, one of the earliest pieces of literatures introducing FSM testing.

There are four classical testing methods based on FSMs: the T method, U method, D method, and W method.

> T method: A FSM is assumed to be strongly connected. The test input sequence corresponds to the state transitions in the statute description and is generated randomly until all state transitions are covered. T method is simpler and has the disadvantage of a large amount of redundancy in the test input sequence, and there may even be loops. It also has a poor error detection capability, as it can only detect the presence of a transition but not the states reached by the transition.

> U method: The premise of the U method is to assume a minimal, strongly connected, and complete FSM. The method requires an identification sequence for each state in the FSM, called a unique input/output sequence (UIO). The UIO sequence uniquely identifies the states in the FSM, and different states cannot have the same UIO sequence. However, not all FSMs have UIO sequences, and if a FSM does not have a UIO sequence, the method cannot be applied to construct a test input sequence. For each change between states in a FSM, a test subsequence for each transition can be generated by (1) inputting r (reset, which is available for each FSM discussed here) to the FSM to return the FSM to its initial state; (2) finding the shortest path $SP(S_i)$ from the initial state to state S_i; (3) inputting a symbol that can cause the FSM to migrate from state S_i to S_j; and (4) input the UIO sequence for state S_j.

> D method: The premise of method D is to assume a minimal, strongly connected, and complete FSM. The method first constructs a distinguishing sequence (DS) for the FSM and then constructs a test input sequence based on the distinguishing sequence. As with the U method, not all state machines have a distinguishing sequence, so the application of this method is somewhat limited.

> W method: The premise of the W method is to assume a minimal, strongly connected, and complete FSM. The method requires first

generating a feature set W of the FSM and then constructing a test input sequence based on the feature set W. The feature set exists as long as the state machine is minimal and complete, so the method is more applicable.

The feature set W is composed of a set of data such that for each state in a FSM, the input $\alpha_1, \ldots, \alpha_k$ in W, the last bit output is different, i.e., $M|S_i(\alpha_1, \ldots, \alpha_k) \neq M|S_j(\alpha_1, \ldots, \alpha_k)$ (M is the FSM), where S_i and S_j are two different states in the FSM.

The principle of applying the W method test is similar to that of the U method, and the feature set W serves to identify each state in the FSM. For the FSM, the test sequence can be generated according to the following steps: (1) construct the feature set W of the FSM, where is an input character; (2) generate the β sequence according to the steps in the U method, with the difference that the UIO sequence of each state should be replaced by the feature set W.

3.2.3 EFSM-Based Software Testing Techniques

1. **Test method based on extended UIO sequences**

    The most commonly used FSM-based test sequence generation method is the UIO method. UIO sequences exist in most state machines, and UIO sequences are a subset of D sequences or W sequences, and their lengths are shorter than the sequence lengths obtained by D and W methods. The direct use of the UIO method for EFSM models generates the unenforceability of test sequences because the precondition of state transition is not considered.

    Chun W, Amer P D. et al. were the first to introduce UIO sequences into the EFSM model, but no definition of executable UIO sequences and generation methods were given. For example, the Context Independent Unique Sequence (CIUS) used in the EFSM-based test sequence generation method proposed by a team considers the executability of the test sequence only during the test sequence generation, and CIUS is used as a state discriminating sequence. CIUS is also a UIO sequence. However, not every EFSM has CIUS, so the applicability of this method is limited.

    Ramalingam, Thulasiraman et al. proposed a method based on transition executability analysis (TEA) called UIO_E (Executable Unique Input Output). Using TEA, a TEA tree is generated using a breadth-first strategy with state configurations as the nodes and executable transitions as the arcs, which is extended to generate an executable sequence of transition tests. This approach addresses the executability of conversions and uses the overlap of unconverted conversions between conversion subsequences to minimize the test sequence. The UIOE method first converts the EFSM to a normalized EFSM, configures the initial state, selects an executable transition to be tested with the current state as the header, and performs a TEA extension to obtain the corresponding UIO_E sequence. By performing TEA expansion, we generate a TEA tree by analyzing the executability of the transformations in the EFSM. Then, according to the principle of "each conversion in EFSM is tested once", the TEA expansion is performed on the other conversions to be tested to generate the corresponding UIO_E sequences until all the conversions are tested. The final test sequence is formed by connecting all the test events. If an EFSM is strongly concatenated and trap-free, then the UIO_E method always yields an executable test sequence.

The limitation of the UIO_E method is the simplification of the EFSM, where only environmental variables (i.e., some internal variables) exist in the model, and the initial values of these variables are constants, so that executability analysis can be performed with symbolic execution, without taking into account the input variables present in each state transition.

2. **Convert EFSM to the corresponding FSM**

To make better use of the existing FSM-based testing methods, some researchers have tried to transform EFSM into its equivalent FSM and then generate executable test sequences using the existing FSM test sequence generation methods. But this transformation is not simple. First, state transition behavior is interrelated with variables; second, state transition interacts with each other through operations on transition and variables. This approach tends to lead to "state explosion".

Duale and Uyar have given a method for EFSM with certain restrictions to automatically generate executable test sequences, pointing out that the difficulty in automatic generation of test sequences based on EFSM stems from the fact that the EFSM model contains unreachable paths, causing unreachable paths due to the presence of so-called contextual variables. The interdependence between variables creates behavioral and conditional conflicts that make certain paths unreachable.

When all conflicts of the EFSM model are eliminated, the existing FSM-based automatic test generation method can be directly utilized. This method generates only reachable paths. However, the method imposes certain restrictions on the EFSM model, such as specifying that the specification consists of a single process and that there are no pointers, recursive functions, or infinite loops. All conditions and behaviors are linear, which also limits the use of the method.

3. **Generate EFSM test sequences based on standards**

EFSM dataflow testing is usually based on a directed dataflow graph. In practice, a criterion is selected that contains the dataflow characteristics of EFSM. The criterion defines the paths to be traversed, which are only a subset of all possible paths in the graph. The selection of EFSM data flow test coverage criteria is a trade-off process: the stronger the criterion chosen, the more thorough the inspection of the IUT (implementation under test), and the weaker the criterion chosen, the smaller the number of test cases required and the relatively lower the testing cost.

The purpose of EFSM's dataflow testing is to discover and test data dependencies between EFSM's state transitions, usually by examining the association between variable definitions and usage. Ural H defines the dataflow coverage standards All-use standard and IO-df-chain standard. The All-use standard requires that each variable be tracked from its definition to its usage association and requires that the variable cannot be redefined during the tracking of the variable. Suppose variable X is defined at node J and variable X is used at node K. To track the association between variable definition and use, a define-clear-use path is constructed, which is the path connecting node J to node K and node J is the only node in the path that defines variable X. If such a define-clear-use path exists, then the association of variable X with nodes J and K are called a define-use pair, also called a du-pair, denoted as du (X, J, K). A test sequence that can cover the define-clear-use path or du-pair of each variable at least once meets the All-use criterion. The Io-df-chain criterion is defined similarly to the All-use criterion. The difference is that the io-df-chain criterion tracks the association between each output and all inputs that affect those outputs.

The control part of EFSM involves state transitions. In practical EFSM-based control flow testing, the test sequence is usually required to cover each state transition in the EFSM at least once. Chen et al. used the coverage criterion as the basis for test sequence generation. This method converts the EFSM into a directed data flow graph, labels the definition and use of variables on the flow graph, defines and selects the data flow test coverage criterion, and selects the test sequence and test data to meet this criterion. Based on this, the test cases are extended to meet the control flow test coverage criteria.

4. **Generate EFSM test sequences based on flow analysis**

Combining the advantages of FSM and EFSM, the control flow part uses the FSM test sequence generation method, and the data flow part uses the EFSM data flow test method, which is also a class of EFSM test sequence generation method that takes into account the comprehensive testing of data flow and control flow.

Sarikaya, Bochmann G et al. applied the functional program testing method to data flow testing of EFSM. The method uses the Data Flow Graph (DFG) to simulate the information flow in the ESTELLE specification and uses decomposition and functional partitioning to obtain the functional modules of the specification's data flow and then tests these modules. This method does not consider the executability of the test sequence, and the resulting test sequence may not be executable. Miller R, Paul S. first transformed the EFSM into an equivalent FSM with modified inputs and outputs, without changing the number of states but increasing state transitions. Then a data flow graph is constructed from this FSM and combined with the control flow graph (CFG) of the FSM to generate a test sequence that tests both control flow and data flow and covers all defined-observation paths. This approach generates executable test sequences, but assumptions about IUT, such as the variables used in IUT are accessible by the tester, are not satisfied in many cases. Chanson S T, Zhu Jinsong proposed the Unified Test Sequences (UTS) method. The method involves four algorithms:

- Algorithm 1 generates test subsequences based on FSM for the control part of the EFSM model, which has the same fault detection capability as the feature sequence.

- Algorithm 2 analyzes the data part of the EFSM model using data flow analysis techniques to obtain the dependencies between EFSM state transitions, denoted as Transition Dependence Graph (TDG), which gives the control and data dependencies between transitions, the du-pair and def-clear paths of all variables, and by merging The TDG graph gives the control and data dependencies between transitions, the du-pair and def-clear paths for all variables, and by merging the concatenated paths, a path through the data stream and containing all I/O dependencies is generated.

- Algorithm 3 merges the first two algorithms to produce a subsequence covering all du-paths and all transformations.

- Algorithm 4 performs an executability check on the subsequence to obtain the final EFSM test sequence. The executability check is done by the Constraint Satisfaction Problem method and conversion loop analysis. This method simplifies the EFSM, and the test sequence executability check is performed after the test sequence is generated.

    Huang C M et al. proposed a test sequence generation method for executable data streams and control streams based on the EFSM model. In the data flow part, probes and tests contain transition paths for variable definition use and output use. An executable test sequence consists of three parts: (1) Executable Switching Sequence (ECSS); (2) Executable DO path (EDO path) or Executable Control Path (EC path), where EDO and EC paths are obtained by extending the TEA tree with the ECSS tail state as the root node; and (3) Executable fallback path (EBP path) is obtained by extending the TEA tree with the EDO sequence tail state as the root node. The DO path is defined as a definition-output path, ECSS is the test prefix, and EBP is the test suffix. All test sequences are executable in this method, but the method is based on EFSM analysis of reachability, so there is a state explosion problem. In addition, the method has to initialize the input parameters to obtain executable test sequences, which makes the resulting test sequences vary depending on the values of the input parameters.

3.2.4 Real-Time Extended Finite State Machine Model RT-EFSM

1. **RT-EFSM Characterization**

Real-time embedded systems often exhibit state-based behavior in whole or in part, so state-based modeling techniques can be used when designing these systems. The modeling process above can lay the foundation for further test design (test sequence and case generation). State-based software testing techniques can fully verify the relationship between events, actions, behaviors, states, and state transitions and using this technique. It is possible to determine whether the state-based system behavior meets the system requirements. The most common, intuitive, and effective approach to modeling the behavior of state-based real-time embedded systems is to use techniques based on FSMs.

From the current technical development, the traditional FSM and EFSM-based testing methods cannot solve the temporal description of state transition in real-time embedded software. They cannot well describe the real-time embedded software real-time, concurrent, cross-linked devices, and I/O interface complexity.

Given the obvious deficiencies of the traditional EFSM in describing the complexity and real-time nature of real-time embedded software, it cannot meet the modeling requirements of real-time embedded software. This book argues that the RT-EFSM must address the following issues (as shown in Table 3.3).

2. **RT-EFSM Definition**

Based on the above analysis, this book adopts the real-time EFSM as the basis of real-time embedded software formal system testing, based on the original EFSM six-tuple (Section 3.2.1), and extends it into an eight-tuple.

TABLE 3.3   Issues that RT-EFSM Should Address

Description	Description
Ability to completely and accurately describe the behavior of real-time embedded software.	Ability to describe complex state transition relationships in real-time embedded software.
Be able to describe the real-time, concurrent characteristics of real-time embedded software.	Ability to provide model validation methods to ensure the correctness of the model.
Be able to describe the temporal characteristics in real-time embedded software state transition.	Provide assurance for subsequent test sequences and automatic test case generation.

Definition 2-1

Real-time EFSM, which can be described as

RT-EFSM=<S^*, S_0, I, O, T, V, E, L>, where

- S^*: the set of non-empty finite states and for $s \in S^*$, we have s=(entry, exit, iact, itran, itevt, It), which
  - 'entry' indicates the entry of state, preceding any internal actions and transitions.
  - 'exit' indicates the exit of the state, after all internal actions and transitions.
  - 'iact' indicates the internal action of the state.
  - 'itran' indicates the internal transition of states, which does not cause state entry and exit actions to occur.
  - 'itevt' indicates the set of time-related events within the state.
  - 'It' indicates the local clock inside the state.
- S_0: the initial state of all states.
- I: the set of input events.
- O: the set of output events.
- T: the set of non-empty state transitions with T=< Head(t), $I(t)$, $C(t)$, act, $O(t)$, Tail(t) >, where
  - Head(t) is the departure state of transition t.
  - $I(t)$ is the input event contained in the input event set I or is empty.
  - $C(t)$ is a precondition for the execution of transition t. It contains variable constraints and time constraints and can be empty. $C(t)=[V_C, T_C]$ where V_C denotes the variable constraint, T_C denotes the transition time constraint, and $T_C = \langle t_S, t_F, t_I \rangle$ means that the transition time is a t_S fixed value and the transition t_F time obeys some distribution function, and t_I denotes that the transition time is some time interval.
  - act is the operation performed during state transition.
  - $O(t)$ is the output event contained in the output event set O or is empty.
  - Tail(t) is the arrival state of transition t.
- V: the set of variables and $V = \langle \text{IV,CV,OV} \rangle$, where IV represents the set of input variables, OV represents the set of output variables, and CV represents the set of environment variables. Variables that are neither input nor output variables can be classified as environment variables and can be null. The tester can control IV, CV and OV are

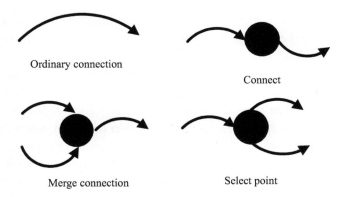

FIGURE 3.6   Extended directed edges of RT-EFSM.

not controlled by the tester, and their values are determined by state transition operation. IV and OV can contain both general variables and temporal variables.

- *E*: the set of non-empty connected directed edges, which is an extension of the ordinary connections between states in the original EFSM, i.e., with the addition of choice points, connections, and merged connections, which can better describe the dynamic behavior of the system, as shown in Figure 3.6.
- *L*: represents the global clock, used to record the time information of system state transition.

Additional notes to the RT-EFSM definition.

- The precondition $C(t)$ *of* transition execution in transition T *is* decomposed into variable constraints and time constraints, which can describe the state transition constraints more effectively; in addition, the time constraint group $T_C = \langle t_S, t_F, t_I \rangle$ of $C(t)$, in three cases, describes the time constraints used to migrate from one state to another, i.e., fixed time, obeying the function distribution or time interval, which can describe the state transition more effectively temporal properties illustrated below.

  - Fixed time means that the time used to perform this transition is the same and is a fixed value, e.g., 50 clock cycles.

  - Obey the function distribution interval means that although each transition time is not the same, but presents a certain law, that is, obey a certain function distribution, common uniform distribution, exponential distribution, etc.

- • The interval time refers to a state transition time for a certain range, i.e., $[t_1, t_2]$, an open interval, a closed interval, or a half-open, half-closed interval.
- *E* is for the complex state transition relationship of real-time embedded software. This book extends the ordinary connection of the original EFSM state transition by adding selection points, connections, and merge connections. A selection point is a connection that executes its list of actions before moving on to the next transition segment. This allows actions to be bound to the first transition segment to be executed before subsequent guardian expression assignments; a join is one in which a number of highest points are used to connect multiple transitions or split a transition into a set of consecutive transition segments. Regardless of the number of connected transition segments, they are executed in a run-to-complete step; a merge connection is also a connection in which multiple incoming transitions can be combined to create an entry or state transition, especially applicable when multiple transitions triggered by different events share an action list and/or guardianship, or arrive together at the same target state. The extension to connection edges makes RT-EFSM more suitable for modeling real-time embedded systems, reducing the number of test cases and increasing test efficiency when automatically generating test cases.
- *L* represents the global clock, which is used to record the time experienced by each system's state from the beginning to the end. Since there is a local clock for each state in the RT-EFSM model, the local clock of each state can be obtained through the corresponding calculation rules for the global clock value of the corresponding dynamic behavior, which can ensure the controllability of the system transition time and meet the real-time embedded system real-time requirements.

The above analysis shows that the RT-EFSM real-time extension solution can effectively solve all the problems that must be solved for real-time embedded software verification, as presented in Table 3.3

3. **RT-EFSM model for UAV flight control system software**

The following is an example of the simplified UAV flight control system (FCS) software state transition to complete the RT-EFSM modeling of this system software.

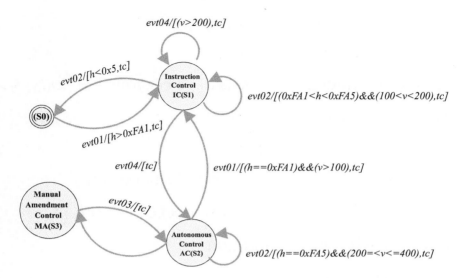

FIGURE 3.7   UAV flight control system software RT-EFSM model.

As a typical avionics real-time embedded software, the UAV flight control software FCS is one of the most important parts of the UAV flight control system. The quality and reliability of the flight control software directly affects the safety and performance of the flight control software the UAV operation. After analyzing the FCS software documentation, Figure 3.7 gives the simplified FCS software state schematic. The FCS software state mainly has the power-on initialization state, Instruction Control (IC), Manual Amendment (MA), Autonomous Control (AC), and other core functions.

Let the initial power-up state be S_0, the IC state be S_1, the MA state be S_2, and the MA state be S_3, and each state transition event be "send state command" (denoted as evt01), "automatic return" (denoted as evt02), "correction return" (evt03), and "automatically enter autonomous control" (evt04), assuming that the global constraint variables are altitude h and velocity v (changes in altitude and velocity values can trigger state transition), and the transition time constraint between each state is t_c ($t_c < 5$ ms), and the transition between states can be described as follows: $T = \{t_{01}, t_{10}, t_{111}, t_{112}, t_{12}, t_{21}, t_{23}, t_{32},\}$ and

$t_{01} = < S_0, \text{evt01}, [h > 0xFA1, t_c], \text{act}_{01}, O(t_{01}), S_1 >$

$t_{10} = < S_1, \text{evt02}, [H > 0x5, t_c], \text{act}_{10}, O(t_{10}), S_0 >$

$t_{111} = < S_1, \text{evt02}, \left[(0xFA1 < h < 0xFA5) \& \& (100 < v < 200) t_c \right], \text{act}_{11}, O(t_{11}), S_1 >$

$t_{112} = < S_1, \text{evt04}, \left[(v > 200), t_c \right], \text{act}_{11}, O(t_{11}), S_1 >$

$t_{12} = < S_1, \text{evt04}, [t_c], \text{act}_{12}, O(t_{12}), S_2 >$

$t_{21} = < S_2, \text{evt01}, \left[(h == 0xFA1) \& \& (v > 100), t_c \right], \text{act}_{21}, O(t_{21}), S_1 >$

$t_{22} = < S_2, \text{evt02}, \left[(h == 0xFA5) \& \& (200 \leq v \leq 400), t_c \right], \text{act}_{22}, O(t_{22}), S_2 >$

$t_{23} = < S_2, \text{evt01}, \left[(h > 0xFA5) t_c \right], \text{act}_{23}, O(t_{23}), S_3 >$

$t_{32} = < S_3, \text{evt03}, [t_c], \text{act}_{32}, O(t_{32}), S_2 >$

Let M be the RT-EFSM model of the FCS, and then we have:

$$S^* = \{S_0, S_1, S_2, S_3\}$$

$$I = \{\text{evt01}, \text{evt02}, \text{evt03}, \text{evt04}\}$$

$$T = \{t_{01}, t_{10}, t_{111}, t_{112}, t_{12}, t_{21}, t_{23}, t_{32}\}$$

$$V = \{x, t_c\}$$

4. RT-EFSM model validation algorithm

To ensure the correctness of the RT-EFSM model, the RT-EFSM model needs to be validated to verify the consistency, determinism, and reachability of the constructed model, where static deterministic validation ensures that the generated RT-EFSM is minimal, dynamic deterministic validation ensures that the RT-EFSM is complete. Reachability validation ensures that the RT-EFSM is strongly connected.

The RT-EFSM model verification algorithm is described below with the RT-EFSM model of a UAV flight control system software.

1. Reachability Verification

The unreachable state means that the RT-EFSM starts from the initial state, and no sequence of events can migrate the system state to a particular target state. The reachability of the RT-EFSM

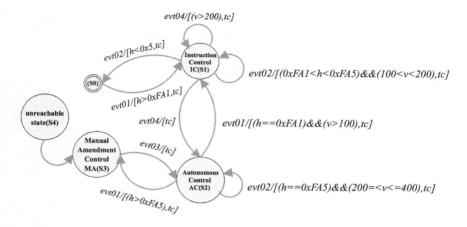

FIGURE 3.8   Example of RT-EFSM unreachable state.

means that there is no unreachable state in that RT-EFSM. An example of an unreachable state can be given by mutating the state in Figure 3.7 state S_4 in Figure 3.8.

Unreachable states are redundant in an RT-EFSM, and these states and the transition associated with them can be removed. Check whether an RT-EFSM contains an unreachable state and if so, eliminate the unreachable state, as shown in Table 3.4.

2. Consistency Verification

The consistency of RT-EFSM means that there is no mutual contradiction and redundancy in the state machine. When modeling the state behavior of real-time embedded software based on RT-EFSM, the range of values of each state variable and the existence of contradictions between state transitions should be considered. Therefore the consistency of RT-EFSM should include the absence of equivalent states, state overlap, and the absence of state transition conflicts (Figure 3.9).

After mutating the states of Figure 3.7 states, state overlap, and the existence of state transition conflicts can be given. The state states S_3 and S_4 in Figure 3.8 are equivalent states, and a model that does not affect the semantic representation of RT-EFSM can be obtained by merging the two states. Figure 3.10 overlaps, i.e., there is an overlap in the determination conditions for velocity in the self-transition of states S_1 and S_2. Figure 3.11 shows state transition conflict, where the determination of velocity in the

TABLE 3.4   Algorithm of Reachability Verification of RT-EFSM Model

Algorithm 3.1 Reachability verification of RT-EFSM model

Input: RT-EFSM model $M = \langle S^*, S_0, I, O, T, V, E, L \rangle$
Output: RT-EFSM model after eliminating unreachable states
$M' = \langle S^{*'}, S_0, I, O, T', V, E', L \rangle$

```
01. RemoveUnreachableState(Sᵢ, tᵢ) {
02.     Sₐ = {S₀}, S_b = {S₀};
03.     while(S_b!= Φ) {
04.         get Sᵢ from S_b;
05.         for_each(tᵢ∈T && Head(tᵢ) == Sᵢ){
06.             if(Tail(tᵢ)∉Sₐ){
07.                 Sₐ = Sₐ ∪ Tail (tᵢ);
08.                 S_b = S_b ∪ Tail(tᵢ);
09.             }
10.         }
11.         remove Sᵢ from S_b;
12.     }
13.     S*' = Sₐ;
14.     T' = {t | Head(tᵢ)∈S*' ∩ Tail(ₜᵢ)∈S*'};
15.     return M';
16. }
```

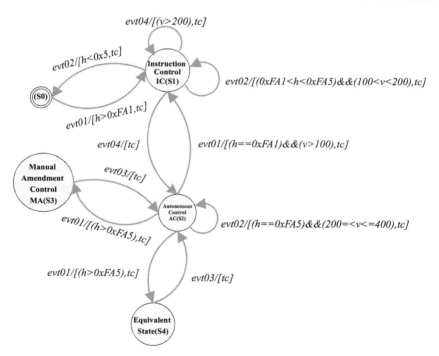

FIGURE 3.9   Example of RT-EFSM Equivalent States.

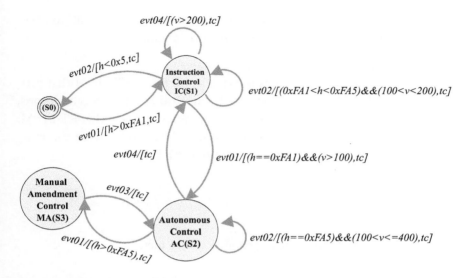

FIGURE 3.10   Example of RT-EFSM state overlap.

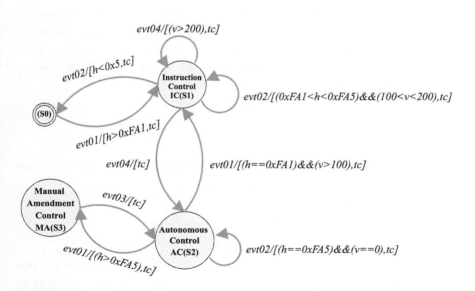

FIGURE 3.11   RT-EFSM state transition conflict example.

self-transition of state S_2 can never be true, then transition never occurs, i.e., there is a state transition conflict.

1. Elimination of equivalence states

   Equivalent states are two states in an RT-EFSM that pro-duce the same target state for arbitrary events and conditions, indicating the existence of redundant states in that RT-EFSM. The following conditions are satisfied to indicate the exis-tence of equivalent states in that RT-EFSM.

   $$\exists S_i \in S^*, \exists S_j \in S^*, t_i \in T(S_i), t_j \in T(S_j)$$

   and the following conditions are met.

   $$\left[\text{Tail}(t_i) = \text{Tail}(t_j) \cap t_i \cdot I = t_j \cdot I \cap t_i \cdot P = t_j \cdot P \cap t_i \cdot o = t_j \cdot o \cap t_i \cdot O = t_j \cdot O\right]$$

   The algorithm to determine the presence or absence of equivalent states in the RT-EFSM model and eliminate them is shown in Table 3.5.

3. Elimination of state transition conflict

   A state transition conflict is a transition with a state as the target state whose transition conditions conflict with the source state itself, making it impossible for the transition conditions to ever be satisfied, i.e., the transition cannot occur. A state tran-sition conflict exists for RT-EFSMs that satisfy the following conditions.

   $$\exists S_i \in S^*, t_i \in T_i\left[(t_i \cdot P \cup t_i \cdot I) \cap S_i \cdot V = \varnothing\right]$$

   The algorithm to check whether an RT-EFSM contains a state transition conflict is shown in Table 3.6.

5. **Deterministic validation**

   1. Static deterministic verification

      The static determinism of RT-EFSM means that the migrated target state is unique for a determined state transition

TABLE 3.5   Algorithm of Equivalent State Elimination Algorithm in RT-EFSM Model

Algorithm 3.2 Equivalent state elimination algorithm in RT-EFSM model

Input: RT-EFSM model $M = \langle S^*, S_0, I, O, T, V, E, L \rangle$
Output: RT-EFSM model after eliminating equivalence states
$M = \langle S^{*\prime}, S_0, I, O, T', V, E', L \rangle$

```
01. RemoveEquivalentState(Sᵢ, Sⱼ, tᵢ, tⱼ){
02.     M' = M;
03.     for_each Sᵢ, Sⱼ∈S* {
04.        T1 = {t | Head(t) = Sᵢ};
05.        T2 = { t | Head(t) = Sⱼ};
06.        for_each tᵢ∈T₁
07.          if (tⱼ∈T₂((Tail(tᵢ) == Tail(tⱼ) && (tᵢ.I == tⱼ.I)
&& (tᵢ.P == tⱼ.P)
                      && (tᵢ.o == tⱼ.o) && (tᵢ.O == tⱼ.O)))) {
08.             remove tⱼ from T₂;
09.          }
10.         if(Φ == T₂){
11.            T3={ t | Head(t) = Sⱼ || Tail(t) = Sⱼ};
12.            remove Sⱼ from S*';
13.            remove T₃  from T';
14.          }
15.      }
16.     return M';
17. }
```

TABLE 3.6   Algorithm of State Transition Conflict Elimination Algorithm in RT-EFSM
Model

Algorithm 3.3 State Transition Conflict Elimination Algorithm in RT-EFSM Model

Input: RT-EFSM model $M = \langle S^*, S_0, I, O, T, V, E, L \rangle$
Output: Set of state transition conflict pairs $ST_{conf} = \{ \langle S_1, t_1 \rangle, \langle S_2, t_2 \rangle, \ldots, \langle S_n, t_n \rangle, \}$

```
01. GetStateTransitionConflict{
02.    for_each Si∈S*{
03.        for_each(tᵢ∈T && Head(tᵢ) = Sᵢ){
04.           if(((tᵢ.P || tᵢ.I) ∩ Sᵢ.V) = Φ)
05.             ST_conf.add (<Sᵢ, tᵢ>);
06.        }
07.        return ST_conf;
08.     }
09. }
```

condition at any one state, i.e., the following conditions should be satisfied.

$$\exists S_i \in S^*, \exists S_j \in S^*, t_i \in T(S_i), t_j \in T(S_j), t_{ij}$$

$$=< S_i, I(t_{ij}), C(t_{ij}), act_{ij}, O(t_{ij}), S_j >, and |t_{ij}| = 1$$

From the above description, it is clear that if the RT-EFSM model is uncertain, it implies that the system can accomplish unpredictable state transition under specific transition conditions, which will undoubtedly make the system modeling a hidden problem and lead to unpredictable execution results (Figure 3.12).

After mutating the states of Figure 3.7 example of state uncertainty can be given. The defective judgment of height in the transition conditions of the states S_2 and S_3 in Figure 3.11 both self-transition of state S_2 *and* transition of S_2 to S_3 when $h ==$ 0xFA5.

The RT-EFSM model static uncertainty determination algorithm is shown in Table 3.7.

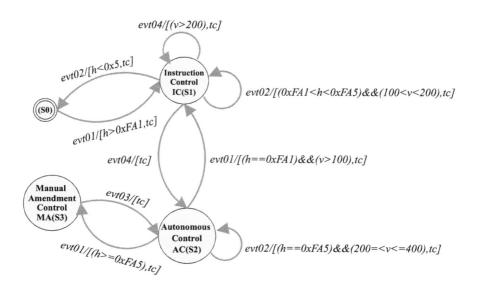

FIGURE 3.12   Example of RT-EFSM state uncertainty.

TABLE 3.7   Algorithm of RT-EFSM Static Uncertainty Determination

Algorithm 3.4 RT-EFSM Static Uncertainty Determination

Input: RT-EFSM model $M = \langle S^*, S_0, I, O, T, V, E, L \rangle$
Output: Returns FALSE when M is indeterminate, otherwise TRUE

```
01. M_Certain(S_i, t_i, t_j) {
02.    for_each S_i∈S*{
03.        for_each t_i, t_j∈T(Head(t_i) == Head(t_j) = S_i){
04.            if((t_i.I == t_j.I) && (t_i.P == t_j.P)
               && (t_i.o == t_j.o)
                  && (t_i.O == t_j.O) && (Tail(t_i)!= Tail(t_j)))
05.            return FALSE;
06.        }
07.    }
08.    return TRUE;
09. }
```

2. Dynamic Certainty

The RT-EFSM model for real-time embedded software proposed in this book is the basis for subsequent model verification. From the definition of RT-EFSM, it is known that V in the RT-EFSM octet is a triple <IV, CV, OV>, where CV represents the set of environment variables. The tester does not control it, and the state transition operation determines its value, then when the state transition in the RT-EFSM model contains preconditions. The preconditions contain internal environment variables. Then there is uncertainty in RT-EFSM, when the next state is related to the current state and input and related to the internal environment variables. This book calls this uncertainty dynamic uncertainty.

For the dynamic uncertainty of RT-EFSM, the treatment is as follows.

1. For RT-EFSM with only input parameters in the precondition, the determinism of the model can be ensured by using Algorithm 3.4.

2. For the RT-EFSM model with input parameters and internal environment variables in the precondition, the state decomposition method can be used to eliminate the uncertainty of state transition caused by the internal environment variables,

TABLE 3.8   Dynamic Uncertainty Handling Algorithm for RT-EFSM Models

Algorithm 3.5 Dynamic Uncertainty Handling Algorithm for RT-EFSM Models

Let M be an RT-EFSM model, the set of states in M be S^*, $S_i \in S^*$, for $t_i \in T_{out}(S_i)$, $T_{out}(S_i)$ is the set of all transitions starting from S_i. If there exists a precondition for t_i and the precondition contains internal environment variables. The precondition can be decomposed into two sub-states and treated as follows.

Let S^* be the set of states in the original RT-EFSM.

1. Take any state S_i from S^*, and let the set of states starting from S_i be $T_{out}(S_i)$.
2. Examining the state transition in $T_{out}(S_i)$ when the precondition is not empty, if there is an internal environment variable for this precondition, S_i can be decomposed into two sub-states S_{i1} and S_{i2}: S_{i1} is the sub-state when the precondition is not equal to TRUE and S_{i2} is the sub-state when the precondition is equal to TRUE.
3. If there is a state transition in $T_{out}(S_i)$ that has not been examined, and the precondition is not empty, the state decomposition continues, i.e., if the value interval of the internal environment variable in a sub-state contains the precondition, the state decomposition continues according to the current precondition.
4. If all the state transitions in $T_{out}(S_i)$ have been examined, let $S^* = S^* - S_i$ and fill in the table of decomposed state transition executable paths with each sub-state and the executable state transition from each sub-state. If $S^* = \varnothing$, the disassembly is finished, otherwise go to step 1.

i.e., to ensure that the transition from any state is not constrained by the internal environment variables. The specific approach is to use the equivalence class division method to divide the state transition constrained by internal environment variables into mutually independent sub-states. The dynamic uncertainty handling algorithm of the RT-EFSM model is shown in Table 3.8.

3.3 TEST CASE GENERATION BASED ON REAL-TIME EXTENDED UML WITH RT-EFSM

3.3.1 UML and OCL Basic Concepts and Techniques

1. UML Concepts

The software crisis of the 1960s led directly to the birth of the ideas and methods of software engineering. The creation and development of object-oriented methods have greatly improved the efficiency and quality of software development. The UML is a milestone in developing object-oriented technology and visual modeling technology, which is a language for specifying, visualizing, creating, and documenting the components of software systems. It combines the basic concepts and advantages of modeling methods such as Booch, OOSE (Object-Oriented Software Engineering), and OMT (Object Modeling Technology). It is widely used in various application areas and widely supported by industry and other industries.

UML was accepted by the American Industrial Standardization Organization (OMG) in 1997, and a standard version of UML was released. After the continuous development of UML version 1.x, the current version of UML has reached 2.x. UML is a standard language for visual representation, detailed portrayal, construction, and archiving of artifacts in software systems. It is also applicable to business modeling and other non-software systems. Compared to other modeling models, UML provides different modeling elements to describe object-oriented software systems from different perspectives and levels, reducing the complexity of modeling and providing flexible expansion mechanisms due to the establishment of a model-based architecture, allowing developers to customize their lead version (Stereotype) to meet different domain requirements, thus making it easy to incorporate new modeling concepts and elements. UML can be used in all phases of software development and can be used for requirements analysis, detailed design, and, more recently, for software development and testing. UML facilitates communication between the various roles in the software development team and provides an intuitive way to demonstrate to users what the software will look like in the future, verify the consistency between the software design and the requirements, and reduce problems during the software development process.

UML is a semi-formal statute language in that it allows for a certain degree of ambiguity and does not fully require completeness. However, suppose the modeler extends the UML appropriately in terms of syntax and semantics. In that case, a complete, consistent, and unambiguous specification can be fully constructed, which is the basic requirement for automated testing.

2. UML Basic Technology

The UML consists of three main components: the UML definition, the rules of the UML, and the public mechanisms of the UML. The UML definition consists of two parts: the UML semantics and the UML representation. The UML semantics describes the precise metamodel definition of the UML. The metamodel provides a simple, consistent, and universal defining description of all elements of UML in terms of syntax and semantics. The UML representation defines a representation of UML notation that provides a standard for developers or development tools to use these graphical notations and text syntax to model systems. Semantically it is an instance of the UML metamodel that can be defined by five types of views (a total of nine graphs). UML's rules are used to integrate UML graphical notation organically, and UML's public mechanisms provide mechanisms and functions for elaborating, modifying, and extending UML.

1. UML semantics

The semantics of UML describes the precise metamodel definition of UML, which is defined in a four-level modeling conceptual framework, with different levels expressing different levels of abstract semantics.

– The Meta-Meta-Model layer, which defines the language of the UML Meta-model, is the basic structure of UML meta-modeling architecture. Meta-Meta-Model layer elements, for example, MOF classes, MOF attributes, and MOF associations.

– The Meta-Model layer, which consists of the basic elements of UML, includes object-oriented and component-oriented concepts, and each concept in this layer is an instance of the Meta-Meta-Model. Examples of Meta-Model layer elements are UML classes, UML state, and UML activities.

– The Model layer, each concept in this layer is an instance of a concept in the Meta-Model layer, which makes up the UML model. It is mainly responsible for defining the language that describes the information domain. The models in this layer are usually called the Class model or Type model. Examples of model layer elements are: component diagrams and use case diagrams for a bank ATM system.

– The User-Object layer, where all elements in this layer are instances of the UML models. Each concept in this layer is

 – Post: <postcondition> indicates postcondition.

   – Several common expressions are described below.

 – Navigation expressions: OCL should represent starting from a context object and getting other objects along the links to determine the required model elements. Since this process requires traversing a part of this object network, the expressions that represent these objects are navigation expressions. The basic form of navigation is a link from one object to another.

 – Package Context Expression.

```
Package Package::SubPackage
context X inv:
… invariant definition …
context X::operationName()
            Pre:
… precondition definition …
Endpackage
```

 – Operation body expressions.

```
Context Typename::operationName(param1:
Type1, …): Return Type
body: - -Some expressions
```

 – Initial and extracted value expressions.

```
Context Typename::attributeName: Type
init: -- expression indicating the initial
value
context Typename::assocRoleName: Type
derive: -- expression extracting the value
```

   – The OCL data types and operation names are shown in Table 3.9.

The model types of OCL include abstract data types and concrete data types, where the abstract data types are mainly collections; the concrete data types are mainly sets, bags, and sequences.

TABLE 3.9   OCL Data Type and Operation

Basic Type	Value	Operation
Boolean	True, false	And, or, nor, not, implies, if-then-else
Integer	1, −10, 1002,……	*, +, −, /, abs(), round(), floor()
Real	3.14, −2.6, ……	*, +, −, /, floor()
String	'just in time'	ToUpper(), Size(), Concat()

3.3.2 UML and Software Testing

The definition, general mechanism and extension mechanism of UML were introduced earlier, and it can be seen that UML has been widely used in industry and research fields. UML provides five types of views reflecting various aspects of software system characteristics from different perspectives. It can be used as a modeling tool for analysis and design in the software development process and to provide solutions for software testing. For example, UML class diagrams can be used to assist in completing unit tests; component diagrams and collaboration diagrams can reflect the interfaces and invocation relationships of software components and the dynamic cooperation relationships of objects and can be used for integration tests; use case diagrams and some dynamic diagrams (state diagrams, activity diagrams, sequence diagrams, etc.) can analyze the functions and dynamic behaviors of the system, and can be used for system testing.

From the perspective of software testing, the UML model is an important basis for obtaining test information. Generating test cases through automatic analysis of the UML model can alleviate much testing work and greatly improve testing efficiency and quality. Due to its complexity, high reliability, and real-time characteristics, embedded software presents new challenges to testing technology. The introduction of UML in the testing of embedded software is the current trend of research and development.

1. **UML-based software testing research status**

    The current research on generating test cases from UML analysis models (use case diagrams, class diagrams, sequence diagrams, cooperation diagrams) is mostly at the theoretical stage. Early research was done by converting or expanding these UML analysis models into other formal descriptions (e.g., FSM, EFSM) and then extracting test cases from them, such as UML state diagrams, activity diagrams, use case diagrams, sequence diagrams, and test cases based on multiple UML diagrams combined testing methods.

2. **The advantages of UML-based software testing**

Through the analysis of the above research on the application of various UML models in software testing, it can be seen that UML models have the following advantages in testing.

- Generality: UML, as a standard modeling language, has broad applicability and is widely adopted by the software development community to guide all phases of software engineering and is supported by many commercially available tools.

- Powerful descriptive capabilities: UML provides various views and models that enable modelers to describe the structure and behavior of software systems from different levels and perspectives.

- Reusability: UML models support the modeling of information about various aspects of the system in all phases of software development. These models facilitate the development of software and guide the design of tests, avoiding the need to construct models specifically for testing, enabling the reuse of models, and integrating the testing of software with the development process.

- Iteratability: Testing activities can be started at the software requirements stage, and the established testing model can be continuously modified and refined as the software design activities are refined. This iterative process allows for early detection of defects in software requirements. It enables testing activities and development activities to be carried out in parallel, allowing testing to be carried out throughout the software development process.

- Powerful management capabilities: UML's view hierarchy mechanism and package mechanism have powerful management capabilities, and these mechanisms solve the problem of state space explosion to some extent.

- Solid theoretical foundation: These foundations have laid the foundation for subsequent related research and provided good support.

3. The disadvantages of UML-based software testing

Despite all of these advantages, UML does not apply to modeling all details in all domains, and software testing based on UML models often suffers from the following disadvantages.

- When modeling systems in the real-time embedded domain, the lack of temporal characteristics of the description lacks the support of a well-defined syntax and semantics and therefore requires real-time extensions to be used for real-time embedded software testing.

- There are many UML models, which models need to be selected for modeling before testing, how to perform software functional division, and model construction need some pre-exploration and research.

3.3.3 UML Real-Time Extensions

Although UML provides powerful description capability and is popular in the industry, there are some shortcomings in ventide real-time embedded software testing, such as the lack of powerful description means for real-time, unambiguity, and other characteristics of embedded software, which are prone to ambiguity and will not be able to meet the requirements of real-time embedded software testing. This section will use the extension mechanism of UML to complete the real-time extension of UML in terms of stereotype, tagged values, and constraints.

1. Real-time extension of UML state diagram

Based on the Harel classical state diagram, UML state diagrams are an extension of the FSM model that emphasizes modeling complex real-time systems while providing descriptions of mechanisms such as hierarchy, concurrency, and broadcasting. They are increasingly used in the field of real-time embedded software testing. UML state diagrams can be expressed as follows

UML state diagram = FSM + nesting + concurrency + broadcast mechanism.

In view of the fact that FSM and EFSM related theories have made considerable research results and have been successfully applied to telecommunications, networks, embedded systems, and other fields, these researches provide good support for real-time embedded software testing techniques based on UML state diagrams and RT-EFSM, so this section uses real-time extensions based on UML state diagrams to complete the modeling process of real-time embedded software systems. The real-time extensions of UML state diagrams are mainly developed from three aspects: improvement and extension of states, improvement, and extension of state transitions, and introduction of time constraint mechanism.

1. Improvement and extension of the state

   In UML representation, the state represents a condition or situation of the object in its lifetime, and the state behavior describes the process of the object activity. In real-time embedded software test modeling, the state of the system under test in the lifetime must be finite. The temporal characteristics of the system behavior in a state are also determined.

   UML state diagrams consist of transitions between states, and in general, the states are classified as follows.

   - Simple states, states without hierarchy, compound, and concurrency.

   - Compound states refer to a state that has several states nested inside it, which means the state diagram contains hierarchical relationships. The states containing other states are called super-states, and the nested states are sub-states.

   - Pseudo states, a special representation of an abstract state, such as the initial and termination states, are pseudo-states.

   In the process of modeling the dynamic behavior of tests based on UML state diagrams, in addition to the initial pseudo-state and termination pseudo-state, this book improves and extends the state in UML state diagram modeling to better describe the system under test, mainly by adding some pseudo-states to define and describe the dynamic behavior of real-time embedded software, Table 3.10 gives the functions of the extended pseudo-states in real-time embedded software testing description.

2. Improvement and extension of state transition

   In the dynamic behavior description of real-time embedded systems using UML state diagrams, traversal along the state

TABLE 3.10   Pseudo States After UML State Extensions

Pseudo State	Description
Branch pseudo state	A set of possible target states, at most one "or state" will be activated in the guardianship condition, which is a combination of guardianship on existing transition segments
Connection pseudo state	Linking multiple state transitions or splitting a transition into a set of consecutive transition segments
Merge connection pseudo state	A type of connected state where multiple incoming transitions can be combined to create an entry or state transition, especially when multiple transitions triggered by different events share an action list and/or guardianship
Select pseudo state	A connection that executes a list of its actions before moving on to the next transition. This state allows actions to be bound to the first conversion segment so that they can be executed before subsequent guardian expressions are assigned
AND state	UML state diagrams use "and states" to represent independent states that can be active concurrently with other states
OR status	UML state diagrams use "or states" to represent independent states that cannot be concurrently active with other states
Broadcast Events	All peer states receive the same event at the same time
Dissemination events	The result of a transformation performed in a "with state" or object that is sent out
IS_IN() operator	The argument in parentheses is a state, indicating that the system is in that state when it is used

diagram is accomplished by receiving events and performing state transition. The state transition is triggered by the reception of an event, while in states where an outgoing transition is specified, the transition is triggered by that event.

In real-time embedded software testing, the types of transition in UML state diagrams are extended to the following four types.

- Self-transition: both the source and target states are the same state.

- Internal transition: internal activity of a state, where the state does not change overall.

- Completion of the transition: transition automatically triggered by the completion of an action within a state.

- Compound transition: a transition that is triggered by a combination of simple transition through branching, determination, concurrency, etc. together.

State transition generally consists of trigger events, parameters, guardians, and actions, etc. State transition can be defined as

event-trigger(parameters)[guard]/action list

Including:

- Event-trigger is the event that triggers the conversion, which, together with the list of parameters, constitutes the identification of the conversion event. If the transition is not marked with an event that triggers the conversion. It means that the transition is carried out automatically.

- Guard is a Boolean expression that indicates the conditions that must be met to trigger state transition, and its value must be TRUE for the transition to be performed. The combination of OCL and UML state diagram will be used in real-time embedded software testing to describe the constraints during the execution of the dynamic behavior of the system under test, i.e., OCL is used to describe the preconditions, guardian conditions, variables, and time constraints in the state diagram transitions.

- The action list is executed as a result of ongoing transformations that will act on certain objects, and the execution of the actions is atomic and non-interruptible. The local clock lt in the real-time extended state will change in response to trigger the transition of entry and exit points.

3. Introduction of time constraint mechanism

In real-time embedded software testing, there are generally time-related events, that is, the timing of events have strict requirements, and these can not be reflected in the original UML state diagram, so it is necessary to provide a time constraint description mechanism by adding OCL constraints, mainly including the following.

1. Introduction of clock variables. The behavior of real-time embedded software is closely related to time, so clocks are needed to record the occurrence and end of state transition. Since the state diagram is described in layers, in order to

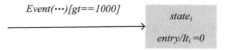

FIGURE 3.13 Global clock and state local clock.

reduce the difficulty of modeling and the coupling between different state diagrams, it is necessary to introduce a global system clock gt and local clocks within each state lt$_i$. The global clock gt *is* used to record the time experienced by the main state diagram from the beginning to the end. The local clock is used to record the time experienced by the transition between each sub-state. The sub-state local clock can be obtained by the corresponding calculation rules for the global clock value of the corresponding dynamic behavior. As shown in Figure 3.13, when an event occurs, and the system clock reaches 1000, the state$_i$ is migrated, and the initialization of the local clock lt$_i$ within the state is performed first after activating the state state$_i$.

In particular, it is important to note that in some cases, the self-transition of states does not require resetting the local clock of the current state. At the same time, since external transitions all activate entry activities, this can lead to resetting the local clock within the state. The solution is to use self-transition. Since there is no target state for self-transition, the transition does not change the current state, and even if there is an action for transition, it does not activate the entry action, thus ensuring that the local clock is not reset.

2. Timeout event constraint means that a state can only be maintained for a specified time, and after the timeout, the system migrates to another state. In the state transition shown in Figure 3.14 in state1 during the timeout time1, and automatically migrates to state2 after the timeout.

3. Operation time-delay constraint means that the operations attached to the state transition need to be delayed for a period of time. In the state transition shown in Figure 3.15 SendData() operation should be delayed for a delay time before execution.

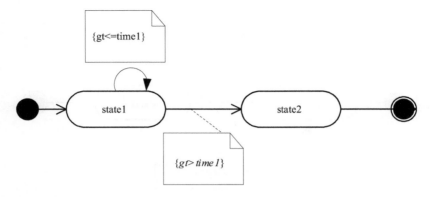

FIGURE 3.14   Timeout event constraint.

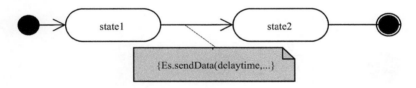

FIGURE 3.15   Operation time constraints.

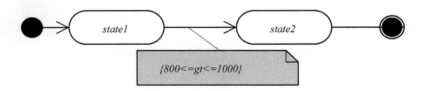

FIGURE 3.16   Example diagram of transition subject to clock constraints.

4. Time-constrained transition means that state transition can only occur in a certain time period. In the state transition shown in Figure 3.16 corresponding transition is allowed to occur within 800–1000 clock cycles.

5. Periodic event constraint means that certain operations are executed periodically, or events and transitions occur periodically in the state diagram. For example, in the state transition shown in Figure 3.17 after the system clock is greater than time1, state2 is automatically migrated to state1 every period time, which occurs x times.

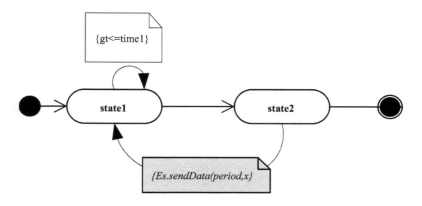

FIGURE 3.17   Periodic event constraint transition.

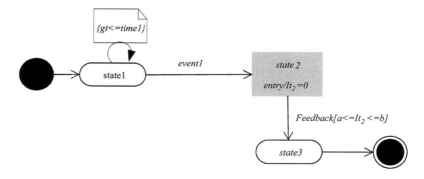

FIGURE 3.18   Feedback time constraint in state transition.

6. Temporal feedback behavior. Real-time embedded systems often have a time feedback problem to external excitation. They must respond within a certain time constraint, so this book gives a way to describe the time feedback behavior. As in the state transition shown in Figure 3.18, feedback time constraint in state transition after state2 receives the event1; the feedback time (local clock within the state lt_2) must satisfy the time constraint: $a \leq lt_2 \leq b$.

Based on the above real-time extension scheme, example of avionics real-time embedded system model based on real-time extended UML gives a model example of an avionics real-time embedded system – inertial/satellite combined navigation system based on the real-time extension UML (Figure 3.19).

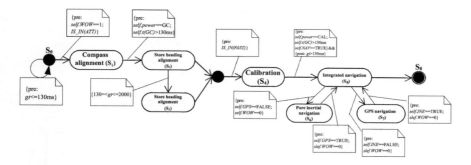

FIGURE 3.19   Example of avionics real-time embedded system model based on real-time extended UML.

2. UML class diagram extensions

The class diagram is the most commonly used diagram in object-oriented system modeling, which shows a set of classes, interfaces, collaborations, and relationships. In real-time embedded software testing requirements analysis, class diagrams represent the relationships between objects in the system and mainly represent the static structure of the software system. The operations and attributes in the class diagram provide the necessary information for transition in the state diagram. They are an indispensable part of the dynamic modeling of the state diagram.

The extension of the UML class diagram mainly completes the static behavior modeling of real-time embedded software. It adds some stereotypes closely related to the embedded system when extending the class diagram. For real-time embedded software testing, the class diagram extension scheme follows the following principles.

- No need to add basic model elements to UML. Semantic and lexical extensions to the original UML model elements.

- The extended stereotypes apply to most real-time embedded systems and allow for a comprehensive representation of the structural characteristics of real-time systems.

The extension of the class diagram in real-time embedded software testing is described as follows:

- Add the stereotypes <<EQUIPMENT>>, which is used to describe the real-time embedded device. Real-time embedded equipment

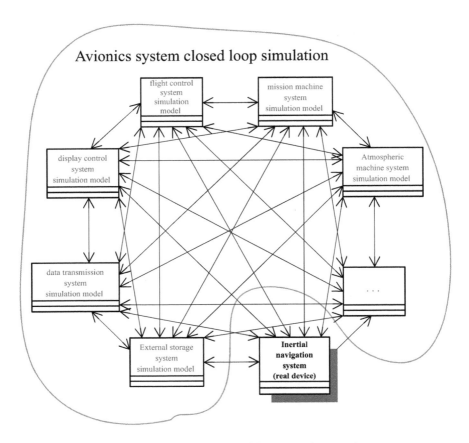

FIGURE 3.20   Schematic diagram of closed-loop simulation of avionics system.

is the object of the system under test and its surrounding cross-linked equipment. In the real-time embedded software simulation test, the simulation model of the cross-linked equipment around the system under test should be constructed according to the system interface control document (ICD), and in the test process, sending and receiving test data during the test in the timing sequence required by the ICD through the test simulation model. Only in this way can we ensure that the system's operating environment under test is consistent with the actual operating environment to complete a realistic real-time, closed-loop, non-intrusive system testing. As shown in Figure 3.20, schematic diagram of closed-loop simulation of avionics system, if the avionics system's inertial guidance system is the system being tested, the surrounding cross-linked equipment, such as flight control system, mission machine system, display control system, atmospheric data computer system, etc. cannot all use real equipment to build a complete closed-loop cross-linked system, so the device simulation should be used to achieve, that is, in the real-time embedded software system testing environment construction, only the system under test is the real equipment. The other devices cross-linked with the system under test are replaced by simulation models.

- The stereotypes <<IODATAVAR>> and <<BLOCK>> are added to describe the type of data transfer between real-time embedded devices. Real-time embedded systems communicate with each other through I/O and data buses, and there are various formats of data protocols, and the bus data is mainly characterized by "block data". To better describe these bus data, the <<BLOCK>> is defined to represent the block data types for communication between real-time embedded systems and their cross-linked devices, such as MIL-STD-1553B, ARINC429, RS232, RS422, AD/DA, DI/DO, and CAN. Figures 3.21–3.23 give the structure of command word, status word, and data word in the bus message of MIL-STD-1553B, respectively.

- Add the stereotypes <<IOLINK>>, which is used to describe the type of I/O bus connection between real-time embedded devices. The devices used to connect real-time embedded systems, and their surrounding cross-linked devices can be divided into two types of connection relationships: unidirectional and bidirectional. Since multiple connections may exist between real-time embedded devices, multiple associations can be established between objects, with different associations indicating different

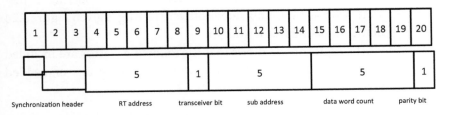

FIGURE 3.21   MIL-STD-1553B bus command word.

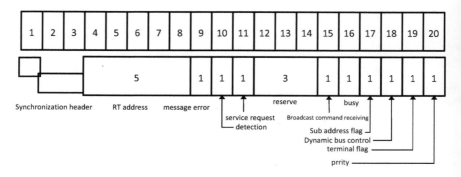

FIGURE 3.22   MIL-STD-1553B bus status word.

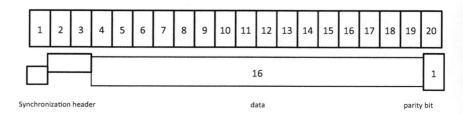

FIGURE 3.23   MIL-STD-1553B bus data word.

types of connection. To indicate the type of data protocol of the connection, the above characteristics are represented by adding tagged values.

IOLINK.TransType=value // indicates the data type of the connection

IOLINK.SrcEqpmt=value // indicates the connected source device

IOLINK.DesEqpmt=value // indicates the connected target device

Based on the above extended ideas, a static modeling framework for real-time embedded software testing is given Figure 3.24 Static modeling framework for

The figure above shows that the following classes are included in the static modeling framework for real-time embedded systems.

- IOVarInfo (belongs to the stereotype IODATAVAR) is an I/O interface data class that belongs to a real-time embedded

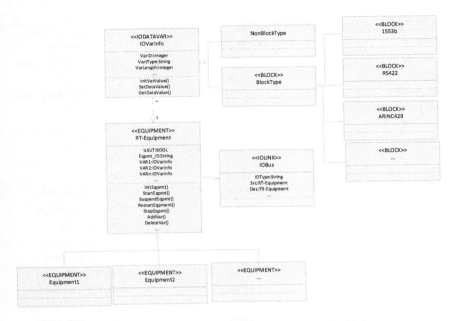

FIGURE 3.24   Static modeling framework for real-time embedded systems.

device, which can derive two subclasses according to the classification of interface data types: NonBlockType and BlockType, where BlockType belongs to the stereotype <<Block>>, indicates the block data type; NonBlockType indicates other common non-block data types, such as double, char, float, int, and long. The BlockType class can also inherit subclasses such as 1553B, ARINC429, and RS422, according to the typical real-time embedded software data transfer protocol type. From the perspective of data transmission, a data variable should include the following characteristics: data source, data destination, data type, data value, data timestamp, and transmission medium. Since different software under test will have different requirements for interface data, including I/O type and data format, take 1553B interface as an example. As shown in Table 3.11, a complete 1553B block information includes the following. Hence, 1553B class needs to add the corresponding attributes to represent this information.

TABLE 3.11   1553B Bus Interface Properties

Name	Properties	Meaning
Variable	int	Variable identification
Source	string	Source model
RT_Source	int	Source model RT value
Target	string	Target model
RT_Target	Int	Target model RT value
SA	string	Sub address
Interface	string	Bus type
PRI	string	Priority
Coment	string	Note information
TransferType	string	Transmission type
Period	int	Periodic value
AllowDelay	int	Maximum latency
WriteProtect	string	Rewriting allows
SystermCondition	string	System status
InterruptAllow	string	Interrupts allowed
DataLeght	int	Data item word length
DataItem	string	The 0th data item
...	...	...

- RT-Equipment (belonging to the stereotype EQUIPMENT) is a generic real-time embedded device class containing the properties and operations shown in Table 3.12.

- IOBus (belonging to the stereotype <<IOLink>>), which indicates the bus connection relationship between devices, can be divided into unidirectional connection and bidirectional connection.

3. **A Study of Real-Time Extended UML Formal Semantics**

The semantics of the state diagram given in the UML standard document is semi-formal and mainly uses natural language combined with OCL to describe the state diagram, which leads to ambiguity and uncertainty and is not conducive to the conversion between UML state diagram and FSM models. To accurately and automatically convert real-time extended UML state diagrams to RT-EFSM models, this section investigates the formal semantics of state diagrams in conjunction with the UML real-time extended scheme. It lays the foundation for the subsequent conversion of state diagrams to RT-EFSM.

TABLE 3.12   RT-Equipment Properties

Classification	Explanation	Type	Description
Property	IsSUT	BOOL	Whether it is the system under test, otherwise it is the cross-linked equipment of SUT
	Eqpmt_ID	Integer	Unique device identification
	VAR1…VARn	Variable	Inter-device communication interface variables are used to store the interface data. The variable types can be classified as complex data type <<BLOCK>> or general data type, and the value range of the variables is indicated by constraints
Operation	InitEqpmt()	BOOL	Initialize the device, return whether the initialization is successful
	StartEqpmt()	VOID	Start the device running and start receiving or sending data
	SuspdEqpmt()	VOID	Hanging devices to wait for specific conditions or messages
	ReStartEqpmt()	VOID	Restarting equipment
	StopEqpmt()	VOID	Stop the device
	AddVar()	VOID	Adding variables
	Delete()	VOID	Delete Variables
	…	…	…

Definition 3.1 Real-time extended UML state diagram RT-SD=$(\rho, \text{tp}, \theta, \text{gt})$, where.

- $\rho: S^* \mapsto 2^{S^*}$ is the state refinement function, which is used to describe the hierarchical relationship between states. Let $\rho(s)$ be the set of sub-states of a state $s \in S^*$, and the 2^{S^*} power set represents all sub-states of S^*. Let $\rho^*(s)$ denote $\forall s \in S^*$, both have $\rho(s) \in S^*$, i.e., $\rho^*(s)$ defines the set of states S^* contained itself and all its sub-states.
- tp: $S^* \mapsto \{\text{smp, AND, OR, psdo}\}$ is a function of the state type, where
  - $tp(s) = \text{smp}$ indicates s a simple state and $\rho(s) \neq \varnothing$;
  - $tp(s) = \text{AND}$ indicates s the AND state.
  - $tp(s) = \text{OR}$ indicates s the OR state.
  - $tp(s) = \text{psdo}$ indicates s a pseudo state.
- $\theta: S^* \mapsto 2^{S^*}$ is the default function, $\theta(s)$ defining the default sub-state contained within $s \in S$, then we have

$$\theta(s) = \begin{cases} \theta(s) = S_{\text{def}} & p(s) \neq \varnothing \wedge tp(s) = \text{OR} \\ \theta(s) = \varnothing & p(s) = \varnothing \wedge tp(s) = \text{AND} \end{cases}$$

- gt is the global clock of the system, which is the timer from the start to the end of the system. When state transition occurs, the local clock lt is reset to 0 at the entrance of each state, and gt is incremented at the exit according to the placement of lt. See the definition of transition structure and time processing method later for the specific algorithm.

Definition 3.2

A parent state $\pi : S^* \mapsto S^*$ is a direct parent state of $\forall s \in S^*$. Let $s' = \pi(s)$, then s be the direct parent state of s', i.e., we have $\forall s \in p(s') \Rightarrow s' = \pi(s)$.

According to the above definition, then the uniqueness of the root node can be expressed as

$$\forall s \in S^*, \exists s' \in S^*, \text{tp}(s') = \text{psdo}, s \in p^*(s') \Rightarrow s' = \text{root}.$$

The uniqueness of the parent state of a non-root node can be expressed as

$$\forall s \in S^*, s \neq \text{root}, \exists s_1, s_2 \in S^*, s_1 = \pi(s) \wedge s_2 = \pi(s) \Rightarrow s_1 = s_2.$$

Definition 3.3 Transition structure

The order $\text{src} : T \mapsto S^*$, $\text{evt} : T \mapsto \text{evt}$, $\text{grd} : T \mapsto \text{grd}$, $\text{act} : T \mapsto \text{act}$, $\text{trgt} : T \mapsto S^*$ indicates the source state, trigger event, guardian condition, action, and target state of the transition $\forall t \in T$, respectively. Then for the transition:

$$s_1 \xrightarrow{\text{evt}[\text{grd}]/\text{act}} s_2$$

There are

$$\text{src}(t) = s_1, \text{evt}(t) = \text{evt}, \text{grd}(t) = \text{grd}, \text{act}(t) = \text{act}, \text{trgt}(t) = s_2$$

The global clock gt and the local clock lt change at this point as follows.

$$\Delta t = \text{lt}(s_2) - \text{lt}(s_1), \ \text{gt} = \text{gt} + \Delta t$$

Definition 3.4 State lattice

Define $\text{conf} : S \mapsto 2^{2^{S^*}}$ is a state pattern function, then for $\forall s \in S^*$, $\exists \text{root} \in S^*$ is the root state, the pattern $C \in \text{conf}(s)$, satisfies:

$$\text{root} \in c$$

$$\forall s \in c : \text{tp}(s) = \text{OR} \Rightarrow \left(\exists s' \in \rho(s) : s' \in C \right)$$

$$\forall s \in c : \text{tp}(s) = \text{AND} \Rightarrow \left(\forall s' \in \rho(s) : s' \in C \right)$$

Definition 3.5 Active states

In the real-time extended UML state diagram, when the system state is migrated from s_1 to s_2, then s_2 becomes inactive. Let $\text{actv} : S^* \mapsto \{\text{TRUE}, \text{FALSE}\}$ be the state active function, then for $\forall s \in S^*$, when $\text{actv}(s) = \text{TRUE}$ means that s is in the active state, when $\text{actv}(s) = \text{FALSE}$ means that s is in the inactive state.

Based on the above definition, it is clear that there are

1. When the combined state s is AND, all sub-states in are active and can be expressed as

$$\exists s_1, s_2 \in S^*, \ \forall s \in S^*, \ \text{tp}(s) = \text{OR}, \ \{s_1, s_2\} \subseteq \rho(s)$$

then there are

$$\text{actv}(s_1) = \text{TRUE} \vee \text{actv}(s_2) = \text{TRUE}$$

2. When the combined state s is OR, only one sub-state in s is active, which can be expressed as

$$\exists s_1, s_2 \in S^*, \ \forall s \in S^*, \ \text{tp}(s) = \text{AND}, \ \{s_1, s_2\} \subseteq \rho(s)$$

then there are

$$\text{actv}(s_1) = \text{TRUE} \wedge \text{actv}(s_2) = \text{TRUE}$$

Definition 3.6 Transition Enable

When the following conditions are met:

- The source state of the transition is active
- Trigger conditions for transition meet current events
- The guardianship condition for transition is TRUE.

Then a transition in a state pattern is enabled. If we make $\text{enb}: \text{CT} \mapsto \{\text{TRUE}, \text{FALSE}\}$ is the transition enable function and we make cur_evt the current event, we have

$$\text{actv}(\text{src}(\text{ct})) = \text{TRUE} \wedge \text{evt}(\text{ct}) = \text{cur\_evt} \wedge \text{grd}(\text{ct})$$

$$= \text{TRUE} \Leftrightarrow \text{enb}(\text{ct}) = \text{TRUE}$$

Definition 3.7 Transition Conflict

Define $\text{conflict}(t_i, \ t_j, \ c)$ to indicate the transition t_i, t_j exit from state pattern c The transition conflict. When there are multiple transitions enabled simultaneously in a state pattern, these transitions must conflict with other transitions and can be expressed as

$$\text{conflict}(t_i, \ t_j, \ c) \Leftrightarrow \text{enb}(\text{ct}_i) = \text{TRUE}, \ \text{enb}(\text{ct}_j)$$

$$= \text{TRUE}, \ \text{ct}_i \neq \text{ct}_j, \ \text{sec}(\text{ct}_i) = \text{src}(\text{ct}_j)$$

Definition 3.8 Transition priority

For $\forall t_i, t_j \in T$, let $\text{prior}(t_i, t_j)$ denote the state transition priority function, and if $\text{prior}(t_i, t_j) = \text{TRUE}$, denote the priority of t_i is higher than t_j. Then we have

- If s_i is a sub-state of the s_j and transition t_i, t_j originate from s_i, s_j respectively, then obviously t_i must have high priority, i.e.,

$$s_i \in \rho^*(s_j) \Rightarrow \text{prior}(t_i, t_j)$$

- If s_i, s_j do not belong to the same state pattern and the transition t_i, t_j originate from s_i, s_j, respectively, then there can be no transition conflict in t_i, t_j, and there is no priority distinction, i.e.,

$$\neg \exists(s_i \in c_i \wedge s_j \in c_j) \Rightarrow \neg \exists \text{prior}(t_i, t_j)$$

Definition 3.9 Transition connection

For $\forall t_i, t_j \in T$, $\text{tp}(\text{src}(t_j)) = \text{psdo}$, and then let $t_i \leftrightarrow t_j$ denote the transition t_i and the default transition t_j to be connected, i.e.,

$$\exists t_i, t_j \in T, t_i \leftrightarrow t_j \Rightarrow \text{trgt}(t_i) = \text{trgt}(t_j)$$

Definition 3.10 Transition division

For $t_i, t_j \in T$, let $t = t_i \otimes t_j$ denote the transition t is divided into transition t_i and transition t_j, and then transition t_i and t_j transition are divided, i.e.,

$$\exists t \in T, t = t_i \otimes t_j \Rightarrow t_i \in T, t_j \in T$$

3.3.4 Test Case Generation Process Based on Real-Time Extended UML and RT-EFSM

1. **Test case generation process**

   With the continuous development of UML ventide techniques and formal methods, combining UML with traditional formal methods has become one of the most important aspects of research in the field of real-time embedded software testing: on the one hand, as a de facto industry standard, UML has gained widespread support since its introduction, and many large companies have joined its camp and launched UML-enabled CASE tools, such as Rose family of tools from Rational, Rhapsody from iLogix. On the other hand, the formal approach enhances the accuracy and consistency of testing. It improves the automation and efficiency of testing due to its ability to eliminate the duality in testing. In summary, combining UML with formal methods is a hot research topic in software testing.

   Real-time embedded software system testing is based on the relevant documents of the software under test, mainly including software mission statement, software requirement specification, interface control document (ICD), and user manual. Through analyzing the structure, function, interface, and state information of the software under test (SUT), clarifying the input and output of the system and its mapping relationship, we can establish static and dynamic models of the SUT and describe the structure and behavior of the system respectively. The test cases are automatically generated by combining the test case generation methods.

   The ventide principle of the test case generation process based on real-time extended UML and RT-EFSM is shown in Figure 3.25

   The test case generation process based on real-time extended UML with RT-EFSM is as follows.

   1. The software under test document analysis: the development unit to provide the real-time embedded software under test documents, such as software development tasks, requirements specifications, ICD, user manuals, and POP manuals, in the document analysis process should be fully communicated with the software developers to obtain relevant information about the software (including functional and non-functional features).

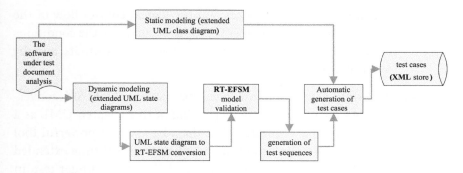

FIGURE 3.25   Test case generation process based on real-time extended UML with RT-EFSM.

2. Static ventide based on extended UML class diagram: the main work is to identify the static information of the input and output of the software under test, including the information of the cross-linked devices around the system under test, the information of the bus and I/O interface variables (elements), the timing requirements of data interaction, and the hardware interface. For example, an extended stereotype is used to describe the system under test and each device cross-connected around it. The block information on the I/O and data bus is described by the stereotype <<BLOCK>>, which generally includes the information block name, description, refresh period, transmission type, transmission period, and receiving object. In addition, you should understand the data exchange and calculation process inside the software, which generally includes block data, signal quantity, analog quantity, and variable information.

3. Dynamic ventide based on real-time extended UML state diagrams. It uses a real-time extended state diagram and OCL language to complete the dynamic behavior ventide of real-time embedded system. The main work is to identify the observable state information presented in the process of system function realization, including precondition constraints, trigger events, transition constraints, corresponding system actions, and expected states. It combines system state transition information, constructs each super state, and sub-state. It also records the test input occurrence conditions and response occurrence conditions

and studies input sequences and the logical control flow of the software, such as the moment of input occurrence, the conditions under which the software system receives specific inputs, and the order of input processing.

4. Real-time extended UML state diagram to RT-EFSM conversion. As mentioned at the beginning of this chapter, UML as a de facto industry standard has the advantage of powerful tool resources. This book recommends the use of real-time extended UML to model the real-time embedded software under test, in order to get RT-EFSM, it is necessary to first convert the real-time extended UML state diagram (including hierarchy, concurrency) into a flat UML state diagram and the flat state diagram can directly correspond to RT-EFSM. In turn, model validation and automatic generation of test sequences and test cases can be completed.

5. RT-EFSM model validation: to ensure the quality of the model, the generated RT-EFSM model needs to be verified for determinism, reachability, and consistency, so that it becomes complete, consistent, and strongly connected, laying the foundation for the subsequent automatic generation of the RT-EFSM-based test cases.

6. Automatic generation of test sequences and test cases based on RT-EFSM. This book introduces the concept of time-area partitioning method and time-constrained transition equivalence class for real-time embedded systems, uses a test scenario tree-based approach to generate test sequences and test cases automatically, and finally stores the test cases in XML format to facilitate testers to convert them into test descriptions identified by specific test platforms to drive test execution.

2. Real-time extended UML statechart to RT-EFSM conversion

For the conversion method between the UML state diagram and FSM, there have been many research results at home and abroad, such as the spreading method based on D. Harel and his STATEMATE tool support, the flattening method based on Y.G. Kim, the gradual improvement based on Petri net to make the hierarchical state diagram into structured, etc. In the following, the existing techniques and methods are extended by combining the formal semantics of RT-EFSM and real-time extended UML state diagrams, and a conversion method of real-time extended UML state diagrams to RT-EFSM is proposed.

Clearly, according to the formal semantics of the real-time extended UML statechart, a simple statechart without hierarchy and concurrency structure can be equated to a finite state machine. Then the (after spreading) RT-EFSM obtained after the transformation of the real-time extended UML statechart can be defined as follows.

Definition 3.11

Real-time extended UML state diagram transformed to obtain (after spreading) RT-EFSM, where *Gstates* is the set of global states, S_0 is the initial state of global states, and *Gtrans* is the set of global transition paths.

1. Build global state

The largest set of states that a system can have at the same time is called a global state, denoted as GS. The rules for constructing a global state GS are as follows:

GS ∈ S and satisfies: (1) GS contains the root state; (2) for every AND composite state *s*, either *s* or its sub-states are in GS, or none of them is in GS; (3) for every OR composite state *s*, either *s* and only one of its sub-states are in GS, or *s* and all of its sub-states are not in GS.

Based on the above properties, the steps for obtaining GS are as follows.

1. Generate a state tree from the UML state diagram in the following steps.

   a. Use the root state of the state diagram as the root state of the state tree.

   b. The breadth-first search of the state graph with its sub-states as child nodes of the root.

   c. Continue operation b on the child nodes until there are no child nodes, i.e., the atomic state is searched.

   d. Refinement of the relationship of sibling nodes in the state tree.

- If the relationship between brothers is or state in the state tree, no change is required.

- If the relationship between brothers is and state in the state tree, treat one of the brothers and all its child nodes as children of all leaf nodes of the other brother.

2. Search all states of the state diagram and find the root state.

3. Perform a depth-first search for all states starting from the root state, and if the state S_i is an atomic state, treat the node together with all its parents as a GS in the RT-EFSM.

The algorithm for obtaining a state tree from a real-time extended UML state diagram is shown in Table 3.13.

2. Build global transition path

From the previous article, it is clear that GS represents the global state and evt represents the event. For $t \in T$, T is said to be triggered for GS about event evt if any transition t in T satisfies $src(t) \in GS$ and $evt(t) = evt$ and any two transitions in T are not in conflict. T is said to be the largest set of transitions valid for GS about evt if all transitions triggered for GS about evt and not contained in T conflict with some transition in T.

The global transition path GT in RT-EFSM can be defined as a five-tuple, $GT = (GS, evt, grd, act, GS')$, representing the transition from

TABLE 3.13 Algorithm for Obtaining RT-EFSM State Tree from UML State Diagram

Algorithm 3.6 Obtaining RT-EFSM State Trees from Real-Time Extended UML State Diagrams

```
INPUT: W(as the Real-time Extened UML Diagram)
OUTPUT: ST(State Tree)
01.  SD_Convert_ST) {
02.      stack=newStack( ):
03.      root=initState;                    //assign the
initial pseudo-state to the root node
04.      while(!W. Empty( )){
05.          e=W. getNextEvent( );          //Take out the
next transition event
06.          w=W. getNextState( );          //Take out the
next target state
07.          if(w. isAtomicState() )        //If atomic state
08.              stack. Push(e, w); //put (e, w) on the stack
09.          else if(w. isORState( )){      //if w is or state
```

(Continued)

TABLE 3.13 (*Continued*)   Algorithm for Obtaining RT-EFSM State Tree from UML
State Diagram

Algorithm 3.6 Obtaining RT-EFSM State Trees from Real-Time Extended UML State Diagrams

```
10.              if(!stack. Empty( )){
11.                  child=newState(stack. popAll()); //produce
all the events and states in the stack
out of the stack
12.                  root.addState(child, e);
//event e as a transition event for connected states
13.              }
14.              Orchild=SD_Convert_ST (w);
//or state, iterative decomposition
15.              root. addState(Orchild, e);
//insert the subtree into the root node
16.          }
17.          else{                              //w is and state
18.              if(!stack. Empty( )){
19.                  child=newState(stack. popAll( ));
//produce all the events and states in the stack out of the
stack.
20.                  root.addState(child, e);
//insert root node, first event as RT-EFSM transition event
21.                  ANDFather=newANDFather( );
//create with intermediate nodes
22.                  for(i=0; i<w. size( ); i++){
// iterate through all sub-states with the state
23.                  ANDchild= SD_Convert_ST (w. substate(i));
//substitute each child state, iterative decomposition
24.                      ANDFather. addANDchild(ANDchild);
//insert with intermediate nodes
25.                  }
26.                  root. addState(ANDFather,e);
//insert the node with the intermediate node into the root
27.          }
28.      if(!stack. Empty()){ //if the stack is not empty
29.          child=newState(stack. popAll());
20.          root. addState(child, e); //insert the state into
the root node, the first event is the transition event of
the state tree
21.      }
22.      return(root);
23.  }
```

one global state GS to another global state GS′. In the UML state diagram, GT is obtained by finding T that satisfies the following conditions.

- The state of GS′ is to convert the source state set in GS to the destination state set.

$$grd = \cup_{t \in T} grd(t)$$

- where $act_1(t)$ is all the actions that occur when all exit events occur, $act_2(t)$ is all the actions that occur when all entry events occur, and $act_3(t)$ is all the actions inside the current state.

The algorithm for finding the global transition path is as follows.

1. Take any GS and GS′.

2. Find $S = \{s \mid s \in GS \cap s \in GS'\}$.

3. Let $S_1 = GS - S$, $S_2 = GS' - S$, search all transitions t in the state diagram and get $T_1 = \{t \mid src(t) \in S_1 \cap trgt(t) \in S_2\}$; search all transitions t in the state diagram and get $T_2 = \{t \mid src(t) \in S_2 \cap trgt(t) \in S_2\}$.

4. $T_3 = \{t \mid t \in T_1 \cap t \notin T_2\}$, then T_3 is the global transition path.

Usually, GT is a series of transitions triggered by an event *evt*. Once the global state and global transition path are obtained, RT-EFSM is generated.

For the transformed RT-EFSM, since the global state is obtained from the UML state diagram considering all combinations of cases, including the unreachable global state, the transformed simple UML state diagram cannot be equivalent to the original UML state diagram in terms of operational semantics, and the test cases generated on this basis contain wrong test cases, which will make some tests not work properly. Therefore, the simple UML state diagram must be processed to remove the unreachable state and the state transition to and from that state.

3. RT-EFSM-based test sequence generation

1. Concepts, Definitions and Assumptions

This book assumes that the tester uses real-time extended UML-based system modeling under test or directly uses RT-EFSM modeling. After that, the UML model has been converted to RT-EFSM model according to the conversion method provided in the book. The generated RT-EFSM model has been verified using the model verification method provided in the book. Finally, as described below, a minimal, strongly connected, and complete RT-EFSM model has been obtained.

- Verification of static certainty and elimination of equivalent states ensures that this RT-EFSM is minimal.

- The validation of reachability and the validation of state transition conflicts ensure that the RT-EFSM is strongly connected.

- Dynamic deterministic validation ensures that this RT-EFSM is complete.

The correct behavior of real-time embedded software depends not only on the input but also on whether the clock processing meets the specified requirements. Therefore the following two core issues must be addressed in the RT-EFSM-based test methodology.

- Time constraints processing issues.

- Test sequence generation problem.

Based on the above analysis, this section will combine the extension of RT-EFSM to firstly propose the definition and assumptions related to time constraints in real-time embedded software test sequence generation (such as time region and time transition equivalence class), and then give the definition of extended test sequences, and finally adopt the test scenario tree-based approach to generate test sequences.

Definition 3.12: Time Region

The global clock L in the RT-EFSM element is the set of all state transition clocks, the value range of is $(0, +\infty)$, and the global clock L is divided into k time regions, then the time points contained in L are expressed as $L_1, L_2, \ldots, L_k$, and $L_1 < L_2 < \ldots < L_k$. Then $\{L_1, L_2, \ldots, L_k\}$ is said to be the time region division of the time constraint ω on L, as shown in Figure 3.26.

FIGURE 3.26   Time zone division.

According to the above definition, then the time constraint $\omega : t_1 < l < t_2$ can determine three time regions: $(0,t_1),(t_1,t_2),[t_2,+\infty]$.

Definition 3.13: Effective Time Region

Let E be the set of state transition events in RT-EFSM, $e \in E$, l_i be a temporal region division on L, $l_i \in L$. If event e occurs within l_i and can trigger state transition, then it is said that l_i is a valid time region for event e.

Definition 3.14: Invalid Time Region

Let E be the set of state transition events in RT-EFSM, $e \in E$, and li be a temporal region division on L, $l_i \in L$. If event e occurs within l_i but cannot trigger any state transition, l_i is said to be an invalid temporal region for event e.

Definition 3.15: Time-Constrained Transition Equivalence Class

In real-time embedded software state transition, in addition to the general state variable (instruction) constraints that can trigger the transition, time constraints are often used as guardian conditions to determine whether transition can be triggered. Based on the temporal region division, Figure 3.27 gives a schematic diagram of state transition with time and variable constraints represented by RT-EFSM.

In the state transition shown below, I is the input that triggers the transition, and the guardianship conditions include the time constraint $(10 < \text{lt} < 20)$ and the input variable constraint $(X == 0x2280)$. When the variable constraint is satisfied $(X == 0x2280)$ is true, if the input I occur in the invalid time region $(0, 10)$ and $[5, +\infty]$, it will not cause the state transition to occur. Only when the variable

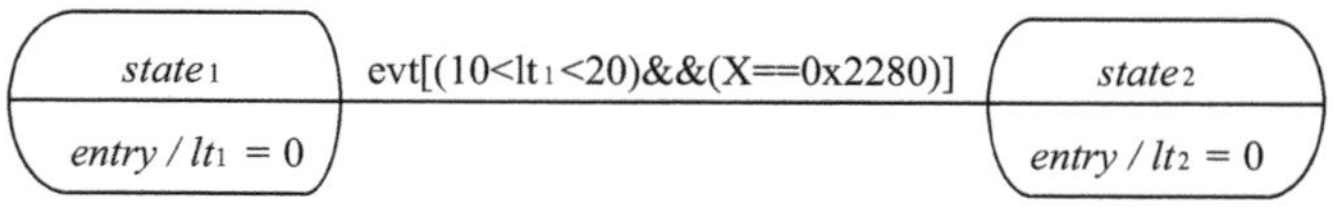

FIGURE 3.27   State transition with time and variable constraints.

constraint satisfies $(X = 0x2280)$ is true in the valid time region (10, 20), and the input event will state transition be triggered.

Based on the above analysis, this book proposes the concept of time-constrained transition equivalence classes, i.e., the state transition is divided into valid time regions and invalid time regions according to time regions, and the transition triggered by events in different time regions is divided into equivalence classes to lay the foundation for subsequent test sequence generation. The formal definition of the time-constrained transition equivalence class is as follows: $\text{timeCTEC} = \left\{ \left(S_{\text{src}} \to S_{\text{trgr}} \right)\_[C]\_?I\_!O \right\}$

- S_{src}: means the source state.

- S_{trgr}: means the target state.

- C: means the guardianship condition under which the transition occurs, and $C = \langle \text{tCnd}, \text{vCnd} \rangle$, i.e., the monitoring condition consists of a time constraint tCnd and a variable constraint vCnd.

- []: means optional and can be omitted when there are no preconditions since not every state transition includes preconditions.

  - ?: means input.

  - I: means the input variables (including clock constraint variables) and operations, and $I = \langle \text{ivVle}, \text{iAct} \rangle$.

  - !: means output.

  - O: means the output variables (including clock constraint variables) and operations, and $O = \langle \text{ovVle}, \text{oAct} \rangle$.

    Figure 3.28 gives a diagram of the time-constrained transition equivalence class. Based on the above definition of time transition equivalence classes, Figure 3.27 can be divided into three time-constrained transition equivalence classes as shown in Figure 3.28 (which can also be described in tabular form) (Figure 3.29).

Definition 3.16 Extended Test Sequence US$_\text{ex}$

According to the definition of time-constrained transition equivalence classes, this book uses a test sequence generation method based on a test scenario tree, which is composed of time-constrained

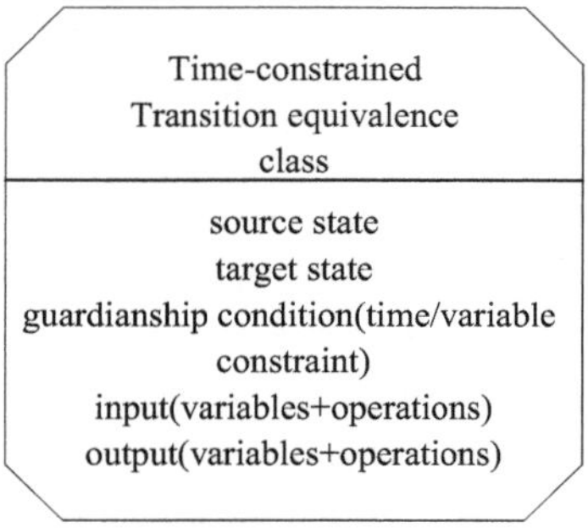

Time-constrained
Transition equivalence
class

source state
target state
guardianship condition(time/variable
constraint)
input(variables+operations)
output(variables+operations)

FIGURE 3.28   Schematic diagram of the time-constrained transition equivalence class.

timeCTEC01

*state*1
*state*2
(0,10]
X==0x2280
...

timeCTEC02

*state*1
*state*2
(10<lt$_1$<20)
X==0x2280
...

timeCTEC02

*state*1
*state*2
[20,+∞)
X==0x2280
...

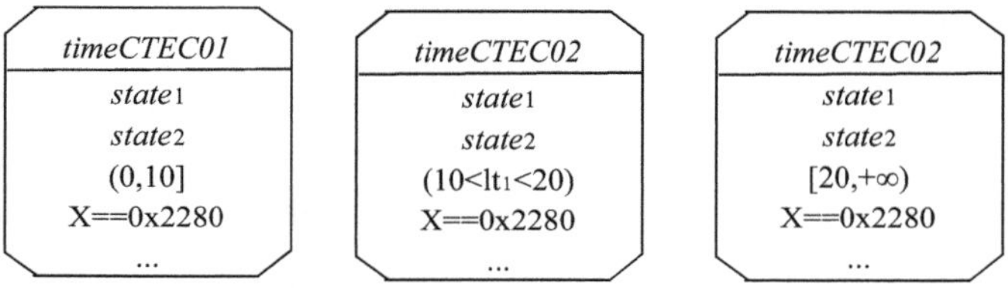

FIGURE 3.29   Example of a time-constrained transition equivalence class.

transition equivalence classes and is a complete description of a test path, so extended test sequences are introduced US_{ex}, which are used to represent the test path, as defined below:

$$US_{ex} = \langle timeCTEC_1 \cup timeCTEC_2 \cup \ldots timeCTEC_{\ldots} \cup \ldots timeCTEC_n \rangle$$

$$= \{\left(S_i \to S_j\right)\_\langle tCnd_{i \to j}, vCnd_{i \to j} \rangle\_?\langle ivVle_{i \to j}, iAct_{i \to j} \rangle$$

$$\_!\langle ovVle_{i \to j}, oAct_{i \to j} \rangle\} \cup$$

$$= \{\left(S_j \to S_k\right)\_\langle tCnd_{j \to k}, vCnd_{j \to k} \rangle\_?\langle ivVle_{j \to k}, iAct_{j \to k} \rangle$$

$$\_!\langle ovVle_{i \to j}, oAct_{i \to j} \rangle\} \cup \ldots$$

where $0 \leq i < j < k \leq n$, n is the maximum state space value of the system, i.e., the extended test sequence is the set of time-constrained transition equivalence classes.

As can be seen from the above definition, the definition of the FSM UIO sequence corresponding to US$_{ex}$ each state transition of the sequence is also not suitable here and should be redefined.

Definition 3.17 Extended Unique Input/Output Sequence

$UIO_{ex} = \{[C]\_?I\_!O\}$, see Definition 3.16 for the meaning of each element in the UIOex sequence.

Definition 3.18 Test Scenario

A real-time embedded software test scenario based on RT-EFSM state transition is a series of state transition processes corresponding to a typical execution path in the RT-EFSM state diagram.

    2. Test sequence generation process

After obtaining the RT-EFSM model, based on the above definitions and assumptions, the RT-EFSM test sequence generation process based on the time-constrained transition equivalence class is shown in Figure 3.30.

Construction of time-bound transition equivalence classes. Time-constrained transition equivalence classes are the basis for test sequence generation, so the RT-EFSM model should be analyzed first to obtain time-constrained equivalence classes, as follows.

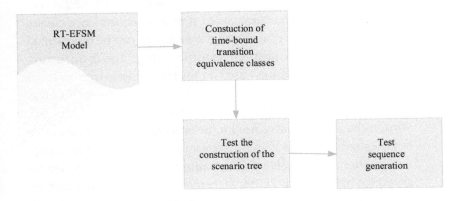

FIGURE 3.30 Test sequence generation process based on time-constrained transition equivalence class.

1. Iterate through the set of states in RT-EFSM S^* and the set of input events I, and for each state $s \in S^*$, obtain the trigger event of $e \in I$.

2. Generate the transition set T^* triggered by event e, select $c \in C^*$ according to the trigger constraints C^* in T^*, and calculate the time region division of c. And according to the time region division to obtain the transition guardianship conditions (usually including time constraints, variable constraints), and clarify the input variables and trigger events, and output variables and output events; if there is no time constraint, the time constraint in the equivalence class is empty.

3. Based on the above analysis, the full-time-constrained transition equivalence classes obtained are listed in tabular form.

Test the construction of the scenario tree. The Test Scenario Tree (TST) is constructed based on the time-constrained transition equivalence class. It is a complete description of the test path that can be used to generate the desired test sequence by traversing the test *scenario* tree. The test scenario tree construction algorithm is given in Table 3.14.

After obtaining the test scenario tree, the depth-first search algorithm can be used to traverse all possible paths of each tree from the root node to the leaf nodes and generate the test sequence based on the information of the equivalence class of the time transition constraints in each path.

Test sequence generation. Each state transition in RT-EFSM corresponds to many time-constrained transition equivalence classes in the test scenario tree, and each test sequence can be represented as a collection of extended test sequences US_{ex}. The construction algorithm of test sequences based on the test scenario tree is shown in Table 3.15. After obtaining the test sequences, the synchronization problems (including the first and second type of synchronization) in the test sequences need to be processed. The test cases can be generated according to the test coverage criterion in the next step.

Synchronization problem of test sequence. For the test sequences generated based on RT-EFSM, there may be synchronization problems in the concurrent transition of states in the test sequences. This book divides the synchronization problems of RT-EFSM state transition into the first type of synchronization problems and the second type of synchronization problems.

TABLE 3.14   Algorithm for Construction of the Test Scenario Tree TST

Algorithm 3.7 Construction of the Test Scenario Tree TST

INPUT: RT-EFSM Model
OUTPUT: TST
STEP01:
01. Let TST contains only the root node of RT-EFSM Model;
// Initialization Process
02. Let the node variable, named Node, point to the root node;
03. Let the current node variable, named curNode, point to the subsequent state of the root node;
STEP02:
04. IF the childNumber of node==0
05.   IF the subsequentState == NULL;
06.   THEN END;
07.   ELSE
08.   curNode point to the subsequent state of node;
09.   construct timeCTEC of curNode;
10.   FOR EACH timCTEC
11.   Back to previous node;
12.   IF timeCTEC is not ventide in back path THEN
13.   Let curNode be the child of node
14.   IF childNumber==0 THEN
15.   Let node point to the parent of curNode, Jump to STEP02;
16.   ELSE
17.   Let node point to the first child of curNode, Jump to STEP02;
18.   END FOR
STEP03:
19.   IF the childNumber of node>0 THEN
20.   FOR EACH child of node
21.   IF child is not visited THEN
22.   node point to the child;
23.   Mark the child as visited, Jump to STEP02;
24.   END FOR
25.   IF (All child nodes have been visited) AND (node==root) THEN END;
26.   ELSE
27.   Let node point to the parent of curNode, Jump to STEP02;

TABLE 3.15   Test Sequence Generation Algorithm Based on Test Scenario Tree TST

Algorithm 3.8 Test Sequence Generation based on TST

```
INPUT: TST
OUTPUT: Test Sequence (TS)
STEP01:
01. Let TS be empty; // Initialization Process
02. Let current timeCTEC, named curNode, point to the root
    of TST;
03. Let evt be the event of the curNode;
STEP02:
04. IF curNode is the root THEN
05.     IF curNode has not been visited THEN
06.         Output the current timeCTEC to TS;
07.         Mark curNode as visited;
08.     FOR EACH child of curNode
09.         IF child has not been visited THEN
10.            Let curNode point to child, Jump to STEP02;
11.         IF All nodes have been visited THEN END;
12.     END FOR
STEP03:
13. IF curNode is not the root THEN
14.     IF curNode has not been visited THEN
15.         Output the current timeCTEC to TS;
16.         Mark curNode as visited;
17.     IF the childNumber of curNode==0 THEN
18.         Output TS;
19.         Let evt of the last timeCTEC in TS be empty;
20.         Bask to the parent node, Jump to STEP02;
21.     ELSE
22.         FOR EACH child of curNode
23.             IF child has not been visited THEN
24.                Let child point to curNode, Jump to STEP02;
25.         END FOR
```

1. The first type of synchronization problem

   The first class of synchronization problems. Let M be an RT-EFSM model, then $M = \langle S^*, S_0, I, O, T, V, E, L \rangle$, t is a state transition $t \in T$ within M_i, S^* is a local state within $M_j (i \neq j)$, and S^* is a synchronized input state of t if there exists $t'(S^* = head(t'))$ and t' and t have the same input, and the set formed by S^* is denoted as $Con(t)$.

   Let t_i, t_j be the transitions within $M_i, M_j (i \neq j)$, respectively, if the sequence of transitions $< t_i \ldots t_j >$ satisfies:

- Tail (t_j) Con (t_j)

- Transition $t_k (k \neq i, j)$ is not a transition within M_i

  Then, the transition sequence is called the first class of synchronous input transition sequence.

  Test sequences containing the first type synchronous input transition sequences have the first type synchronization problems. The input sequence corresponding to a test sequence R with a first type synchronization problem may result in a different test sequence R' than R being executed. To avoid the first synchronization problems, they should be solved by adding a synchronization lock statement.

```
Check Lock L;  // Check if L is 0
Lock L;             // L++, L becomes 1,
synchronous lock L is locked
Unlock L;    // L--, L becomes 0
```

Lock L executes operation L++, Unlock L executes operation L--, and Check Lock L checks if L is 0. The execution of Lock L and Unlock L is non-blocking. If the synchronous lock L is locked (), the execution of Check Lock L is blocked. Otherwise, it is not blocked.

The test sequence generation algorithm for solving the first synchronization problem is given in Table 3.16.

2. The second synchronization problem. t_i, t_j are transitions within M_i, $M_j (i \neq j)$ respectively, if the sequence of transitions $< t_i ... t_j >$ satisfies:

- Head $(t_j) \in$ Con (t_j)

- Transition $t_k (k \neq i, j)$ is not a transition within M_j, then the transition sequence is called the second synchronous input transition sequence.

  This book will contain test sequences with second synchronous input transition sequences that have second synchronization problems.

  The input sequence corresponding to a test sequence R with a second type synchronization problem may lead to the execution of a test sequence R' different from R. Table 3.17 gives the algorithm for generating a test sequence to avoid a second type synchronization problem.

TABLE 3.16   Algorithm for Solving RT-EFSM First Type Synchronization Problems

Algorithm 3.9 Solving RT-EFSM First Type Synchronization Problems

Input: set $T(T_1, T_2, \ldots, T_n)$ of continuous state transition sequences of RT-EFSM
Output: test sequence R.
Step 1: Create a synchronous lock queue Q. For t for which $\text{Con}(t)$ is not empty, define a synchronous lock $L_i = 0$ for t if there exists $S \in \text{Con}(t)$ that is traversed by T.
Step 2: Empty each T_i.
Step 3: For each transition t in E :
  1. If t is a transition in the synchronous lock queue Q, add the statement Check Lock L_i before all statements corresponding to t.
  2. If $\text{Tail}(t)\ \text{Con}(t')$, t' is a transition in the synchronous lock queue Q whose corresponding synchronous lock is L_j, then add the declaration Lock L_j to t.
  3. If the input of M_i's transition t is global input A, add "InputA" to the end of T_i's queue.
  4. If the input of M_i's transition t is the local input B from M_j, then add "Receive B from M_j" to the end of T_i's queue.
  5. If the output of M_i's transition t is a local output C to M_j, add "Send C to M_j" to the end of T_i's queue.
  6. If $\text{Head}(t) \in \text{Con}(t')$ and t' is a transition in a synchronous lock queue Q whose corresponding synchronous lock is L_j, add the statement Unlock L_j after all statements corresponding to t.
Step 4: Process each statement in T. If all statements corresponding to a local transition are processed, the transition is output to the test sequence queue.

TABLE 3.17   Algorithm for Solving RT-EFSM Second Type Synchronization Problems

Algorithm 3.10 Solving RT-EFSM Second Type Synchronization Problems

Input: set $T(T_1, T_2, \ldots, T_n)$ of continuous state transition sequences of RT-EFSM
Output: test sequence R.
Step 1: the same as steps 1~4 in Algorithm 3.9.
Step 2: If the generated test sequence contains a second type of synchronous input transition sequence $< t_i \ldots t_j >$, mark the transition t_j such that the migrated input is not generated when the corresponding input sequence is generated.

4. **Test case generation**

1. Test sequence traversal

Based on the generated test sequences, by traversing the test sequences (generated based on the TST), we can obtain. The time-constrained transition equivalence classes involved in each test sequence are obtained. Then test cases are generated according to certain adequacy coverage criteria (see later), test cases can be generated. The process of traversing the test sequences is as follows.

First, a stack STACK(x) is set to hold the information of the state nodes NODE(x) and transition TRANSPORTATION(x, y) experienced by the test scenario SCENARIO(x), and a hash table HASH(x) is set to hold the information of the state transitions that have been visited from the judgment node in the test sequence. In addition, during the test sequence traversal, the start node is noted as A, the target node is noted as B, and the intermediate node is noted as C. The specific search process is described as shown in Table 3.18 Iteration algorithm for the test sequence.

2. Test case generation

Based on traversing the test sequence, information of all time-constrained transition equivalence classes, such as time regions, guardianship conditions, and input/output information of state transition, is obtained. By instantiating time constraints, variable constraints, input/output information, etc. in time-constrained transition equivalence classes and combining with certain test case coverage guidelines, test cases can be automatically generated. In FSM-based testing methods, the commonly used and more mature test coverage guidelines are generally studied from state coverage, transition coverage, Boolean coverage, full predicate coverage, conversion pair coverage, etc. Different coverage guidelines generate different sets of test cases with different abilities to reveal errors. Given that these coverage criterion algorithms are relatively mature, only a brief description is given below.

State coverage criterion: The generated test case set is required to test every state, i.e., it should be such that every state in RT-EFSM is visited at least once. The state coverage criterion is the simplest and most easily satisfied test criterion and often requires the fewest test cases.

The test sequences generated by the algorithm in Section 3.3.4 can cover all states and transitions, based on which. Based on this, we can generate test cases that meet the requirements of state coverage and transition coverage criteria by assigning appropriate values to variables. The method is relatively simple.

TABLE 3.18   Iteration Algorithm for the Test Sequence

Algorithm 3.11 Test the Traversal Algorithm of a Sequence

Input: Test sequence (based on TST)
Output: State transition information obtained by traversal

Step 01:
```
01. ACK(s), (∃h)HASH(h), (∃c)SCENARIO(c),
```

Step 02:
```
02. CTIVITYDGRM(g) ∧ (∃a)STARTNODE(a, g)
03. → COPY(a, c) ∧ RECORD(a, A) ∧ PUSH(a, s),
04. P1:
05. (∃B)(TRANSPORTATION(B, A) ∧ JUDGENODE(B))
06. → SETFLAGTRUE(B),
07. (∃C)(TRANSPORTATION(C, B) ∧ FLAGFALSE(C))
08. → SETFLAGTRUE(C) ∧ COPY(C, c),
09. INSTEAD(A → B → C, A → B, B, B → C),
10. COPY(A → B → C, c),
11. PUSH(A → B, s), PUSH(B, s), PUSH(B → C, s), PUSH(C, s),
12. SAVE(B → C, h),
13. RECORD(C, A),
14. P2:
15. (∃B)(TRANSPORTATION(B, A) ∧ ¬JUDGENODE(B))
16. → COPY(A → B, c) ∧ COPY(B, c),
17. PUSH(A → B, s), PUSH(B, s),
18. RECORD(B, A),
```

Step 03:
```
19. (∃a)NODE(a, g) ∧ ¬END(a, g) → P1 ∨ P2, (∃a)NODE(a, g) ∧
    END(a, g) ∧ (∀n)INSTACK(n, s)
20. → STACKTOPPULL(n, s),
21. (∃a)NODE(a, g) ∧ END(a, g) ∧ (∀i)INSTACK(i, s)
22. → STACKTOPPULL(i, s),
```

Step 4:
```
23. ISSTACKTOP(n, s) ∧ CORRENT(n) ∧ JUDGE(n) → (P1 ∨ P2) ∧ P3,
24. ISSTACKTOP(n, s) ∧ CORRENT(n) ∧ ¬JUDGE(n)
25. →STACKTOPPULL(n, s).
```

Transition coverage criterion: It is required that the generated test case set causes each transition of RT-EFSM to be activated at least once. The system is first brought to a certain state (current state). If a transition "event" is accepted and the value of the transition "condition" is true, then the transition is activated. The transition coverage criterion is a simpler and more easily satisfied test criterion and often requires fewer test cases.

Boolean override: Requires that all migrated Boolean conditions of RT-EFSM take TRUE or FALSE once each. The transition coverage test guideline simply tests whether the statutes' transitions are implemented; it does not guarantee that every transition is implemented correctly. To effectively test each transition in RT-EFSM, it is necessary to have corresponding test cases to test when the value of the ventid condition (precondition) in the transition is true or false; if the value of the Boolean condition is true, the system state is migrated to the corresponding next state according to the transition relation. Otherwise, the system does not execute the transition relation, and the system stays in its original state.

Full predicate coverage criterion: When there are multiple Boolean conditions in the transition relation, the coverage criterion is called the full predicate coverage criterion for transition conditions. That is, each Boolean condition is required to take TRUE or FALSE once. The Boolean coverage criterion is a special case of the full predicate coverage criterion.

Transition pair coverage criterion: Requires that each state be considered independently and that the input transitions of each state match its output transitions, i.e., the combination of these input and output transitions of the state is used to create test cases.

In addition to the above coverage criterion, this book combines the time-constrained characteristics of real-time embedded software and proposes a time-conditional coverage criterion, that is, for each state transition in RT-EFSM, in addition to satisfying the full predicate coverage or Boolean coverage criterion, the time used for transition must satisfy the time constraint, which can be specifically divided into fixed time, obeying some distribution function or time interval for processing respectively, and this coverage condition is defined as follows.

Definition 3.19

Time-conditional coverage criterion, defined as follows.

$$\exists S_i \in S^*, \exists S_j \in S^*, \forall t \in T\left\{S_i \to S_j\right\}$$

and satisfies

$$t = \left\{t \mid t = t_S \| t \le t_F \| t \in t_I\right\}$$

According to the above guidelines, all migrated time-related Boolean conditions of RT-EFSM must take TRUE or FALSE once each. Both those satisfying the time constraints and those not satisfying the time constraints have corresponding test sequences for testing to ensure that the automatically generated test sequences can satisfy the adequacy requirements.

The test case generation algorithm based on the temporal conditional coverage adequacy determination criterion is shown in Table 3.19.

TABLE 3.19   Test Case Generation Algorithm Based on Time-Conditional Coverage Criterion

---

Algorithm 3.12 Test Case Generation Based on Time-Conditional Coverage Criteria

Input: extended test sequence US_{ex}
Output: set of test cases that satisfy the time-conditional coverage criterion
StateTo(s): the state of arrival s
transitionOut(s): the set of transitions out of the state
event(s'): the event that triggers the s' state
ventideon(s'): the precondition of s', divided into variable constraints and imposed constraints
Follow(s'): the next state of s'
ExpectedState – the post-converted state
ValueTransPara(s'): assigns a value that raises the trigger event when the precondition variable for s' is satisfied
timSimple(F): sampling according to the time-constrained distribution function F
ExpressionParse(exp, value): get the value of the variable in the expression from the syntax analysis of the expression exp

(*Continued*)

TABLE 3.19 (*Continued*)   Test Case Generation Algorithm Based on Time-Conditional Coverage Criterion

Algorithm 3.12 Test Case Generation Based on Time-Conditional Coverage Criteria

```
01 TimeConstraintCoverageTestCaseGen (Usex)
02. BEGIN
03      TestcaseSet = EMPTY;
04      FOR EACH source state in Usex // traverse the test
sequence
05          Get StateTo(s);
06          Get transitionOut(s);
07          FOR EACH outgoing transition ∈ transitionOut(s)
08              ExpectedState = Follow(s');
09              ValueTransPara(s') = EMPTY;
10              Get event(s') and 82ventide8282on(s');
11              FOR EACH conditioni in 82ventide8282on(s')
12                  IF(conditioni. varConstrain == TRUE))
13          IF(conditioni. timeConstrain.type == tS) //
            time constraint is a fixed time value
14                              IF(ValueTransPara(s') ≤
conditioni.timeConstrainValue)
15                                  TestcaseSet = TestcaseSet ∪
{StateTo(s), ValueTransPara(s'), ExpectedState}; //variable
instantiation
16                      END IF
17          END IF

18          IF(conditioni.timeConstrain.type == tF) //
            time constraint is the distribution function F
19                          ValueTransPara(s') =
timSimple(F) //sample the values
20                              IF(ValueTransPara(s') ≤
conditioni.timeConstrainValue
21                                  TestcaseSet =
TestcaseSet ∪ {StateTo(s), ValueTransPara(s'),
22                                      ExpectedState};
23                      END IF
24                  END IF
25              IF(conditioni.timeConstrain.type == tI) //
                time constrained interval
26                  ValueTransPara(s') = timSimple(F)
27                  IF(ValueTransPara(s') ≥ conditioni.
timeConstrain.minValue&&
28                      ValueTransPara(s') ≤ conditioni.
timeConstrain.maxValue)
```

(*Continued*)

TABLE 3.19 (*Continued*)   Test Case Generation Algorithm Based on Time-Conditional Coverage Criterion

---

Algorithm 3.12 Test Case Generation Based on Time-Conditional Coverage Criteria

```
29                     TestcaseSet = TestcaseSet ∪
{StateTo(s), ValueTransPara(s'), ExpectedState};
30                  END IF
31              END IF
32                  BEGIN
33                      IF(a condition variable var ∈
StateTo(s),.
34                          var.name == conditioni.name ∧
var.value == conditioni.value)
35                          ValueTransPara(s') =
ValueTransPara(s') ∪ {conditioni.name, conditioni.value};
36                      END
37                      ELSE((conditioni.varConstrain ==
expression) && (conditioni.timeConstrain == time)
38                      BEGIN
39                          IF(a condition variable exp ∈
StateTo(s),
40                              exp.name == conditioni.name ∧
exp.value == conditioni.value)
41                              ExpressionParse(exp.name, exp.
value);
42                              ValueTransPara(s') =
ValueTransPara(s') ∪ {vari.name, vari. Value};
43                          END
44                      END IF
45              END FOR
46              ValueTransPara(s') = ValueTransPara(s') ∪
{event(s').name, event(s').afterValue};
47              TestcaseSet = TestcaseSet ∪ {StateTo(s),
ValueTransPara(s'), ExpectedState};
48              ExpectedState = current state;
49              FOR EACH variable var in ValueTransPara(s')
// traversal, all variables instantiated
50                  ValueTransPara(s') = ValueTransPara(s')
- {var.name, var.value};
51                  var.value = var.value;
52                  ValueTransPara(s') = ValueTransPara(s')
∪ {var.name, var.value};
53                  TestcaseSet = TestcaseSet ∪ {StateTo(s),
ValueTransPara(s'), ExpectedState};
54              END FOR
55          END FOR
56      END FOR
57 END TimeConstraintCoverageTestCaseGen
```

---

3. Description of test-type support

Real-time embedded software system testing based on the black-box testing method requires different test types to verify different characteristics of the software under test. The test sequences and test case generation methods provided in this book can generate normal functional test cases and test types such as exception, boundary, performance, interface, safety, and strength. The specific descriptions are as follows.

Normal function test cases: these can complete the examination of the normal workflow situation of the system. By traversing the time-constrained equivalence classes in the test sequence, selecting the normal equivalence classes of variable constraints and time constraints, and testing them according to the normal workflow of the system, test cases for normal functions can be generated.

Abnormal test cases: these can complete the examination of the functional implementation in the abnormal situation of the system. In the test sequence and test case generation method proposed in this book, the design of abnormal test cases can be accomplished by artificially setting unreachable state transition, state transition of wrong timing sequence, variation testing in the case of multi-variable constraints, etc., or by selecting use cases in the range of non-normal equivalence classes for variables and time constraints.

Boundary test cases: these can complete the examination of the system's functional implementation in the boundary case, can include the test of the boundary or endpoint of the system input or output domain, the test of the boundary or endpoint of state transition, the test of the boundary or endpoint of functional boundary, the test of the boundary or endpoint of performance boundary, and the test of the boundary or endpoint of the capacity boundary. In the test sequence and test case generation method proposed in this book, the design of boundary test cases can be completed by analyzing the number of variables and time constraints in the time-constrained transition equivalence class and selecting the boundary point (value) use cases for state transition, function, and performance.

Performance test cases: these can be completed to examine the accuracy of program calculation (processing accuracy) when the system obtains quantitative results, the time characteristics of the system and the actual time to complete the function (response time), the amount of data processed by the system to complete a specific function, or the system's ability to handle concurrent things and concurrent user access. The test sequences and test case generation methods proposed in this book are fully capable of accomplishing the examination mentioned above of system performance, i.e., they can support the generation of performance test cases.

Interface test cases: these can complete the test of all system's external interfaces, including the examination of the format normality and content correctness of the interface communication protocol, need to test each external input/output interface of the system for normal and abnormal conditions. In real-time embedded software system testing, interface testing is one of the core elements of testing. According to the book's support mechanism for ventide the system and its surrounding cross-linked devices and the definition of time-constrained transition equivalence classes, It is obvious that the test sequences and test case generation methods proposed in the book are fully capable of generating interface test cases.

Security test cases: these can be completed to test the system's ability to prevent dangerous states from occurring, to handle and protect the system under abnormal conditions, to handle failure modes and safety-critical operation errors. In the test sequence and test case generation method proposed in this book, the design of abnormal test cases can also be completed by artificially setting unreachable state transition, state transition of wrong timing, and other variant tests.

Intensity test cases: these can be completed for the maximum amount of information processed by the system, the data capacity of the saturation experiment indicators and continuous prescribed, continuous uninterrupted testing. Obviously, in the test sequence and test case generation method proposed in this book, the design of intensity test cases can be achieved by applying a large amount of interface data to all system interfaces under test in a given time and increasing the long-time examination of system operation.

In addition to the test mentioned above types, the test case design of the recovery test, data processing test, and other types of test cases can be completed by using the test sequence and test case generation methods proposed in this book. In addition, after extension, it can support the design of reliable test cases.

4. XML-based test case storage

The test cases generated using the method provided in this chapter are independent of the specific test platform. To make the generated test cases easily convertible into test descriptions (or test scripts) supported by the specific test platform, they must be expressed in the form of a common, easy-to-grasp intermediate language for testers so that the readability of the test data can be achieved and the computer recognition can be facilitated. On the basis of this intermediate language form of test case data, test descriptions (or test scripts) supported by a specific test platform can be generated through further processing.

With the continuous development of computer technology, markup languages have become an important means of data storage and conversion in the software field. XML (Extensible Markup Language) is a markup language that provides a structured metadata representation with the platform and semantic independence, openness, and extensibility. Due to the self-explanatory nature of XML, structured data can be easily read and saved. Therefore, the generated test cases are saved in XML format to support subsequent automatic conversion to test descriptions (scripts) supported by the test platform.

In real-time embedded software testing, the test cases generated based on RT-EFSM describe a complete execution process of system activities. The test cases should be saved as follows.

- Test case index information <TC: IndexInfos>, which can be subdivided into test case number information <TC: SNInfo>, test case person information <TC: PersonInfo>, test case time information <TC: DateInfo>, test case version information <TC VersionInfo>, and so on.

- Software under test information <TC: SUTInfos>, software under test name <TC: SUTNameInfo>, software under test version information <TC: SUTVersionInfo>, software development unit under test information <TC: SUTDeveloperInfo>, etc.

- Test case static information <TC: StaticInfos>, which can be subdivided into emulation device information <TC: SequipmentInfo>, bus type information <TC: IOBusInfo>, variable information <TC: VarDataInfo>, etc.

- Test case dynamic information <TC: DynamicInfos>, which can be subdivided into state information <TC: StateInfo>, constraint information <TC: ConstraintInfo>, state transition information <TC: StateTransition>, input information <TC: InputInfo>, output information <TC: OutputInfo>, etc.

The hierarchy of the test cases stored in XML format is shown in Table 3.20.

An example of storing test cases for UAV flight control software in XML format is given below.

```
<TC: TestCase20091210>
    <TC: IndexInfos >
        < TC :SNInfo >T01-GN-101</ TC :SNInfo >
        <TC: PersonInfo >HEEJUN</ TC: PersonInfo >
        <TC: DateInfo>2010/12/10</ TC: DateInfo>
        <TC: VersionInfo> V1.0</.TC: VersionInfo>
    </TC: IndexInfos >
    <TC: SUTInfos>
        <TC: SUTNameInfo>UAVFCS</ TC: SUTNameInfo>
        <TC: SUTVersionInfo>V3.45</ TC: SUTVersionInfo>
        <TC: SUTDeveloperInfo>CCTC</ TC:
SUTDeveloperInfo>
    </ TC: SUTInfos>.
    <TC: StaticInfos>
        <TC: SequipmentInfo>NULL</ TC: SequipmentInfo>
        <TC: IOBusInfo>
                    <IOBus001> MIL-STD-1553B </
IOBus001>
                    <IOBus002> RS-422</ IOBus002>
                    <IOBus003> RS-232</ IOBus003>
        </ TC: IOBusInfo>.
        <TC: VarDataInfo>
                    <VarData001>
                        <VarData001Name>A1</
VarData001Name >
                        <VarData001Type>Int</
VarData001Type >
        <VarData001>
                • • •
```

TABLE 3.20   XML Storage Structure for Test Cases

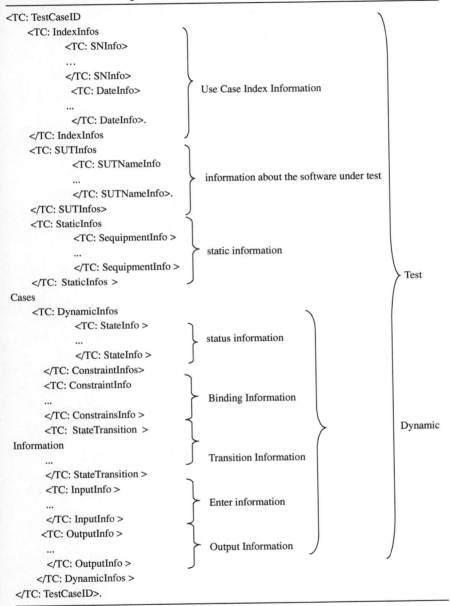

```
<TC: TestCaseID
    <TC: IndexInfos
            <TC: SNInfo>
            ...
            </TC: SNInfo>
            <TC: DateInfo>                    Use Case Index Information
            ...
            </TC: DateInfo>.
    </TC: IndexInfos
    <TC: SUTInfos
            <TC: SUTNameInfo
            ...                               information about the software under test
            </TC: SUTNameInfo>.
    </TC: SUTInfos>
    <TC: StaticInfos
            <TC: SequipmentInfo >
            ...                               static information
            </TC: SequipmentInfo >
    </TC: StaticInfos >
Cases
    <TC: DynamicInfos
            <TC: StateInfo >
            ...                               status information
            </TC: StateInfo >
    </TC: ConstraintInfos>
    <TC: ConstraintInfo
    ...                                       Binding Information
    </TC: ConstrainsInfo >
    <TC: StateTransition >
Information
    ...                                       Transition Information
    </TC: StateTransition >
    <TC: InputInfo >
    ...                                       Enter information
    </TC: InputInfo >
    <TC: OutputInfo >
    ...                                       Output Information
    </TC: OutputInfo >
    </TC: DynamicInfos >
</TC: TestCaseID>.
```

```
                    <VarData006>
                          < VarData006Name>C1</
VarData006Name >
                          <VarData006Type>Int</
VarData006Type >
              <VarData006>
        <TC: VarDataInfo>
     </ TC: StaticInfos>.
     <TC: DynamicInfos>
        <TC: StateInfo>
           <TC: State001>
             <StateID>MA</ StateID>
             <StateName>ManualAmendment </ StateName>
             <StateDescribe>NULL</ StateDescribe>
             <StateAttribute> ManualAmendment</
StateAttribute>
           </ TC: State001>
           . . .
           <TC: State006>
             <StateID>CRC</ StateID>
             <StateName> CarriageRemoteControl </
StateName>
             <StateDescribe>NULL</ StateDescribe>
             <StateAttribute> CarriageRemoteControl </
StateAttribute>
           </ TC: State006>
        </ TC: StateInfo>
        <TC: ConstrainsInfo>
           <varConstraint>{ (C1= =1)&&(A2= =1,vg=
=552.8)}< varConstraint >
           <timeConstraint>{gt>0&&lt<=20ms}<timeConstra
int
        </ TC: ConstrainsInfo>.
              <TC: StateTransition>
           <StateTransitionID>AC-MA</ StateTransitionID>
           <SourceState>AC</ SourceState>
           <DestState>MA</ DestState>
           <ventide>event1</ ventide>
           < VarDataInfo >C1</ VarDataInfo >
           < VarDataInfo >A2</ VarDataInfo >
           < VarDataInfo >vg</ VarDataInfo >
           < ConstrainsInfo >
```

```
        <varConstraint>{(C1= =1)&&(A2= =1,vg=
=552.8)}< varConstraint >
        <timeConstraint>{gt>0&&lt<=20ms}<timeConstr
aint>
        </ ConstrainsInfo >
        <TransitionActivityList>NULL</
TransitionActivityList>
    </TC: StateTransition >
    <TC: InputInfo>
        <VarData001Name>A2</VarData001Name >
        <VarData001Type>Int</ VarData001Type >
        <VarData003Name>vg</VarData003Name >
        <VarData003Type>Double</ VarData003Type >
        <VarData006Name>C1</VarData006Name >
        <VarData006Type>Int</ VarData006Type >
        <eventInfo>
            <ventide>event1</ ventide>
        <event>
            ReceiveData(C1, 1, STATE_OF_OPERATION, 1);
                GetGlobalTime(gt);
                GetLocalTime(lt);
                ConstraintCAL(C1,A2,vg,gt,lt);
        <event>
        </ eventInfo>
    </ TC: InputInfo>.
    <TC: OutputInfo>
            <VarData005Name>B2</VarData005Name >
            <VarData005Type>Int</ VarData005Type >
        <eventInfo>
            <ventide>event2</ ventide>
        <event>
            SendData(A2, vg, STATE_OF_OPERATION, 0);
        <event>
        </ eventInfo>
    <</ TC: OutputInfo>
    </ TC: DynamicInfos>
    </TC: TestCase20091210>
```

3.4 SUMMARY

The introduction of formal methods helps improve the automation of real-time embedded software testing and is the future trend and direction in software testing. In this chapter, we systematically introduce the embedded software system testing techniques based on formal methods. Firstly, a comprehensive summary and sorting out of software formal testing techniques is given, and the testing techniques based on FSM and EFSM are highlighted. A real-time EFSM model RT-EFSM is given, and the model verification techniques are studied in depth to lay the foundation for the subsequent test case generation based on RT-EFSM.

CHAPTER 4

Real-Time Embedded Software Automation Test Description Technology

T HE TEST DESCRIPTION (SCRIPT) in embedded software system testing is the core element driving automated testing. How to design and implement a test description language that meets the characteristics of embedded software is directly related to the success or failure of subsequent automated test environment construction, and this chapter will explain and illustrate the real-time embedded software test description technology in detail.

4.1 TEST DESCRIPTION CONCEPT AND CLASSIFICATION

4.1.1 Test Description Concepts

With the development of the modern software industry, the scale of software is increasingly large, and for a long time, the traditional software testing used manual methods with low efficiency. Obviously, when the software is very large, the number of test codes is very impressive, which will inevitably lead to software testing costs and an increase in the number of software testing cycles. The establishment of maintainable, effective

DOI: 10.1201/9781003390923-5

software testing can greatly reduce the cost of engineering. Therefore, the software testing automation requirements are also increasingly urgent.

Real-time embedded software, due to its complex operating environment and interface cross-linking relationships, requires high real-time test input and feedback processing, making it difficult to ensure the effectiveness of traditional manual testing. Therefore, more and more research studies introduce automation testing techniques into the field of real-time embedded software testing.

Real-time embedded software automation testing is essentially based on user programming testing, so the introduction of test description technology is an effective means to realize test automation technology, which can reduce the workload of testers and improve the maintainability of software testing. At the same time, by enhancing the portability of the test description language, it is conducive to the realization of cross-platform, which can improve the reusability of the test code and the repeatability of the test.

The purpose of the test description is to: (1) define the test case running scenario; (2) allow testers to customize their own test "metadata"; and (3) facilitate running on a specific test platform. Test description is mainly the description of test cases. From the results of current literature research, there is no standard or specification for test description.

The test description is a standardized description of a sequence of software test events and test instructions. Test descriptions and test scripts are closely related. Testers can express the test process and test intent through graphical or non-graphical test descriptions and then generate test scripts from the test descriptions to drive the tests. The method of test description directly affects the efficiency and difficulty of user-constructed tests. Therefore, a good test description method must have the following characteristics:

- Accuracy and clarity without ambiguity;

- Both graphical and non-graphical test descriptions are supported by a set of normalized languages;

- Graphical test descriptions should have mechanisms for automatic generation of normalized language;

- With a certain specification, test descriptions are generally able to reuse.

4.1.2 Test Description Classification

The classification of test descriptions can be classified in terms of usage, description means, and so on.

1. By usage, test descriptions can be divided into the following categories:

   - For the auxiliary use of software development and design process, such as in the test-based software development model, the test design should precede the software implementation, when the test description is used to assist test development, help programmers sort out the development intention and improve the correctness and effectiveness of development.

   - It is used for test case execution, which aims to improve the automation of testing, and mostly uses test scripts to store and execute test cases to drive the testing process and achieve the purpose of automated test execution.

   - For test design and test execution, such as Testing and Test Control Notation 3 (TTCN-3), which uses a combination of tree table notation to guide the software development process and can complete the automated execution of test cases.

2. By means of description, test descriptions can be classified into natural language description methods, structured table methods, descriptions based on formal methods, and test language descriptions.

   - Natural language description method. It is mainly applied to the traditional manual testing process, which generally uses manual operation to complete the test data input, and its advantage is that the testers are intuitive and clear. However, the quality and granularity of this description depend entirely on the use case designer, which cannot be recognized by the computer. In addition, natural language is ambiguous, so this description method is prone to misunderstanding between the test designer and the test executor.

   - Structured form approach. It refers to the method of form customization, in which the test content is filled in columns in a pre-customized form so that the test cases can be understood at a glance. In the test design phase, this is a frequently used form of description. It also has the inherent drawbacks of natural language descriptions since the content of the form filling is still natural language.

- Description based on formal methods. This approach mostly describes only the language of test input, including the generation of test input data and self-defined data based on formal statutes. The form of the test cases generated in this way depends on the form of the requirement statute and the algorithm of the use case generation based on mathematical theory, as its form is also abstract and incomprehensible to the computer, and the algorithm is complex and does not facilitate the communication among testers. In addition, the test data generated based on the formal statute still needs to be further transformed into a language that can be processed by the computer before the test can be executed.

- Test languages. With the continuous development of automated testing technology, international testing organizations, i.e., test tool vendors, have been exploring new techniques for test description languages, and numerous test languages have emerged one after another with increasingly wide applications. These test languages can be divided into two categories:

  - Specialized test languages, such as TTCN-3, ATLASGOAL, PLACE, ELATE, and DIMATE.

  - Extensions based on existing general-purpose programming languages such as TeCL, TestTalk, ESSTSL, test scripting languages based on Basic, C++, Java, Tcl/tk, perl, and python extensions, etc.

4.2 CHARACTERISTICS OF REAL-TIME EMBEDDED SOFTWARE TEST DESCRIPTION

4.2.1 Real-Time Embedded Software Testing Features

The characteristics of real-time embedded software determine the special nature of its testing. Test methods, test strategies, and test tools have unique properties that other software does not have. This is reflected in the following aspects:

1. **Highly targeted testing methods**

   As a component of a large system, real-time embedded systems often have a wide variety of interfaces and complex types, which directly leads to the test methods for real-time embedded software is usually carried out only for a certain type or even a typical system and often need to be developed specifically for its supporting test tools, but these tools are difficult to apply to the testing of other embedded systems, that is, poor generality.

2. **Large number of test cases and complex situations**

   Due to the complex cross-linking relationship of real-time embedded systems, generally run in a specific hardware environment, and often there is real-time communication with the surrounding cross-linking devices and has strong responsiveness and real-time, which leads to a large scale of software input, real-time, and timing relationship and complexity, in order to fully test must increase the number of test cases and improve the quality of test cases.

3. **Special emphasis on system testing**

   Due to the large amount of hardware information in real-time embedded software and the high degree of software hardware coupling. Testing the software separately before it is integrated with the hardware environment is often insufficient. It is often inadequate (e.g., when the actual operation of the system under test in real-time feedback and timing relationship is difficult to truly simulate), so the real effective test is in the real-time embedded system integration (hardware-software integration of the real environment) after the system-level testing, and often using software requirements-based dynamic testing is the main approach.

4. **Dependence on test tools (environment)**

   System testing of real-time embedded system software must rely on test tools to provide automated test inputs as well as collect output information in real time. Therefore, the testing of real-time embedded systems requires a high and dependent test environment.

5. **Strong demand for automated testing**

   As the application of embedded systems continues to spread, it often takes less time, cost, and manpower to complete the testing of a real-time embedded system, especially when the system is upgraded more frequently and the delivery time is limited, which requires test cases and test environments with high versatility and reusability, so there is a strong demand for automated testing, and more and more test tools (environments) introduce automation test descriptions (scripts).

4.2.2 RT-ESTDL Design Principles

Based on the above analysis, it can be concluded that the real-time embedded software test description language (RT-ESTDL) should follow the following design principles:

1. **Easy for testers to understand and master**

   The purpose of RT-ESTDL is to provide testers with an intuitive, easy to write and easy to maintain test description language for real-time embedded software emulation testing, so it is necessary to ensure the simplicity and clarity of RT-ESTDL, with a good design structure, so that testers can easily understand and master.

2. **Meet the real-time embedded software requirements for real-time**

   As a specialized test description language for real-time embedded software automation testing, RT-ESTDL must be able to support the real-time requirements of real-time embedded software and be able to handle the description of real-time, concurrent input of test inputs. It should also be able to support the processing of real-time feedback from tests during the testing of real-time embedded systems.

3. **With good generality and portability**

   Real-time embedded software test platforms are often built on top of real-time operating systems (RTOS) (e.g., VxWorks, μC/OS, and RT-Linux). The portability of RT-ESTDL can be understood as porting across different testing platforms (or RTOS), meaning that the test descriptions generated by testers can be run in any running environment equipped with the RT-ESTDL language execution system.

4. **With good test platform adaptability**

   As a more general test description language, RT-ESTDL and its execution system should have good test platform adaptability and should ensure that when porting from one test platform to another, the adaptation to the new platform can be done quickly without or with only a few changes.

5. **Support real-time embedded system cross-linked environment modeling and inter-device communication**

   The real-time embedded system under test often exists around the cross-linked devices. In the real-time embedded software simulation test, the modeling of the system under test and its surrounding cross-linked devices should be completed based on the interface control document (ICD), and the description of the real-time communication between the devices should be supported during the test.

6. **With better reusability**

   RT-ESTDL should be designed in a more general programming language extension, which can make the test description developed by the tester without or only need to make a few changes to quickly organize a new round of testing in the case of upgrading the software under test, ensuring that the test description has good reusability, facilitating the saving of testing time, and improving testing efficiency.

7. **With good encapsulation and scalability**

   RT-ESTDL should have good encapsulation and scalability in the following two aspects:

   - The grammar of the language can be easily extended to better suit the needs of different real-time embedded software test descriptions according to the different needs of testing.

   - RT-ESTDL should encapsulate the test functions commonly used for real-time embedded software testing so that testers can describe complex test logic with fewer statements. In addition, these encapsulated test library functions should be easy for testers to add or modify, that is, the test function library has good scalability.

8. **Have good reliability and robustness**

   As a specialized test language, RT-ESTDL should have good reliability and robustness, as evidenced by:

   - Having a complete grammar and semantics;

   - Test descriptions written using the RT-ESTDL must be able to give accurate and reproducible test results and not allow problems in the test due to defects in the RT-ESTDL and its implementation system itself;

- When tests are run, avoid illegal exits or terminations if unexpected circumstances arise and make every effort to give as many prompts as possible;

- The mutual independence between test descriptions should be ensured as much as possible to reduce their dependencies and prevent the occurrence of abnormal test termination due to the failure of one or several test descriptions.

4.2.3 Status and Role of RT-ESTDL

In the automated real-time embedded software semi-physical simulation testing, RT-ESTDL play is the core element that drives the test execution process. Figure 4.1 gives the status and role of RT-ESTDL in automated real-time embedded software emulation testing; see Chapter 6 for the specific real-time embedded software emulation test environment design.

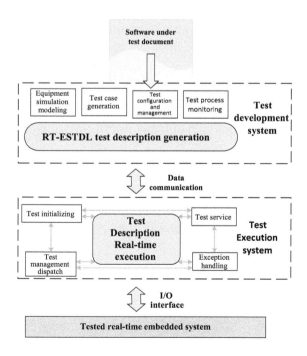

FIGURE 4.1   Status and role of RT-ESTDL.

4.3 DESIGN OF REAL-TIME EMBEDDED SOFTWARE TEST DESCRIPTION LANGUAGE

In real-time embedded software automation testing, the test description language is a very critical factor. Compared with the general-purpose programming language, the test description language is generally implemented based on the extensions and improvements of the general-purpose programming language, that is, it is extended on the basis of the general-purpose programming language to add some descriptions and implementation methods suitable for real-time embedded software testing, such as the description of the system under test modeling, the control of the test flow, the description of test cases, real-time, concurrent, and test feedback processing. The purpose of RT-ESTDL is to provide testers with an intuitive, easy to write, easy to maintain dedicated test language for real-time embedded software simulation testing.

4.3.1 Lexicon of RT-ESTDL

RT-ESTDL mainly refers to C and C++ language in lexicography and syntax. According to the characteristics of real-time embedded software testing, it eliminates the language elements not needed for real-time embedded testing in C and C++ language, introduces object-oriented thinking, and increases the elements necessary for real-time embedded software testing, such as adding support for objects to facilitate real-time embedded software device modeling; allowing testers to customize test primitives; adding support for avionics bus block type data; adding support for device communication; and eliminating explicit declaration of data types so that testers can focus more on the test case description itself.

A brief description of the lexicon of the RT-ESTDL language is given below (see Appendix 2 for details).

For the language itself (simplified C/C++ language format):

- Global variables, local variables, functions and procedures with parameters
- Numeric constants, string constants
- C, C++ and shell format comment statements
- include statement, using statement
- if statements, if-else statements

- new statement (for device object construction)
- switch-case statement, for statement, while statement, do statement
- continue, break, return statements
- Common standard library function support (extensible)
- Commonly used arithmetic/bitwise operators, operators
- Support for user-defined functions

For the characteristics of real-time embedded software simulation testing, on the basis of the above, the following features are introduced:

- Representation and reference to the global clock in the test
- Construction of equipment simulation model
- Description and operation of device simulation models and their variables
- Communication between device simulation models
- Time waiting function
- Standard signal generation functions, etc.

In addition, all symbols (tokens) of the RT-ESTDL language are shown in Table 4.1.

4.3.2 Syntax of RT-ESTDL

BNF (Backus-Naur Form) representation is a grammatical representation commonly used in programming languages nowadays. It was first introduced by John Backus and Peter Naur to describe the symbol set of computer language grammar, which can strictly represent the grammar rules and facilitate the definition of the grammar rules of programming languages. The RT-ESTDL proposed in this book is based on the general-purpose language, adding support for bus data types commonly used in real-time embedded software, increasing the clock description mechanism, and improving and extending the language grammar to make it more suitable for completing real-time embedded software test description. The following only gives the syntax description of RT-ESTDL (please refer to Appendix 2 for the specific semantics and usage).

TABLE 4.1   RT-ESTDL Language Symbol Classification Table

Category	Description					
Keyword	*var*	*const*	*procedure*	*include*	*using*	*equipment*
	static	*string*	*array*	*object*	*function*	
	resource	*if*	*else*	*switch*	*for*	
	do	*while*	*break*	*continue*	*return*	
	case	*default*	*new*	*bool*	*int*	
	float	*complex*	*vec2*	*vec3*	*vec4*	
	mat2	*mat3*	*mat4*			
Operator	Arithmetic operators: +, -, *, /, power (^), modulo (%), etc. Relational comparison operators: >, >=, < and <=, sameness comparison operators == and! =					
Identifier	Such as variable names, constant names, procedure, and function names, the first character must be a letter; underscores are also treated as letters; upper and lower case letters are sensitive; identifiers can be of any length					
Constant	Numeric constants and string constants					
Boundary	Such as commas, semicolons, and parentheses					

The syntax description of RT-ESTDL (based on BNF) is as follows:

```
Terminals:
        identifier
translation-unit:
        (procedure-definition
        | declaration)+
procedure-definition:
        declaration-specifiers? declarator
declaration* block
declaration:
        declaration-specifiers init-declarator% ";"
declaration-specifiers:
        (type-specifier)+
type-specifier:
        ("var"
        | equipemnt-specifier
        | procedure-specifier
        | function-specifier)
equipemnt -specifier:
        ("equipemnt ") (identifier
        | dentifier "::" equipemnt -specifier)
equipemnt variable -specifier:
        equipemnt -specifie "." dentifier
```

```
procedure-specifier:
        ("procudure ") (identifier? "{" field-
declaration+ "}"
        |identifier)
function -specifier:
        ("function ") (identifier? "{" field-
declaration+ "}"
        |identifier)
init-declarator:
        declarator ("=" initializer)?
field-declaration:
        (type-specifier)+ field-declarator%
field-declarator:
        declarator
        | declarator? ":" constant-expression
declarator:
        (identifier
        | "(" declarator ")") ("(" parameter-type-list
")"
        |"(" identifier%? ")")*
parameter-type-list:
        parameter-declaration% (", " "...")?
parameter-declaration:
        declaration-specifiers (declarator
        | abstract-declarator)?initializer:
assignment-expression
        | "{" initializer% ", "? "}"
statement:
        ((identifier
        | "case" constant-expression
        | "default") ":")* (expression? ";"
        | block
        | "if" "(" expression ")" statement
        |"if" "(" expression ")" statement "else"
statement
        | "while" "(" expression ")" statement
        | "do" statement "while" "(" expression ")"
";"
        | "for" "(" expression? ";" expression? ";"
expression? ")" statement
        | "continue" ";"
        | "break" ";"
```

```
      | "return" expression? ";")
    block type:
       ("var"
       | "1553BBLOCK"
       | "ARINC429BLOCK"
       | "ARINC629BLOCK"
       | "RS422BLOCK"
       | "RS232BLOCK"
       | "RS485BLOCK")
block:
          "{"[block type*]declaration* statement* "}"
expression:
       assignment-expression%
assignment-expression:
         (unary-expression ("="
       | "*="
       | "/="
       | "%="
       | "+="
       | "-="
       | "@="
       | "@="
       | "&="
       | "^="
       | "
       |="))* conditional-expression
conditional-expression:
       logical-OR-expression ("?" expression ":"
conditional-expression)?
    constant-expression: conditional-expression
    logical-OR-expression:
       logical-AND-expression ("||"
logical-AND-expression)*
    logical-AND-expression:
       inclusive-OR-expression ("&&"
inclusive-OR-expression)*
    inclusive-OR-expression:
       exclusive-OR-expression ("|"
exclusive-OR-expression)*
    exclusive-OR-expression:
       AND-expression ("^" AND-expression)*
    AND-expression:
```

```
      equality-expression ("&" equality-expression)*
   equality-expression:
      elational-expression (("==" | "!=")
relational-expression)*
   relational-expression:
      shift-expression (("<"
      | ">"
      | "<="
      | ">=") additive-expression)*
   additive-expression:
      multiplicative-expression (("+" | "-")
multiplicative-expression)*
   postfix-expression:
       (identifier
      | string
      | "(" expression ")") ("[" expression "]"
      | "(" assignment-expression% ")"
      | "++"
      | "--")*
   systemClock: "::"gt
   number: 0 | 1 | 2 | 3 | 4 | 5 | 6 | 7 | 8 | 9
   letter: a | b | c | … | z | A | B | C | … | Z
```

4.4 RT-ESTDL SUPPORT MECHANISM FOR REAL-TIME EMBEDDED SOFTWARE TESTING

4.4.1 Support for Real-Time Embedded Device Modeling

According to the extension of UML class diagram in Section 3.3.3.2, RT-ESTDL uses the technique based on object-oriented thinking to complete the modeling of real-time embedded devices, and testers can use inheritance and polymorphism to complete the static modeling work of real-time embedded software and its surrounding cross-linked devices through the real-time embedded software static modeling framework (see Figure 3.24). The following is an example of avionics real-time embedded device modeling based on the application of extended UML class diagrams in RT-ESTDL.

As an important component and nerve center system of aircraft, avionics equipment is a core component for aircraft to complete flight attitude control, mission management and weapon management as well as an important factor to determine the combat effectiveness of warplanes.

Avionics software is the computer software applied in the avionics system to realize the functions of data acquisition, data interpretation, automatic control and data interaction, which generally has the characteristics of real-time, embedded, high reliability, and high security.

The modern integrated avionics system is a distributed computer network system based on the aviation data bus. For the subsystems with a large amount of equipment and complex functions, the secondary integration is realized through the subsystem control and management computer. The structure of a typical avionics system and subsystem is shown in Figure 4.2.

It is particularly important to emphasize that the important basis for avionics static modeling is the ICD between avionics devices, which is the standard document for avionics data bus interface definition and the basis for avionics device modeling. The data block description is the typical format of avionics bus data, which generally includes source device, destination device, and data update cycle. Each data block also includes several data elements, and each element has its own format definition and description. Table 4.2 gives the format and content of a typical avionics system ICD file.

Based on the above analysis, the avionics class (CAVIEqpmt) is introduced in RT-ESTDL for describing avionics devices (derived from the generic device class CEQUIPMENT), and correspondingly the avionics I/O interface data class CAVIIODATAVAR (derived from the generic

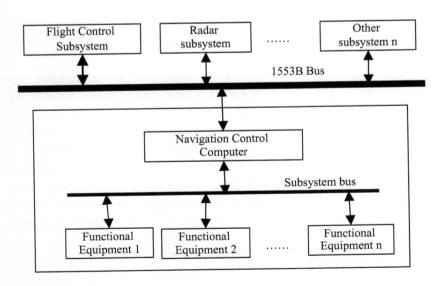

FIGURE 4.2   Typical avionics system architecture.

TABLE 4.2   Format and Content of a Typical Avionics System ICD File

BLOCK NAME:	Block Name
SOURCE:	Source
DESTINATION:	Purpose
COMMUNICATION:	Communication format
PRIORITY:	Priority
TRANSMISSION:	Type of transmission
REFRESH CYCLE:	update period
MAXIMUM:	Maximum delay
OVERWRITE PERMITTED:	Allowed override flag
SYSTEM STATE:	System status
INTERRUPT:	whether to allow interrupts
SIZE:	Size
BLOCK REMARKS:	Block description
BLOCK ELEMENTS:	Block elements, containing the name of each signal
SIGNAL NAME:	Signal name
SIGNAL LABEL:	Signal label
SIGNAL TYPE:	Signal type
SIGNAL SOURCE:	Signal source
DISTRIBUTION:	signal distribution
SIGNAL FORMAT:	Signal format
SIGNAL RANGE:	Signal range
COMPUTATION RATE:	Rate of operation
DATA BIT DESCRIPTION:	Data bit description
(Example:)	
BIT 0 STATIC-PRESSURE—BU USED	
BIT 1 STATIC-PRESSURE—BU USED	
...	
ACCURACY:	Precision

interface data class CIODATAVAR) is introduced for describing real-time embedded devices. The avionics bus connection class CAVIIOLINK is introduced to describe the type of I/O bus connection between real-time embedded devices (derived from the general bus connection class CIOLINK). At the same time, C1553BBLOCK, CARINC429BLOCK, CARINC629BLOCK, CRS422BLOCK, CRS232BLOCK, and other derived classes are introduced to describe the bus data connection between avionics devices. The static modeling of avionics equipment software derived based on the real-time embedded software static modeling framework is shown in Figure 4.3.

Based on the above analysis, the RT-ESTDL description of the static modeling of a typical combined avionics system inertial/satellite navigation system I/GNS is shown in Table 4.3.

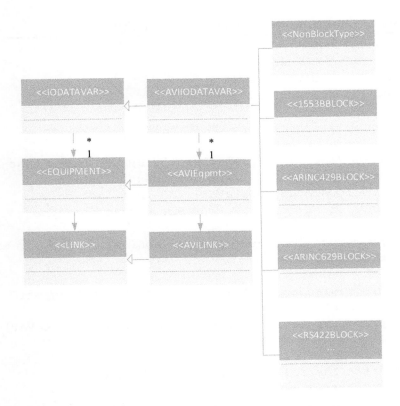

FIGURE 4.3   Static modeling diagram of avionics equipment software.

4.4.2 Support for Real-Time Embedded Software Testing Time Constraints and Concurrent Processing

RT-ESTDL uses real-time scheduling to complete the processing of multiple real-time embedded software test tasks. In addition, the test task action sequence allows references to the system clock, all of which can ensure real-time software test time constraints and concurrent processing. The specific analysis is as follows:

1. The design of RT-ESTDL is based on the description method of time-constrained migration equivalence classes, which can better complete the description of the temporal characteristics of each state migration in the real-time embedded software testing process.

2. By using real-time task scheduling algorithm (based on SBRMS scheduling algorithm, see Section 6.5.3 in Chapter 6), the RT-ESTDL

TABLE 4.3 RT-ESTDL Description of a Typical Avionics System Model

```
// avioniceqpmt.mdl
using "RT-ESTDL.mdl"
using "aviiodatavar.mdl"
using "1553bBlock.mdl";

CAVIEqpmt AvionicEqpmt::CEQUIPMENT
{
    BOOL IsSUT;        //Whether the system under test
    var Eqpmt_ID;       //Device identification
    CAVIIODATAVAR ioDataVar; /IO interface data
    CAVIIOLINK ioLink;   / / Bus connection type
    ...
    procedure InitEqpmt(ioData, ioLink);
    procedure StartEqpmt()

    procedure SendDataValue (srcEqpmtID,dstcEqpmtID,
ioData, sndVar);
    procedure GetDataValue (srcDevID,ioLink, recVar);
    ...
}
/******** The following is the I/GNS model
*************/
// IGNS.module
IGNSMDL :: AvionicEqpmt
{
    IsSUT = TRUE;
    Eqpmt_ID = "IGNS";
    ioLink.ioType = "MIL-STD-1553B";
    var APP;
    var WOW;
    1553BBLOCK  B_ADIN_01_00;
    1553BBLOCK  B_DCIN_00_00;
    1553BBLOCK  B_DCIN_01_01;
    1553BBLOCK  B_DCIN_01_02;
    . . .
}
```

execution engine can complete concurrent execution between different test tasks and can support real-time scheduling of test tasks with different priority order.

3. The RT-ESTDL design introduces a reference to the system (global) clock and a time waiting mechanism, such as by calling the encapsulated function *GetCurTestTime()*, which can be obtained to obtain the current global clock value (since the start of the test timing), by calling the function *wait()*. In this way, the test process can be ensured that the clock is unified and coordinated, ensuring that the test process is fully controllable.

4. The design of the RT-ESTDL execution engine allows users to customize the execution priority of online test tasks, so that the actual requirements of testers can be met to the maximum extent while ensuring minimal interference with the running timing of the test execution system.

4.4.3 Support for Real-Time Communication of Real-Time Embedded Device Models

In the RT-ESTDL design, after the modeling of each device model is completed, if each device model is visible and accessible to each other, the real-time communication between devices can be completed by means of function calls, and its implementation process is shown in Figure 4.4.

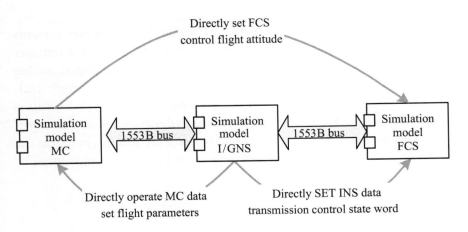

FIGURE 4.4   Real-time embedded device model real-time communication schematic.

The advantage of this approach is that the interaction is direct, simple, and fast, which can better meet the real-time communication and simplify the complexity of the system.

4.4.4 Support for Reuse of Existing Device Models and Test Descriptions

RT-ESTDL supports pre-compilation mechanism, which can well realize the reuse of real-time embedded device models and existing test descriptions. Through this reuse, the existing test resources can be reused to the maximum extent to improve test efficiency and shorten test time. Specific analysis is as follows:

1. The *using* statement can pre-include the established real-time embedded device model to realize the reuse of the existing device model. In addition, in this case, if the tester wants to develop a new device model based on the existing model, he only needs to make a few changes to complete the development of a new device model, which greatly improves the efficiency of modeling.

2. The *include* statement can be used to pre-include the test description sequence that has already been created. Similarly, the tester only needs to make a few changes to complete the programming of a new test statement sequence.

4.5 SUMMARY

Based on the formal testing theory in Chapter 3, this chapter presents the characteristics and design principles of real-time embedded software test description and comprehensively summarizes the common testing methods for real-time embedded software. The concept of generic real-time embedded software test tasks is given, and on this basis, the real-time embedded software test description language is designed and implemented, and the grammar and semantics of the language are studied, as well as the analysis of the real-time embedded software test support mechanism.

CHAPTER 5

Testing Technology of Intelligent Terminal Application Software System

ANDROID APPLICATION IS ONE important class of embedded software, especially for consumer electronics devices. The huge market needs, the limited time-to-market pressure, and the diverse hardware platforms make it challenging to ensure the quality of Android applications. In this chapter, we will cover typical testing techniques for Android applications, including test case generation, regression testing, and stress testing.

5.1 BASICS FOR ANDROID APPLICATIONS

5.1.1 Android Operating System

Android operating system is an open-source mobile operating system based on Linux released by Google on November 5, 2007. It mainly targets mobile devices such as mobile phones and tablets. Android operating system was originally developed by Andy Rubin to support mobile phones since 2003 in the USA. In 2007, Google and 84 companies including hardware manufacturers, software providers, and telecommunication providers build the open handset alliance and released the improved Android

DOI: 10.1201/9781003390923-6

system. The alliance supports the Android system and its applications. Then, Google released the source code of Android under the Apache license.

In 2008, Google released Android 1.0. The first Android mobile phone is released in October 2008. Android operating system has extended its usage into many consumer electronics areas such as TV, digital camera, game, and smartwatch. In the first quarter of 2011, the mobile market share of Android exceeded the Symbian system to be the top mobile operating system. In the fourth quarter of 2013, the market share of Android platform reached 78.1%.

The Android operating system has evolved into a whole software stack for mobile devices including the OS kernel, middleware, UI framework, and applications. As shown in Figure 5.1, the architecture of Android operating system includes the application layer, application framework, libraries, runtime, and Linux kernel.

The application layer is the top layer of Android operating system. It is used to interact with the end users. The application layer includes the built-in application of Android and third-party applications. The end users can use these applications to make calls, write notes, watch videos, and play games. The end users can install or uninstall these applications with flexibility.

The application framework layer is under the application layer. It provides a different system, API, for developers for building applications. The main modules of the application framework layer are:

- Activity Manager: Managing the life cycle of different applications.

- Window Manager: Managing all windows applications.

- Content Provider: Managing the sharing of content among applications.

- Package Manager: Managing the installation, upgrade, and uninstall of applications.

- Notification Manager: Managing the notification of system.

The system runtime layer lies between the application framework layer and the Linux kernel layer, and it is composed of the system libraries and Android Runtime. The system library contains the Surface Manager, SQLite Library, Media Framework, OpenGL/ES library, and FreeType.

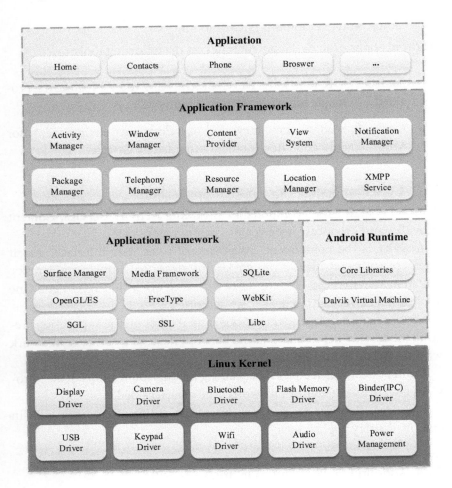

FIGURE 5.1   Android system architecture diagram.

It is responsible for 2/3D drawing, multimedia, databases, etc. The Android Runtime is composed of the core library and the Dalvik virtual machine. The former is implemented in Java to provide core APIs for application development. The latter is a register-based Dalvik virtual machine to ensure each application has its independent process without interfering with other applications.

The Linux kernel is at the bottom of the Android system. The kernel layer provides drivers for Android mobile devices. It also provides security management, power management, memory management, process management, network driver, graphics card driver, etc.

5.1.2 Android Development Environment

Android application development relies on the following tools:

- Android SDK (Software Development Kit): the API libraries provided by Google for application development.

- Android Studio: the integrated development environment for Android application development provided by Google.

5.1.3 Core Components for Android Application

Android contains four components, including Activity, Service, Content Provider, and Broadcast Receiver.

Activity is the component composing of basic user interface, and it interacts with end users through UI interfaces to fulfill certain tasks. Different activities can communicate with each other through Intent. One application can contain one or more activities.

Service has no independent process, and it relies on the application creating the service. Service also has no user interface, so it can continue work when switched to background.

Content Provider realizes data sharing among applications. It also provides a security mechanism to protect the data accessed.

Broadcast Receiver receives the broadcast notifications from built-in and third-party applications.

5.1.4 Android Emulator and ADB Tools

The Android Emulator simulates Android devices on your computer so that you can test your application on a variety of devices and Android API levels without needing to have each physical device. The emulator offers the following advantages:

Flexibility: In addition to being able to simulate a variety of devices and Android API levels, the emulator comes with predefined configurations for various Android phones, tablets, Wear OS, and Android TV devices.

High fidelity: The emulator provides almost all of the capabilities of a real Android device. You can simulate incoming phone calls and text messages, specify the location of the device, simulate different network speeds, simulate rotation and other hardware sensors, access the Google Play Store, and much more.

Speed: Testing your app on the emulator is in some ways faster and easier than doing so on a physical device. For example, you can transfer data faster to the emulator than to a device connected over USB.

Android Debug Bridge (adb) is a versatile command-line tool that lets you communicate with a device. The adb tool is included in the Android SDK Platform-Tools package. The adb command facilitates a variety of device actions, such as installing and debugging apps, and it provides access to a Unix shell that you can use to run a variety of commands on a device. It is a client-server program that includes three components. A client is used to send commands. The client runs on your development machine. You can invoke a client from a command-line terminal by issuing an adb command. A daemon (adbd) can run commands on a device. The daemon runs as a background process on each device. A server is responsible for managing communication between the client and the daemon. The server runs as a background process on your development machine.

5.1.5 Android UI

The base class for all elements in Android UI (User Interface) are class View or class ViewGroup. The View class draws the UI contents for interaction with end users. The A ViewGroup is a special view that can contain other views (called children). The view group is the base class for layouts and view containers. All the widgets in the view form a tree-style hierarchical layer.

Widget is an important concept for Android UI design, and it is the basic element of Android application UI. The Input widget is used to interact with the end users to acquire user input information. As shown in Figure 5.2, other frequently used widgets include Button, Check Box, TextField, Slider, and Switch Button.

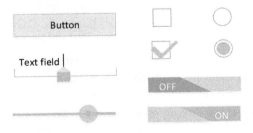

FIGURE 5.2   Basic widgets in Android UI.

Layout is an important concept in Android UI design. It is used to define the user interface that holds the UI controls or widgets that will appear on the screen of an Android application or activity screen. A user can define the layout of an Android application in two ways. One is to use XML file to define UI layout while another is to directly program the UI objects with code. Using XML file to define UI layout is preferred because the UI and program logic can be decoupled. Developers can build an application for different Android versions and different UI layout, which can significantly improve the reusability of the code.

The Android system will receive input events when the end users have interacted with the application user interface. There are a set of callback functions in the View class to handle Android UI events. Handling events based on listener mechanism is the recommended way in the Android system. The core concepts are Event Source, Event, and Event Listener. The Event Source are widgets user can interact to trigger events, including buttons, slide bars, and images. The Events are the messages generated through the interaction between the user and the UI widget. And the event listeners are the callback interfaces provided by the Android View class, which are responsible for handling the events. For example, the onClick() method is within the View.OnClickListener. When an end user clicks a button, it will be invoked.

5.1.6 Android Log System

Android Log system provides the logging facility for Android applications. Logging is useful for Android application development, testing, and debugging. Developers can use the logging system to locate the bugs within the application. Each line of log contains the Tag, Time stamp, Log level, and Log info.

The Android Log can be classified into six levels: Verbose, Debug, Info, Warn, Error, and Assert. Verbose is at the lowest level in the logging system with the most complete information for diagnosis. Debug level is used to print debugging information and is only valid for the Debug version. The Info level prints the common reminder information. The Warn level can print warning information to remind the developers of possible programming bugs. The Error level is of relatively higher priority, and it is used to print the error message during program crash. For example, the exception information is captured in the try-catch mechanism. Assert level is the highest level in the logging system, and it will output information related to fatal errors. The size of log can be very large: an application execution usually generates MegaBytes of logs.

The logs can also be classified into Application log, Event log, and System log based on usage. The Android system generally uses System log to differentiate from the application logs.

5.1.7 Code Coverage for Android Application

Code coverage is an important metric for software testing. During testing, we often care about whether the source code is covered. The percentage of code covered during execution is called code coverage rate. When talking about code coverage for source code, we may have different granularities:

- Line Coverage (Statement Coverage): It checks whether each executable statement in the program has been covered during execution. Line coverage is the most frequently used metric.

- Branch Coverage: It checks whether each branch of the program is covered.

- Function Coverage: It checks whether each function of the program is covered.

  Here we introduce some code coverage tools for Android applications:

  1. Emma is an open-source code coverage tool for Java. Emma is implemented in Java and can be integrated into IDEs such as Eclipse, Android Studio easily. Emma performs code instrumentation at the bytecode level. Whenever the instrumented code is executed, it will send coverage information to BroadcatReceiver, which in turn is responsible for writing the code coverage information into the coverage.cc file. Emma can log the code coverage information at the statement, branch, and function level.

  2. Ella is another open-source Android application code coverage tool. Different from Emma, Ella performs instrumentation at the bytecode level. Therefore, it can be applied to collect code coverage information on third-party Android application without source code. Ella is written in Python and can be used with command-line user interface. The code coverage of Emma is relatively coarse, and it can only get function-level code coverage.

3. Jacoco is developed by the same team as Emma. Jacoco can be integrated into IDEs such as Eclipse, Gradle, and Maven. Similar to Emma, Jacoco also performs instrumentation at the byte-code level and returns the code coverage information through BroadcastReceiver. Jacoco supports the collection and generation of code coverage information at instruction, line, and branch level.

4. Clover is a code coverage tool for Java developed by Cenqua. Clover is based on source code instrumentation. Apart from reporting code coverage information, Clover can also track the change of code coverage such that developers can track whether the new test cases can trigger uncovered code before.

5.1.8 Android GUI Testing Frameworks

1. **UI Automator testing frameworks**

   UI Automator is a UI testing framework suitable for cross-app functional UI testing across system and installed apps. The UI Automator APIs let you interact with visible elements on a device, regardless of which activity is in focus, so it allows you to perform operations such as opening the Settings menu or the app launcher in a test device. Your test can look up a UI component by using convenient descriptors such as the text displayed in that component or its content description. The UiAutomator Viewer provides a set of APIs for dynamically querying the user interface of applications. The APIs can retrieve the UI widget tree of the application under test to get the detailed UI state. Furthermore, the class UiDevice can get the state information of the target device and change device state by sending key events. UiAutomator is useful to serve as the underlying library to develop a new Android testing framework.

2. **Instrumentation testing framework**

   An instrumentation test provides a special test execution environment where the targeted application process is restarted and initialized with basic application context, and an instrumentation thread is started inside the application process VM. Your test code starts execution on this instrumentation thread and is provided with an Instrumentation instance that provides access to the application context and APIs to manipulate the application process under test.

The instrumentation framework can create test cases, send UI events and system events to Android application, check the runtime state of application, and control the lifecycle of Android application. Different from black-box testing techniques, instrumentation framework can directly invoke the method of UI widgets and modify the attributes of widgets. The limitation of the Instrumentation framework is that it requires the source code of the application under testing. This makes it more suitable for developer testing rather than third-party testing.

5.2 TEST CASE GENERATION TECHNIQUES FOR ANDROID APPLICATIONS

When performing Android application testing, designing the test cases is the most time-consuming activity. A complex application usually involves many different usage scenarios. Therefore, it may require nontrivial efforts to design test cases to cover even the most important scenarios. To improve the efficiency of testing, we need effective automatic test case generation techniques. A large number of automatic test case generation techniques for Android applications are based on GUI state traversal. These techniques differ from each other in terms of GUI state equivalence criteria, the state search strategy, and waiting time between two events.

However, the effect of different factors used in a GUI traversal algorithm has not been systematically explored. In this section, we report a controlled experiment on 33 real-world applications to expose their real failures to systematically study three major factors that are commonly observed in testing tools for this class of applications. They include the notion of GUI state equivalence, the state search (or exploration) strategy, and the amount of time to wait between two input events. Our experimental results clearly show that different notions of GUI state equivalences have significantly different effects on failure detection rate and code coverage, randomized search is comparable to systematic search, and different choices of waiting time strategies do not make significant differences in terms of testing effectiveness.

5.2.1 Test Case Generation Tools for Android Application

There are many popular test development environments and tools, such as MonkeyRunner, Robotium, and UIAutomator. These test development platforms usually provide a set of APIs for the testers to write test scripts based on their own test requirements.

MonkeyRunner is a testing tool within the Android SDK. It provides API interfaces in Python for the testers to interact with the device, to simulate user inputs, and to get testing results for verification. The script is interpreted by the MonkeyRunner to interact with the application under test. Moreover, it also provides a mechanism to capture screens and compare images to support the test oracle procedure. Robotium uses the Android instrumentation framework to support black-box automated testing by extending those instrumentation classes. UIAutomator allows testers to craft test scripts to send input events to UI widgets rather than screen coordinates. Appium uses the WebDriver protocol to test iOS, Android, and Windows apps. It also supports several programming languages so that testers can easily adopt it for use.

There are also many popular automatic Android test case generation tools.

Monkey is a widely used stress-testing tool within the Android platform. It can generate pseudo-random sequences of user events to an app under test. Furthermore, many improved fuzzing tools over Monkey are also widely used. They either use widget-level interaction or have enhanced failure diagnosis ability.

The SwiftHand tool aims at maximizing the code coverage of the application under test while minimizing the number of restarts during testing to save testing time. It builds a finite state model of the app for exploration to generate inputs dynamically. During the testing process, the tool will also dynamically improve the model based on the testing data.

A3E is a GUI traversal–based test generation tool with two complementary exploration strategies: *A3E-Depth-First* and *A3E- Targeted*. The former strategy performs DFS on a dynamic model of the app where the dynamic model defines each activity as a distinct GUI state. The latter strategy is more complicated. It applies static taint analysis to build an activity transition graph of the app and then uses the graph to efficiently generate intents.

Dynodroid realized a randomized exploration strategy. It is able to generate system events relevant to the app through analysis. It can also either generate events that have been least frequently used or take the contexts into account. In other words, it can bias toward those events that are relevant in selected contexts.

Stoat is a guided, stochastic model-based GUI testing technique for Android applications. It combines static analysis and dynamic analysis to first build the GUI model of the application. Then it mutates and refines the stochastic model to guide the test generation process. The results show that the technique is effective to achieve high code coverage and to trigger crash for Android application testing.

Sapienz is a search-based test case generation tool. It takes failure detection rate, code coverage, and test case size as factors in optimizing its test cases during the search process. Their evaluation results show that Sapienz can be effective in generating smaller test cases and these test cases can result in high failure detection rate and high code coverage.

ACTEve is a testing tool based on dynamic symbolic execution. Based on source code instrumentation, it performs concrete and symbolic execution to systematically generate test inputs. However, the requirement to instrument the application limits its applicability to application with source code only. Furthermore, it can only output test cases with 4 input events at most due to the state explosion problem.

PUMA [11] is an extensible framework for dynamic analysis and GUI traversal–based test case generation. Both its dynamic analysis component and its component for the exploration of a UI transition model can be customized.

Figure 5.3 shows the overview of the PUMA workflow. Developers should first provide a PUMAScript code and the binary code of an Android

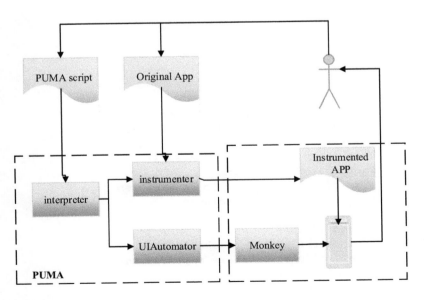

FIGURE 5.3 PUMA workflow.

application to PUMA where PUMAScript is a language implemented as a Java extension. Next, the PUMA interpreter interprets the given PUMAScript code, and translates the code instructions into monkey-specific directives (via UIAutomator) and app-specific directives. PUMA's app instrumenter statically analyzes the application to determine the parts of the code relevant to analysis and instruments of the application. The output is an instrumented version of the given application that satisfies the app-specific directives specified through the given PUMAScript code. Finally, a programmable monkey configured with the monkey-specific directives specified in the PUMAScript code executes the instrumented version of the application. Upon the completion of the program execution, PUMA generates logs which contain outputs specified in the app-specific directives, as well as outputs generated by the programmable monkey.

5.2.2 A GUI Traversal–Based Test Case Generation Framework

Table 5.1 presents the pseudo-code of a general GUI Traversal–Based Test Case Generation Framework, which is also proposed by PUMA.

TABLE 5.1   Generic Algorithm for Test Generation Based on GUI

Algorithm 5.1 Generic GUI Exploration-Based Test Case Generation Framework of PUMA
1: **while** not all apps have been explored **do**
2:      pick a new app and start the app
3:      S←empty stack
4:      push initial page to S
5:      **while** S is not empty **do**
6:        pop an unfinished page si from S
7:        go to page si
8:        pick next clickable UI element from si // **Factor 2: Search strategy**
9:        perform the click
10:      wait for next page sj to load // **Factor 3: Waiting time**
11:      flag←sj is equivalent to an explored page // **Factor 1: State equivalence**
12:      **if** not flag **then**
13:          add sj to S
14:          update finished clicks for si
15:      **if** all clicks in si are explored **then**
16:          remove si from S
17:      **if** S is empty **then**
18:          terminate this app

The underlined part is the configuration points (i.e., parameters stated in Section I), which can be extended in the test case generation framework. In the algorithm, s represents a GUI state and S represents the set of GUI states. Each state is associated with a set of clickable UI elements. If there is any clickable UI element not yet receiving an input (click) event, the state is called unfinished, otherwise, finished.

The algorithm first selects an application from the application set under the test and starts the application. Then, it puts the initial page of the application into the GUI state set, which is empty initially. Next, it selects an unfinished state from the GUI state set, picks a clickable UI element, and clicks on it. Third, it waits for a certain period of time so that the next UI page can be loaded, then compares the new state with those explored states one by one to determine whether the new state is equivalent to an explored state. If there is no match, the algorithm puts this new state into the GUI state set. If all the clickable UI elements have been explored by clicking on them, the finished state is removed from the GUI state set. The above procedure then repeats until the state set is empty.

The code lines (lines 8, 10, and 11) with underlined comments in the algorithm are the locations of three major factors to be studied in our controlled experiment. In the next section, we describe our design of the factor levels of these design factors at these three configuration points.

1. **GUI state equivalence strategy**

    The first design factor to be studied is how to characterize a GUI state and how to consider two GUI states to be equivalent.

    We aim to explore the factor levels that have been proposed separately in different previous works. The main purpose is to critically examine whether there is any significant difference in test effectiveness, which, to the best of our knowledge, the present work is the first one to report it.

    Specifically, three state equivalence criteria chosen in our controlled experiment as three factor levels of state equivalence are as follows: the cosine similarity used by the DECAF and PUMA, the UI hierarchy used by SwiftHand, and ActivityID used in A3E.

2. **Cosine similarity strategy**

    In DECAF, a feature vector is used to represent a UI hierarchy. This feature vector extracts the type, the level in the DOM tree and the text from each visible UI element in the DOM tree of the UI

TABLE 5.2   Vectorization Algorithm of GUI State

Algorithm 5.2 Vectorization Algorithm for GUI State

```
1.    node←get root node in current state
2.    L←empty set
3.    while node is not null do
4.         type←node's classname
5.         level←node's height in DOM tree
6.         count←number of the node of the same type at
           current level
7.         text←node's text
8.         keyMatch←string of type@level@count@text
           //build a string with type, level, count, and text
9.         put keyMatch into L
10.        node←current node's childnode
11.   end-while
12.   return current node set L
```

hierarchy. For instance, a button can be expressed as (Button@2, "red", "Dial") in the feature vector, which represents that the UI element is a red button with text "Dial" at level 2 of the DOM tree of the UI hierarchy. A state is a set of UI hierarchies that every pair of UI hierarchies in the same state are similar to one another based on the cosine similarity coefficient with a default threshold (0.95) used by PUMA. In this paper, the cosine similarity is expressed by the eigenvectors of the UI widgets. We also adopt the same default threshold in our controlled experiment.

As shown in Algorithm Table 5.2, the type of the widget (Type), the level of the control within the DOM tree, the sequential number of the widget within all widgets of the same type in the same level, and the text of the widget are used as one dimension of the vector. The comparison of states uses cosine similarity of vectors. Suppose we have two vectors representing two GUI states: $V = \langle v_0, v_1, v_2, \ldots v_n \rangle$ and $U = \langle u_0, u_1, u_2, \ldots u_n \rangle$. The cosine similarity is calculated as

$$\mathrm{Cosine}(V, U) = \sum_{i=1}^{n} v_i u_i \left/ \left(\sqrt{\sum_{i=1}^{n} v_i^2} \times \sqrt{\sum_{i=1}^{n} u_i^2} \right) \right.$$

The value of cosine similarity lies between [−1,1]. When its value is close to 1, the two states are considered equivalent. We use a

TABLE 5.3　Algorithm for Calculating Cosine Similarity

Algorithm 5.3 Cosine Similarity Algorithm

```
1.   get state s2 and s1
2.   U←empty set
3.   feature←s1's node set //Vector for state s1
4.   feature2←s2's node set //Vector for state s2
5.   put union elements in feature and feature2 into U //
     U is the union of s1 and s2
6.   N1,N2,dot ← 0
7.   while U has next element do
8.       int v1 ← (if feature has the element)? 1 : 0
9.       int v2 ← (if feature2 has the element)? 1 : 0
10.      dot ← sum of dot and v1*v2
11.      N1 ← sum of N1 and v1*v1
12.      N2 ← sum of N2 and v2*v2
13.  end-while
14.  cosine←Cosine similarity calculation(dot / (sqrt(N1)
     * sqrt(N2))) //Cosine Similarity
15.  return cosine
```

threshold 0.95 to determine whether two states are equivalent or not. The algorithm to calculate cosine similarity is shown in Table 5.3.

3. Jaccard strategy

Based on the feature vector representation of the GUI state as Cosine, we can calculate the distance between two GUI state with Jaccard similarity. Given two feature vector $V=<v_1,v_2, ..., v_n>$ and $U=<u_1,u_2, ..., u_n>$, the Jaccard similarity is defined as:

$$\text{Jaccard}(V, U)=|V \cap U|/|V \cup U|$$

The Jaccard similarity gives a value in the range from 0 to 1. The value 1 means the two vectors are exactly the same. In our controlled experiment, we also set the threshold value as 0.95. The algorithm to calculate Jaccard similarity is shown in Table 5.4.

4. Hamming strategy

Given the feature vector representation of the GUI state such as *Cosine*, we can calculate the distance between two GUI state using the *Hamming* distance. Given two feature vector $V = <v_1,v_2, ..., v_n>$

TABLE 5.4   Algorithm for Calculating Jaccard Similarity

Algorithm 5.4 Similarity Calculation for Jaccard Similarity

```
1:   get state s2 and s1
2:   U←empty set
3:   feature←s1's node set //Vector of State s1
4:   feature2←s2's node set //Vector of State s2
5:   put union elements in feature and feature2 into U
     //U is the union of s1 and s2
6:   N1,N2,dot ← 0
7:   while U has next element do
8:        int v1←(if feature has the element)? 1 : 0
9:        int v2←(if feature2 has the element)? 1 : 0
10:       dot ← sum of dot and v1*v2
11:       N1 ← sum of N1 and v1*v1
12:       N2 ← sum of N2 and v2*v2
13:   end-while
14:   jaccard←Jaccard calculation(dot / (N1 + N2
      - dot)) //Calculating Jaccard Similarity
15:   return jaccard
```

and $U = <u_1, u_2, ..., u_n>$, their *Hamming* distance is the number of positions where the two feature vectors are different. We normalized the *Hamming* distance in between 0 to 1 after distance calculation. We set the threshold value as 0.95 for Hamming distance in this work (Table 5.5).

5. **UI Hierarchy strategy**

For UI hierarchy strategy, a GUI state is represented by the hierarchical structure of its widget tree without considering the detailed properties of GUI widgets. Each GUI widget in a UI hierarchy is modeled by its widget type. For instance, a textbox widget located at the third level in the DOM tree of a UI hierarchy is represented as "TextBox@3". Two GUI states are equivalent if their corresponding vectorized widgets tree representations are identical (Table 5.6).

The GUI state similarity algorithm based on the UI hierarchy strategy is shown in Table 5.7.

TABLE 5.5   Similarity Calculation for Hamming Strategy

Algorithm 5.5 Similarity Calculation for Hamming Strategy

```
1:   get state s2 and s1
2:   U←empty set
3:   feature←s1's node set //Vector of State s1
4:   feature2←s2's node set //Vector of State s2
5:   put union elements in feature and feature2 into U //
     U is the union of s1 and s2
6:   N1 ← 0
7:   N2 ← U's length
8:   while U has next element do
9:        int v1←(if feature has the element)? 1 : 0
10:       sint v2←(if feature2 has the element)? 1 : 0
11:       if v1 equals v2 then
12:           N1 ← N1 + 1
13:  end-while
14:  ham←Hamming normalization (N1/N2)
15:  return ham
```

TABLE 5.6   Vectorization Algorithm of UI Hierarchy Strategy

Algorithm 5.6 Vectorization Algorithm of UI Hierarchy strategy

```
1:   node←get root node in current state
2:   L←empty set //L stores all the nodes information for
     current state
3:   while node is not null do
4:        type←node's classname
5:        level←node's height in DOM tree
6:        count←number of the node of the same type at
          current level
7:        key←string of type@level@count //
          build a string with type, level, and count
8:        put key into L
9:        node←current node's childnode
10:  end-while
11:  return current node set L
```

6. ActivityID strategy

If the ActivityIDs of two GUI states are the same, then the two states are deemed equivalent. ActivityID is the identifier of each activity in Android OS and this notion of GUI state equivalence is easy to implement. For instance, the ActivityID of an activity can be

TABLE 5.7   Similarity Calculation for UI State Hierarchy

Algorithm 5.7 Similarity Calculation for UI State Hierarchy
1:   get state s2 and s1
2:   feature←s1's node set //*Vector of State s1*
3:   feature2←s2's node set //*Vector of State s2*
4:   U←empty set
5:   put union elements in feature and feature2 into U // *U is the union of s1 and s2*
6:   **while** U has next element **do**
7:       int v1←(if feature has the element)? 1 : 0
8:       int v2←(if feature2 has the element)? 1 : 0
9:       **if** v1 equals v2 **then** //*The two states are equivalent when the two vector are equal*
10:          continue
11:      **else return** false
12: **end-while**
13: **return** true

returned by *getCurrentActivityName()* in PUMA, and a string comparison of two ActivityIDs can determine the equivalence. When using ActivityID to determine the equivalence of GUI states, the number of states within the GUI transition graph will be very small for simple applications.

7. **State search strategy**

Search strategy determines the order of widgets within a GUI state to interact with. We can construct the widget tree by collecting all clickable widgets reachable from the root widget. As presented in Figure 5.4, different orders of interacting with these widgets in

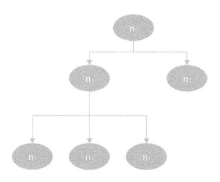

FIGURE 5.4   An exemplified GUI widget tree.

the same widget tree determine the traversal order of the GUI state model. For instance, upon clicking the chosen widget, the app under test may transit to a new or an existing state, which will be the next GUI state to explore.

Note that the target of the whole test case generation algorithm is the traversal of all clickable widgets. Different search strategies (BFS, DFS, and Random) will only affect the order of clickable widgets to traverse. All clickable widgets will be traversed based on the test case generation algorithm, finally.

8. **BFS strategy**

Table 5.8 presents the BFS search strategy. In our study, our tool traverses the GUI widget tree with a queue data structure. Firstly, the algorithm enqueues the root node into an empty queue. Next, it deques the first widget and inserts it into the list *ret*. Then, it enqueues the children of this widget into the queue. The process repeats until the queue becomes empty. Finally, the returned ordered list determines the order of the widgets to interact with the corresponding GUI state. Figure 5.2 presents an exemplified GUI widget tree where nodes denote clickable widgets while edges denote their parental relationship. For BFS traversal, n_0 enqueues first. Then, it is moved from the queue to the returned list. Next, n_1 and n_2 are put into the queue and then moved to the list in turn. Finally, n_3, n_4, and n_5 are put into the queue and then moved to the list in turn.

TABLE 5.8   BFS Strategy

Algorithm 5.8 BFS Strategy
1.   get root clickable UI element in current app state
2.   Q←empty queue
3.   ret←empty list as clickable UI element list // ret stores the list of clickable UI widget
4.   put root into Q
5.   **while** Q is not empty **do**
6.   qto←queue Q's head element
7.   take qto, add it to clickable list ret
8.   put the children clickable UI elements of qto into Q
9.   **end-while**
10.   **return** current clickable list ret

TABLE 5.9   Deep First Search

Algorithm 5.9 Deep First Search Strategy
1. `get root clickable UI element in current app state`
2. `S←empty stack   //Use stack to realize DSF`
3. `ret←empty list as clickable UI element list //` `ret stores the list of clickable UI widget`
4. `push root into S`
5. **`while`** `S is not empty` **`do`**
6. `sto←the top element of stack S`
7. `pop sto, add it to clickable list ret`
8. `push the children clickable UI elements of sto into S`
9. **`end-while`**
10. **`return`** `current clickable list ret`

9. **DFS strategy**

The DFS next-click algorithm is presented in Table 5.9. This algorithm is similar to the BFS algorithm, except that it uses a stack instead of a queue. We also use the tree in Figure 5.2 for illustration purpose: it first places n_0 into the stack. Then, it clicks on n_0 and pops it out from the stack. Next, it places n_1 into the stack followed by clicking n_1 and popping it out from the stack. The processing on n_3, n_4 and n_5 are similar. Finally, the algorithm places n_2 into the stack and clicks n_2.

10. **Random strategy**

The Random Strategy just randomly select one widget from the set of operable widgets in the current Activity to click. The implementation of random search strategy is straightforward with the support of Java APIs.

11. **Waiting time strategy**

The waiting time factor determines the time to wait between sending two consecutive input events. Different waiting times may result in different following up GUI states to interact with. One option is to wait until the next GUI state is stable, while the other options are setting fixed time intervals for waiting. The choice of waiting time is a trade-off. On one side, a short waiting time may lead to unnecessary ANR (application not responding) or unexpected application behaviors. On the other side, a long waiting time may waste precious testing time.

In this empirical study, we choose four typical factor levels of waiting time because they were used in existing GUI traversal–based test case generation tools. The first one is to use the waitForIdle() method of the UIAutomator API in PUMA, whose functionality is to wait until the execution of the app becomes idle. This API call checks nothing notable on the GUI happening for a certain amount of time. We refer to this strategy as **wait-for-idle**.

Other Android testing tools adopt different strategies for timing control. In our controlled experiment, we studied the following waiting time periods: (1) 200 ms as in Shauvik et al. to control the Monkey tool in their experiment, (2) 3000 ms as in ACTEve, and 5000 ms as in SwiftHand. We refer to them as wait200 ms, wait3000 ms, and wait5000 ms, respectively, and collectively call them as **wait-for-a-while**.

12. **Summary of strategies**

Table 5.10 presents a summary of the factor levels for each factor studied in this work. For GUI state equivalence, the 5 levels are Cosine, UI hierarchy, ActivityID, Jaccard, and Hamming. For search strategy, the 3 levels are BFS, DFS and Random. For waiting time, the 4 levels are waitForIdle, wait200 ms, wait3000 ms, and wait5000 ms.

Our experiments have revealed several interesting results for the choice of factor levels. First, the choice of state equivalence can cause StateTraversal techniques to produce significantly different testing effectiveness. Second, applying Random and applying BFS or DFS on the same widget trees can be comparable in terms of testing effectiveness.

TABLE 5.10   Three Factors and Their Levels

Factor Level	State Equivalence	Search Strategy	Waiting Time
0	Cosine Similarity	BFS	waitForIdle
1	UI Hierarchy	DFS	wait200 ms
2	ActivityID	Random	wait3000 ms
3	Jaccard	—	wait5000 ms
4	Hamming	—	—

Third, if a test session is long enough (i.e., 1 hour in our controlled experiment), the choice between the wait-for-idle strategy and the wait-for-a-while strategy is immaterial. Also interestingly, if the test session is more limited in length, applying the wait-for-idle strategy and Random was observed to achieve the best failure detection rate in our study.

5.3 REGRESSION-TESTING TECHNIQUES FOR ANDROID APPLICATION

With the prevalence of smartphones and mobile operating system (e.g., iOS & Android), mobile applications are becoming an indispensable part of our life. From the point of view of mobile application developers, those mobile applications serve as a crucial interface of their business services to end users. Many popular mobile applications (e.g., Facebook and WeChat) have hundreds of millions of active end users, which is the key to the business success of the company. Indeed, a low-quality mobile application will seriously impact user experiences. Thus, mobile developers strive to ensure the quality of their mobile applications to avoid user loss.

A key characteristic of such a mobile application is that their software components undergo rapid evolution. In another word, newer versions of the same mobile application are released frequently. For instance, Firefox is planned with tens of official releases (versions 45.8–52.7) and another tens of developer releases (versions 53.0–62.0) in 2017. Furthermore, a survey on Android Play store reports that such a period is around 10 days for apps with more than 100K+ downloads. Therefore, in such a short period, not only the source code of an app is modified but also all the testing should be completed toward the release of the new version.

Regression testing is the activity of testing changed software to provide confidence that the changed parts of the software behavior as expected and that the unchanged parts of the software have not been adversely affected. There are many regression-testing techniques studied in literature. One important technique is regression test selection (RTS), which selects a subset of test cases (denoted as test suite A) for regression testing, rather than re-testing all these test cases (denoted as test suite B), on a newer version based on some notions of equivalence. For instance, if test cases in A and B both pass through the same set of edges in the same control flow graph of a version of an app (called the original version in RTS), then test suite A may be selected to test a new version of the app for the regression testing. Furthermore, if the control flow graphs of the two app versions are available, then the set of nodes (i.e., program statements) and the edges of the control flow graph of the original version can be labeled to indicate that these nodes and edges are impacted by changes between the two control flow graphs. The test suite A can be further reduced to merely include test cases that pass through these edges impacted by change. This process is known as change impact analysis.

5.3.1 Safe Regression Test Selection Techniques

In regression-testing research, the retest-all strategy is to execute all the test cases in an existing regression test suite over the modified software. Regression Test Selection (*RTS*) is to select a subset of test cases from a given test suite (*T*). The regression test selection essentially consists of two major activities:

1. Impact Analysis: Identification of the unmodified parts of the program that are affected by the modifications.

2. Test Case Selection: Identification of a subset of test cases from the initial test suite T which can effectively test the affected parts identified by the previous activity.

Rothermel and Harrold formally defined the regression test selection problem as follows: Let P be an application program and P' be a modified version of P. Let T be the test suite developed initially for testing P. RTS technique selects a subset of test cases T' of T to be executed on P', such that every error detected when P' is executed with T is also detected when P' is executed with T'.

A test case t of T is considered failure-revealing for P and P', if and only if it produces different outputs for P and P'. A test case t of T is said to be modification-traversing for P and P' if and only if the execution traces of t on P and P' are different. If traces are the same, then the outputs will be the same. They define a test case selection algorithm as safe if it selects all test cases that are modification revealing. In this work, we consider a test case selection technique **safe** if all failure-revealing test cases have been selected for a program version. Furthermore, we consider one RTS technique is **safer** than the other if the former can select more failure-revealing test cases than the latter on a program version.

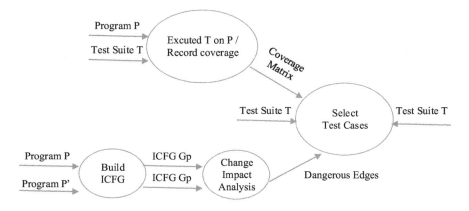

FIGURE 5.5   The workflow of ReTestDroid.

5.3.2   Workflow for Regression Testing of Android Applications

In this section, we present the workflow of our regression test selection system (ReTestDroid), which is shown in Figure 5.5.

Given an Android app with two versions P and P' as well as a test suite T, ReTestDroid statically builds two ICFGs G_p and G_p' for P and P', respectively. After that, ReTestDroid performs change impact analysis on G_p and G_p' to label a set of edges on G_p as dangerous. Then, ReTestDroid executes P over T to generate the coverage matrix of T on P with respect to G_p to indicate which edges in G_p have been exercised by which test cases in T. This coverage information is usually collected after the testing of previous program versions in practice. Finally, ReTestDroid selects a subset T' from T based on the coverage matrix and the labeled dangerous edges. Note each edge in the *ICFG* of P that is modified in P' is called a ***dangerous*** edge.

5.3.3   Control Flow Graph Construction for Android Application

The ICFG constructed by ReTestDroid significantly enhances the ICFG built by FlowDroid. As discussed in previous sections, an ICFG built by FlowDroid includes the modeling of component lifecycles, callback edges, multiple entry points, as well as the Object-Oriented features of the Android apps under analysis. The ICFG of FlowDroid provides a solid yet basic framework for static analysis. ReTestDroid further enhances the ICFG built by FlowDroid with the following improvements:

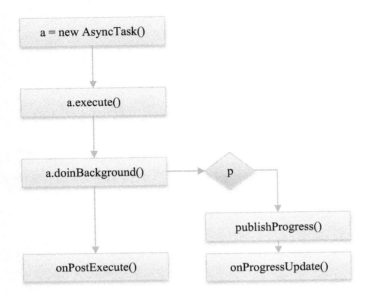

FIGURE 5.6   Sub-ICFG modeling asynchronous tasks.

1. it handles the calls to Android framework APIs related to asynchronous tasks.

2. its ICFG handles the lifecycle of Fragments;

3. it handles the native code built with *Android NDK*.

In our preliminary study, these features are frequently used in Android application programming. In the next three subsections, we present how ReTestDroid achieves these improvements.

1. **Handing asynchronous tasks**

An asynchronous task is used by an Android app to perform background operations and publish results on the UI thread without having to use threads or handlers Figure 5.6. It is in fact the recommended way in Android for multi-threading. For asynchronous tasks, ReTestDroid connects the *execute()* method of each AsyncTask module with the *doInBackground()* callbacks implemented by that AsyncTask module. The *doInBackground()* method may optionally call the publishProgress() method, which will lead to the invocation

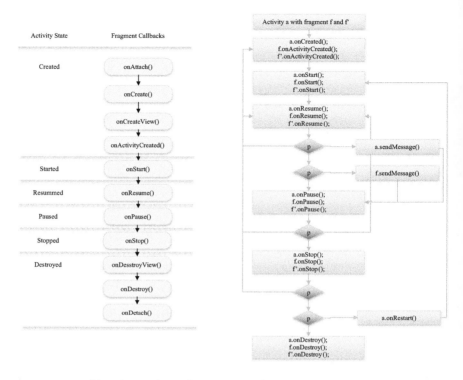

FIGURE 5.7 (a) Relationship of Fragment lifecycle and its containing Activity state. (b) Part of a sample Fragment-aware control flow graph generated by ReTestDroid.

of *onProgressUpdate()*. When *doInBackground()* returns, *onPostExecute()* will be called. ReTestDroid added all these edges within the lifecycle of *AsyncTask* in its ICFG. An exemplified sub-ICFG modeling of the asynchronous tasks is shown in Figure 5.2 where *p* is a predicate in the graph. All these sub-ICFGs are incorporated into the ICFG of ReTestDroid to enable precise impact analysis on application code with asynchronous tasks.

2. **Handling life cycles of fragments**

In Android, a Fragment is a module of code that holds part of the behavior and/or UI of an Activity and is subservient to an Activity. Figure 5.7a shows the relationship between Fragment lifecycle and its containing Activity state. Each invocation of each callback method of the containing Activity triggers an invocation of the corresponding callback method of an underlying Fragment module (e.g., onStart, onResume, onPaused, onStop, onDestroy). For instance, the onActivityCreated() callback of a Fragment module is invoked when the onCreate() method of its containing Activity module is returned. Different Fragment modules may invoke different callbacks of other Android components in different lifecycle method invocations.

The lifecycle of a Fragment is dependent on the Activity containing it. To model it, ReTestDroid inserts the call to the callbacks of Fragments right after each call to the corresponding callback of its belonging Activity. For example, when the onCreate() method of an activity is put into the ICFG, the onActivityCreated() methods of its dependent fragments will be inserted right after it. Other lifecycle methods of fragments are inserted into the ICFGs similarly.

Most importantly, those event handlers of the Fragment are also inserted into the ICFGs in between the lifecycle method of onResume() and onPause(). For example, for the class *ListFragment*, the *onListItemClick()* method will be added into the ICFGs. In contrast, in the ICFGs of FlowDroid where the Fragment class is not modeled, the fragment event handler is nowhere to go. If changes happen in those fragment-related event handlers, those modification-revealing test cases covering them will not be selected since the change is not reflected anywhere in the ICFGs of FlowDroid. However, with the ICFGs of ReTestDroid, the problem is addressed.

Figure 5.7b shows a sub-ICFG modeling an example Activity with two Fragments generated by ReTestDroid. The *a.sendMessage()* represents arbitrary fragment-related event handlers realized in the application.

3. **Handing native code**

The Android platform supports programming in native code (C and C++) using Android Native Development Kit (NDK). Precise analysis of Android apps written with native code is nontrivial. Since the SOOT framework used by FlowDroid is targeted at analyzing Java bytecode, we have to adopt a static analysis framework for C/C++ programs to perform the required analysis. To the best of our knowledge, existing analysis framework on Android application only handles the Java code and treats all calls to the native code as a system call symbol in their graph model.

Therefore, ReTestDroid first generates an ICFG for the native code portion. Then it connects this ICFG for the native code to the ICFG for the Java code portion to construct a combined ICFG. To generate an ICFG for the native code portion, ReTestDroid generates the call graph of the whole native code written in C/C++ as well as the intra-procedural control flow graph of each function with LLVM compiler framework. Then it connects the call graph to all the Intraprocedural CFGs of all the functions to build the ICFG of the native code portion. Finally, ReTestDroid identifies each Java Native Interface (JNI) call site in the ICFG of the Java code portion and adds an edge from that call site to the ICFG of the native code.

5.3.4 Impact Analysis Algorithm

The idea of the *impact analysis algorithm* realized by ReTestDroid is an adaptation of the impact analysis algorithm for procedural program proposed by Rothermel et al. Table 5.11 for Obejct-Oriented programs. They both try to avoid further traversal beyond a call node if all tests become modification traversal if analyzed within the called method. However, the efficient algorithm in Table 5.12 is just for procedural programs, and it takes no consideration of the OO features such as polymorphism. In contrast, our algorithm accommodates the virtual calls appropriately, which are frequently used in OO and Android application.

As shown in Table 5.11, this efficient algorithm caches the "selectsAll" tag to skip unnecessary impact analysis of follow-up nodes after a called node is analyzed. The flag "selectsAll" represents that all its successor nodes are impacted and there is no need to traverse more. Both methodStatus

TABLE 5.11   Impact Analysis Algorithm

Algorithm 5.11 Impact Analysis Algorithm

Inputs: N : entry node in the ICFG for original program P
                 N' : entry node in the ICFG for
                 modified program P'
Output E: a global set of dangerous edges for P
methodStatus: has status ("unSelected", "selectsAll") to
                 represent method impact info.
methodTable: is a global map (methodName, methodStatus)
                 which contain methods status
procedure compare(N, N')

(Continued)

TABLE 5.11 (*Continued*)   Impact Analysis Algorithm

Algorithm 5.11 Impact Analysis Algorithm

```
begin
01    mark N as "N'-visited"
02    foreach(call edge or virtual edge e' in
      N'.leavingEdges){
03        e = N.match(e') //get edge e with the same
          property as e'
04        m and m' are entry nodes of the targets method of
          e and e', respectively
05        if (m exist and not in methodTable)
          { compareMethod(m, m') }
06    }//foreach
07    if(All target methods of N are already set
      "selectsAll")
08        return  //No more analysis is need for the current
          method
09    foreach (normal edge e in N'.leavingEdges){
10        e = N.match(e')  //Get the edge that has the same
          property as e'
11        if(e!=null){  //Compare the destination nodes of
          the two edges
12          c = e.getTarget()
13            c' = e'.getTarget()
14            if(!e.equals(e')){
15                  E = E∪e
16                }// Add 'e' to the set of dangerous edges 'E'
17            else{
18                  compare(c, c')
19                }//Iterative invoke, compare, Compare the next
                  set of nodes
20          }//Otherwise, 'e' is the new edge, Continue
21    }//foreach
22    foreach(edge e in N.leavingEdges and e has no matched
      e'){ //'E' can be any kind of edge
23        E = E∪e
24    }//foreach
end
procedure compareMethod(N, N')
Input: N, N': entry nodes of two methods
begin
01    m is the method name for node N
02    put m in methodTable and set methodStatus
      ("unSelected")
03    compare(N, N')
04    if (None of the exit nodes of m is visited)
05            set methodStatus ("selectsAll") for m
06 end
```

TABLE 5.12   Safe Test Case Selection Algorithm

Algorithm 5.12 Safe Test Case Selection Algorithm

```
Input:    E: {e₁, e₂,...} ← get a dangerous edges returned
             from Impact Analysis Algorithm
          C: {c₁, c₂,...} ← coverage matrix of each test
             case on the original program P
          T: {t₁, t₂,...} is a set of test cases for P
Output:   T': {t₁, t₂,...} is a set of selected test cases
             for P'
begin
01    foreach(ci in C){
02       if(ci covers ej in E){
03          T' = T'∪ti
04       }//end if
05    }//foreach
end
```

and methodTable are hash tables to keep the impact analysis status for a method. The efficient impact analysis algorithm starts by invoking ***compare()***, and its core idea is to handle different types of nodes in different ways (lines 2–6). If a node N has any call edges or virtual edges, their target node must be an entry node of a method, and so it invokes ***compareMethod()*** to perform impact analysis on that method (lines 6). If every target method of *N* are marked as "selectsAll", then no more analysis is needed for the current method (line 7 and 8). Apart from call and virtual edges, node *N* may also have ordinary edges.

It then iterates each edge of *N'* with a matched edge of *N*, and checks whether their target nodes are equal or not (lines 11–14). If their target nodes match, this algorithm will recursively invoke ***compare()*** to traverse the two graphs (line 18). Otherwise, a dangerous edge is identified and added to the set *E* (initially an empty set). Finally, a loop finds whether there is any leaving edge *e* of *N* that does not have any matched edge *e'* of *N'* and adds every such edge e to set *E* (lines 22–24). This algorithm ends after traversing the whole *ICFG* of *P*.

The method ***compareMethod()*** accepts the two entry nodes of two methods, it records the method status into *methodTable* (line 26) and traverses the *CFG* by recursively invoking ***compare()*** (line 27). Only if none of the exit nodes of a method is visited, this method is set as "*selectsAll*" (lines 28–29).

The test case selection process is intuitive. We first recall that by executing the program P over the test suite T, the set of edges on the *ICFG* exercised by each test case is recorded, which forms a coverage matrix. As shown in Table 5.12, the test case selection algorithm accepts the set of dangerous edges, the coverage matrix, and the whole test suite as its inputs. It returns the set of selected test cases for P'. Based on the coverage matrix, it checks whether a test case covers any dangerous edges identified by an impact analysis algorithm. If this is the case, that test case is added to the set of selected test cases.

5.4 STRESS TESTING OF ANDROID APPLICATION

The testing engineers expressed that stress testing of Android applications requires setting up the resource available for the applications to use. We run an agent service on the Android device to control and monitor the resource utilization levels of various resources. With the agent service, we realize a set of strategies to control memory, CPU, network, and USB usages of an Android device.

5.4.1 Resource Usage Query

The testing engineers specify that there are five typical kinds of resource information on an Android system that they need to know in order to test Android applications in their industrial environment: memory usage statistics, CPU usage statistics, network usage statistics, USB storage usage statistics, and operating system (OS) information.

We thus realize the profiling functions within our agent services. Our agent wraps the Linux commands "cat /proc/meminfo" and "top" to retrieve the CPU and memory information. To get the network usage information such as the uplink and the downlink network speeds, our tool uses the Android API *android.net.TrafficStats* class to get the data sent and received per second and calculate the current network speed (by adding up these two values) accordingly. Our tool further invokes the methods of the Android API android.os.*Environment* and android.os.StatFs classes to get the path of a USB device as well as its total space and available space. Finally, our tool directly uses the Android API *android.os.build* class to get the operating system information.

```
      /*Function for consuming the CPU usage */
1     Input: the percentage of the CPU to consume.
2     Output: The CPU usage are consumed as required.
3     void consumeCPU(int percentage){
4     /*get the current CPU Usage */
5        float currentPercent = getCPUUsage();
6        float toConsume = percentage – currentPercent;
7        if( toConsume > 0){ /* need to consume resouces */
8           int num = numofCores();   /* get the number of cores */
9           /* start a thread for each core */
10          for(int i=0; i<num; i++)
11             new CPUServiceThread(toConsume).start();
12       }/*if*/
13    }/* end of ConsumeCPU */
14    private class CPUServiceThread extends Thread {
15    private int tPercent;
16    private boolean stop;
17    public CPUServiceThread(int percent) {
18          stop = false;
19          tPercent = percent;
20          }
21    public void run() {
22       long time;
23       /* if not yet stopped by the script*/
24       while (!stop) {
25          time = System.currentTimeMillis();
26          while (System.currentTimeMillis() - time < 10);
27             try {
28             Thread.sleep(10 * (100 - tPercent) / tPercent);
29             } catch (InterruptedException IException) {}
30                }/* while*/
31       }/* run*/
32    public synchronized void stopThread() {
33             stop = true;
34    }
```

FIGURE 5.8   Algorithm consumeCPU() for controlling CPU usage.

5.4.2 Memory Stress Testing

To keep the memory consumption at a specified level (e.g., 90% of all memory), the agent service actively allocates and de-allocates memory blocks via Linux's native memory management library through the Java Native Interface so that it bypasses the memory usage restriction imposed by the Android OS on the agent service. A memory usage control is valuable in testing memory-intensive applications such as games. For instance, it is critical to test whether an application runs or shuts down correctly even in an execution environment with a small amount of available memory.

```
     /*Function for consuming the network bandwidth*/
1    Input: the percentage of the network bandwidth to consume.
2    Output: The network bandwidth is consumed as required.
3    void consumeNetwork(int percentage){
4       /*calculate the number of network consumer threads */
5       int num=MAX_NETWORK_THREADS*percentage/100;
8       /* start the threads accessing files on USB storage */
9       for(int i=0; i< num; i++)
10          new NetworkAccessThreads(i).start();
11   }/*end of consumeNetwork*/
12      private class NetworkAccessThreads extends Thread {
13         private int idx;
14         private boolean stop;
15         public NetworkAccessThreads (int aIndex) {
16            stop = false;
17            idx = aIndex;
18         }
19      public void run() {
20         /* if not yet stopped by the script*/
21         while (!stop)
22         /* even numbered thread send data*/
23         if(idx % 2 == 0)
24            Post data to Web server with HTTP client;
25         else /* odd numbered thread receive data*/
26            Get data from Web server with HTTP client;
27      } //run
28      public synchronized void stopThread() {
29            stop = true; } /* stopThread*/
30      } /* end of NetworkAccessThreads*/
```

FIGURE 5.9   Algorithm consumeNetwork() for controlling network usage.

5.4.3 CPU Stress Testing

An Android device is typically equipped with a multi-core processor (CPU). Figure 5.8 shows the *consumeCPU()* algorithm to control the CPU usage. The algorithm first estimates the total amount of additional CPU loads to be consumed (lines 5–6). Then, it starts the same number of threads as the number of CPU cores (lines 8–11) For each thread, the algorithm uses a busy loop and the sleep system call to consume a certain percentage of the CPU processing capability and release the consuming CPU capability, respectively (lines 25–28). We have found that in our industrial case study, this algorithm can effectively control the CPU usage between 10% and 98% when testing an Android application. This is extremely useful for stress testing a computationally intensive application such as playing or recording a video. In an environment with low CPU availability, these applications should either degrade their quality of services or quit gracefully instead of crashing or becoming non-responsive to users.

5.4.4 Network Stress Testing

Figure 5.9 shows the *consumeNetwork()* algorithm to help stress testing the network. In essence, to control the network bandwidth usage, the algorithm starts several threads, each sending and receiving data via the http client API to communicate with a Web server (in the testing lab) to consume the network bandwidth. The variable MAX_NETWORK_ THREADS is the number of network threads needed to consume 100% of the available network bandwidth. Then, it controls the network bandwidth consumption by starting a portion of such threads, i.e., MAX__USB_THREADS×percentage÷100.

TAST also provides an API to determine a value for MAX_NETWORK_ THREADS, which simply allocates an increasing number of threads (initially 1) until all the available network bandwidth has just been consumed. This algorithm is useful for testing network-dependent applications such as online music players, online video streaming applications or Web browsers. Instead of freezing and buffering endlessly, these applications should either reduce their bandwidth requirement or stop gracefully under adverse network conditions.

5.5 SUMMARY

In this chapter, we first discussed the characteristics of Android applications. Then, we systematically discussed the test case generation technique, the regression-testing techniques, and the stress-testing techniques. The authors are encouraged to customize and build their own testing tools most suitable for their target Android application.

CHAPTER 6

Real-Time Embedded Software System Testing Environment Construction Technology

B UILDING AN EFFECTIVE EMBEDDED software system testing environment is the basis for realizing real-time, automated closed-loop testing. This chapter will introduce virtual machine technology, explore the design ideas and methods of test virtual machine specification, and propose real-time embedded software simulation test environment construction technology, specifically including architecture design and test execution engine, to provide technical support for realizing a common real-time embedded software simulation test environment construction. The proposed technology includes architecture design and test execution engine, and provides technical support to realize a common real-time embedded software simulation test environment.

6.1 ANALYSIS OF EXISTING TEST ENVIRONMENTS FOR REAL-TIME EMBEDDED SOFTWARE SYSTEMS

According to the characteristics of real-time embedded software, the current system testing methods for real-time embedded software are mainly based on the following three ways:

DOI: 10.1201/9781003390923-7

1. Real test environment. Real test environment is to directly establish a real connection between the whole system (including hardware platform and embedded software) and its cross-linked physical devices to form a closed loop for testing.

2. Semi-physical simulation environment. Semi-physical simulation environment is to establish a connection between the embedded system (software/hardware, called the target system) and its simulated cross-linked system and cross-linked physical devices (if available) to form a closed-loop test of the target system. Typical products using this approach are the ValidorGold system from B-TREE, USA, and the ADS2 system from Tech SAT, Germany.

3. All-digital simulation environment. All-digital simulation environment means stripping the code of embedded software and implementing an integrated simulation environment (also called digital platform) for testing the software with all-digital simulation technology. It implements embedded software testing on the host HOST by developing simulators for CPU instructions, common chips, I/O, interrupts, clocks, etc. At present, the method is adopted by E-SIM system developed by Prosoft of USA for C language programs.

Based on the comparison of the above three testing methods, a comparative analysis of the three testing methods is given in Table 6.1.

TABLE 6.1   Comparison of Three Real-Time Embedded Software Testing Methods

Serial Number	Category	Advantages	Disadvantages
1	Real Testing Environment	Fully guarantee real-time and authenticity, reliable and credible test results, with great reference value	High cost of building and running environment, high loss in case of error, and poor security
2	Semi-physical simulation environment	Good generality, interchangeability of models, real-time assurance, moderate cost, both test results and security	Poor flexibility, inadequate testing in some cases, and potential pitfalls
3	Full digital simulation environment	Low cost, short development cycle, high effectiveness, better support for test cases, good cross-platform, good transparency and controllability of the environment	Poor applicability, great difficulty in simulating cross-linked systems, difficulty in securing uniform and accurate system clocks and rationalizing timing relationships

According to the comparison of the above three testing methods, engineering practice has proven that the use of semi-physical simulation environment is currently the most effective method, generally known as Real-time Embedded Software Testing Simulation Environment (RT-ESSTE).

Definition 6.1 Real-time embedded software simulation test environment

RT-ESSTE is a computer system for real-time embedded software testing. Testers can organize the input of the software under test, drive the operation of the software under test, and receive the output results of the software under test by configuring various test resources of the system according to the requirements of the software under test, so as to conduct automatic, real-time, non-invasive closed-loop testing of real-time embedded software.

In general, RT-ESSTE generally consists of a non-real-time component and a real-time component, with the data communication pipeline being the connector between these two components:

1. The main function of the non-real-time component is to describe the test cases and test environment using the test language, forming test files that can be recognized and executed by the real-time component, including the cross-linked environment, simulation model, and test tasks of the system under test. The non-real-time component runs on a GUI workstation, and the operating system can be a general-purpose operating system.

2. The main function of the real-time component is to form a test environment and execute tests based on each file pair generated by the non-real-time node. Most of the real-time components run on real-time nodes with real-time operating systems, such as VxWorks, UC/OS-II, and RT-Linux.

A schematic diagram of the basic components of RT-ESSTE is shown in Figure 6.1.

From the literature research, the current real-time embedded software test environment is mostly a dedicated test environment established for specific areas or specific needs, and its real-time, generality, portability and other aspects are inadequate, as shown in:

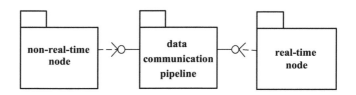

FIGURE 6.1   Schematic diagram of the basic components of RT-ESSTE.

1. Poor real-time: many existing real-time embedded software test environment only users simple timing simulation and functional verification and did not introduce a real-time operating system, such as some based on DOS or Windows and other non-real-time operating systems, some based on microcontrollers, DSP and other operating environments, these directly lead to the inability to meet the real-time embedded software test data complex, large amounts of data, high real-time requirements (usually for milliseconds) requirements.

2. Poor versatility: Since dedicated RT-ESSTEs all have their own unique test development systems, the organization of the tests is not exactly the same, resulting in a test environment with little versatility.

3. Poor portability: For different development languages and running environments of real-time embedded systems, the test descriptions (programs) developed by the dedicated RT-ESSTE cannot run under different test environments, resulting in poor portability of test resources.

4. Poor maintainability: The strong correlation between RT-ESSTE and the system under test makes any modification or upgrade of the real-time embedded system under test may lead to large-scale changes in the test environment and may even require a redesign of the test environment, which will result in the developed test description (program) not being reusable and almost not maintainable.

6.2 VIRTUAL MACHINE TECHNOLOGY AND REAL-TIME EMBEDDED SOFTWARE TESTING

In recent years, virtual machine technology has received extensive attention and made great progress, such as virtual computing environments based on virtual machines, Java virtual machines, HEC virtual machines, communication virtual machines, and real-time Java virtual machines.

In general, the core of virtual machine technology is to intercept the upper layer software's call to the underlying interface through a new virtual middle layer and reinterpret and re-process the call to achieve shareable and manageable resources in a heterogeneous environment. Through virtual machines, a virtual computer can be emulated on the original hardware resources and operating system, so that the software runs directly in the virtual machine without modification. Virtual machine technology reduces the coupling between the user development environment and the program runtime environment and is a very effective way to improve system versatility, portability, and maintainability.

In the development of virtual machines, a variety of virtual machines have emerged for different application requirements, and virtual machines can be classified according to a variety of criteria, one of which is a virtual machine model classification as follows:

1. IBM virtual machine model: A virtual machine running on the IBM S/390. A single computer system can be implemented to simulate multiple computers with different operating systems through the IBM virtual machine model.

2. Program porting virtual machine model: The program porting virtual machine model satisfies the need for programs to run on multiple platforms and is more typical of program porting virtual machines such as the Java virtual machine and the HEC virtual machine.

3. Extended virtual machine model: The extended virtual machine model addresses the problem of providing services and functions at the operating system level that do not exist in the system hardware.

Virtual machines that address the portability and generality of programs are inherited from the program portability virtual machine model. Although Java and HEC virtual machines have excellent designs in terms of portability and generality, they do not fully meet the needs of real-time embedded software testing due to deficiencies in execution speed, memory management mechanisms, task management, data collection and concurrent execution.

This book introduces virtual machine technology into the construction of RT-ESSTE, and its purpose is to solve the problems of real-time, generality and portability of test descriptions (programs), i.e., to solve the problems of test descriptions (programs) running on different test execution systems.

After analysis, this book considers that the program porting virtual machine with real-time extensions is suitable for solving the above problems.

6.3 DESIGN OF A VIRTUAL MACHINE SPECIFICATION FOR REAL-TIME EMBEDDED SOFTWARE SIMULATION AND TESTING

In the design of the virtual machine-based real-time embedded software simulation test environment, direct data transfer between the test development system and the test execution system is avoided due to the virtual machine, making it possible for the m test development systems of RT-ESSTE to communicate with the n test execution systems with a maximum of $n + m$ communication channels instead of $n \times m$. At the same time, in terms of generality, a formal statute language is used to describe real-time embedded software tests, and test descriptions (programs) written by testers on following the virtual machine specification can be executed on all RT-ESSTEs that support this virtual machine, thus greatly improving efficiency and maintainability.

Typically, a virtual machine is defined by a set of specifications. A virtual machine is not a particular software implementation, but a set of rules that constitute a specification, and constructing a specific virtual machine implementation requires compliance with the corresponding specification. A virtual machine can be implemented in any programming language on any kind of operating system or hardware platform, but only if its specifications are followed. Based on the in-depth study of the basic technical research of virtual machine, this book completes the definition of the specification for real-time embedded software test virtual machine, such as the design of data types and memory management, the classification of test commands and test data, the introduction of real-time task scheduling mechanism, the division and definition of the test instruction system, at the same time, the test virtual machine specification and the test description studied in the subsequent chapters of this book closely with the test descriptions studied in the subsequent chapters of this book, which enables the accurate implementation of virtual machine-based testing.

Definition 6.2 Real-time embedded software emulation test virtual machine specification

The Real-time Embedded Software Simulation Testing Virtual Machine Specification (RT-ESSTVMS) is a program migration virtual machine specification for real-time embedded software simulation test. It defines the data type, memory management, task management, instruction system, test description file and other requirements necessary for real-time embedded software simulation test, so that the test description (program) based on the specification can be executed on all RT-ESSTEs that support the specification.

Due to the limitation of space, this book only provides a brief description of the real-time embedded software simulation and testing virtual machine specification.

6.3.1 Data Type

To enhance platform independence, the data types of RT-ESSTVMS and their operations must be strictly defined.

In RT-ESSTVMS, data types are divided into basic types and reference types. To improve the real-time performance of RT-ESSTVMS, almost all data type checks are done at compile time.

1. Basic types specify the range of values for each data type, but do not define their bit widths, and the occupancy widths required to store the values of these types are determined by the design of the specific virtual machine implementation. RT-ESSTVMS basic data types include two categories: numeric types and return address types:

   - Among the numeric types, there are integer types, floating-point types and block data types: integer types include byte, bool, char, short, int and long types, floating-point types include float and double; block data types are determined according to the real-time embedded software bus data types. Numeric type implementation mechanism can be changed appropriately according to the compiled program requirements.

   - The return address type is used as the test task return type and is only used inside the RT-ESSTVMS implementation.

2. RT-ESSTVMS reference type is mainly a reference to the simulation model instance variable type, pointing to the location of this simulation model instance variable in the variable index table of the runtime area of RT-ESSTVMS, and the real value of this type is obtained by reading the data area of the simulation model variable index table.

6.3.2 Memory Management

Considering the real-time and efficiency issues, RT-ESSTVMS adopts the manual memory management method to manage the runtime data area, giving the right to allocate and use memory to the testers. The specific memory allocation and management can use a table-driven algorithm, sequential table matching algorithm or isolated storage algorithm, etc. This book recommends using the sequential table matching algorithm, which has higher performance and reliability and is relatively simple to implement. RT-ESSTVMS runtime data area is shown in Figure 6.2.

1. Downstream test command area: The downstream test command area stores the test command queue downloaded from the test development system to the test execution system and the test command information downloaded online by the testers during the test execution.

2. Downlink test data area.

   • During test initialization, the downlink test data area holds the test description file information downloaded from the test development system to the test execution system;

   • During the test execution, the downlink test data area holds the test data sent to the system under test by the real-time embedded device simulation model (a virtual device model built based on the cross-linked devices around the system under test). The test data is arranged in the order requested by the system under test. In each scheduling cycle, the downstream test data area sends the

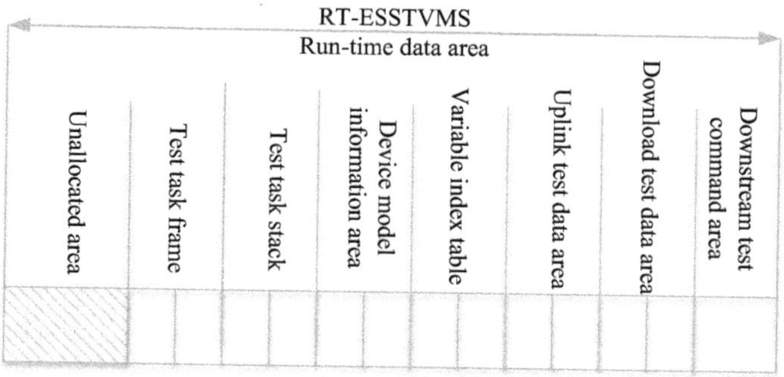

FIGURE 6.2   Memory allocation scheme as defined by RT-ESSTVMS.

test data of this scheduling cycle to the system under test until the end of the test.

3. Uplink test data area: It stores the device simulation model and the output data of the system under test, which can be sent to the tester during the test, or after the test, so that the tester can verify the test results.

4. Variable index table: The variable index table records all the variable index information of the device simulation model and the system under test in the downstream and upstream test data areas. During the test process, you can get the information of any device simulation model variables through this table, and according to the length and type of the variables, you can get the data blocks from the data area, and then carry out the corresponding data communication and test feedback operations.

5. Device model information area: When test initialization, if there is device simulation model information in the test file, the system will read out the simulation model information and open a separate memory area for all device simulation models in the RT-ESSTVMS memory domain to store the device simulation model information into the device model information area.

6. Test task stack: Store information about all test tasks in the runtime of RT-ESSTVMS. All tasks that need to get executed during the run-time when the test is initialized are recorded in the test task stack.

7. Test task frame: It is the test task activity area of RT-ESSTVMS. Whenever a new test task is started, the system allocates a test task frame to it. The test task frame consists of three parts: local variable area, operand stack and frame data area. The test task frame is the smallest scheduling element in the test process.

6.3.3 Test Task Management

Test task management is a key factor in realizing automated and real-time testing in real-time embedded software simulation testing. In consideration of the complexity of real-time embedded software, RT-ESSTVMS provides only the system clock management scheme necessary for the test environment, and at the same time provides several test task scheduling methods and synchronization methods, so that testers can choose the corresponding task management strategy according to the specific test needs when building the test environment.

1. Test clock

To ensure synchronization among test tasks during real-time embedded software simulation testing, the test execution system starts timing from test execution, all test tasks use absolute timestamps starting from the zero moment and running throughout the test, and the data transmission of test tasks is carried out strictly according to the time sequence.

The relationship between Scheduling Time, Testing Time, and Scheduling Period in RT-ESSTVMS is as follows:

$$\text{Testing Time} = \text{Scheduling Times} \times \text{Scheduling Period}$$

At a certain scheduling time, the system completes the calculation of the test time and determines whether there is a test task to be executed at that moment, and if so, activates it for execution.

2. Test task scheduling

In RT-ESSTVMS, the core of test task management is the problem of selecting a task scheduling strategy, because the task scheduling strategy directly affects the efficiency of the system and even the implementation of the function, there are many scheduling strategies available, but most of them evolved from two scheduling strategies, namely, the single rate scheduling strategy (RMS: Rate Monotonic Scheduling) and the earliest Deadline First scheduling (EDF: Earliest Deadline First). The analysis is as follows:

- RMS is a static scheduling policy, which is one of the earliest scheduling policies proposed for system development and is still widely used today, mainly for scheduling static periodic tasks; RMS specifies the priority according to the period, which is inversely proportional to the period, and tasks with shorter periods have higher priority.

- EDF is a more commonly used dynamic scheduling strategy. It determines the priority based on the size of the task deadline, with the task closest to the deadline having the highest priority and the task furthest from the deadline having the lowest priority, so the priority must be recalculated after each task is finished.

TABLE 6.2   Comparison of RMS and EDF Scheduling Strategies

Comparison Items	RMS	EDF
Dispatchability	Static Optimal Scheduling	Dynamic scheduling is better
Certainty of execution	High certainty	Low certainty
System real-time	Slightly lower	Higher
Applicable system types	Cyclical tasks predominate	Episodic and off-cycle tasks predominate
Implementation Complexity	Low	High

A comparison of RMS and EDF scheduling strategies is given in Table 6.2.

RT-ESSTVMS only provides principles for selecting task scheduling strategies, and users can select the required scheduling strategy according to the requirements of specific test environment implementations, but RT-ESSTVMS gives preference to RMS or RMS evolution-based test strategies, for the following reasons.

- RMS can guarantee deadlines for all tasks and can guarantee the stability and predictability of the system, which is one of the conditions that must be met by formal real-time embedded software testing.

- Compared with EDF, RMS is a bit simpler to implement, which helps improve the reliability of the RT-ESSTE execution system, because RT-ESSTE requires testers to be visible to the scheduling strategy in order to organize the test process according to their test intent while implementing a simple RMS scheduling strategy facilitates the user's understanding and control.

3. Test task synchronization and mutual exclusion

RT-ESSTVMS provides a choice of synchronization and mutually exclusive policies between test tasks, providing a protection mechanism for accessing the downstream test data area, simulation model information area, variable index table and upstream test data area during testing. Similarly, RT-ESSTVMS does not provide restrictions on task mutexing and the user can select the required algorithm according to the specific RT-ESSTE implementation requirements. RT-ESSTVMS provides the following synchronization and mutexing selection strategies.

- When the RT-ESSTE implementation has a very large amount of shared memory data, the more efficient semaphore approach can be used to solve task synchronization and mutual exclusion problems.

- When the system requires high reliability, the message queue method can be chosen.

6.3.4 Instruction System

The instruction system is the core of RT-ESSTVMS. To improve portability, ESSTVM eliminates low-level hardware control instructions, reduces the dependency on the host platform, and adopts a concise design principle in instruction design, where each instruction contains the corresponding instruction type, instruction parameters, and the corresponding instruction reference data. The RT-ESSTVMS specifies that the test instruction system consists of test task instructions and system service instructions, and the instruction system composition is shown in Table 6.3.

TABLE 6.3   Instruction System Specified by RT-ESSTVMS

Category	Instruction Type	Function Description
Testing task instruction	Test data operation instruction	Supports both integer and floating-point instructions
	Test data type conversion instructions	Test data type conversion
	Process Control Transfer Instructions	Instruction to jump conditionally or unconditionally
	Test data loading and storage instructions	Data transfer between local variables and runtime data area
	Task call and return instructions	Test task invocation and return
Systems service instructions	I/O operation instructions	I/O operation for the system under test
	Test task control commands	Control of the test task execution process
	Simulation Model Instructions	Creation, acquisition, verification and destruction of simulation device models
	System class service instructions	Loading and unloading of system and IO interface drivers; system time-related instructions
	Test Data Service Instructions	Transmission, collection and storage of test data
	Exception Handling Instructions	Handling of exceptions in the testing process

6.3.5 Test Description File

Before starting real-time embedded automation simulation testing, testers should first use the test development system to generate a test description RT-ESTDL file according to the RT-ESSTVMS specification. The test description file specified by RT-ESSTVMS should include device simulation model information, test configuration information, test cases, etc. These test description files will be downloaded to the test execution system after test initialization and preprocessed and generate a sequence of test instructions that can be recognized by the test execution system.

6.4 RT-ESSTVMS BASED REAL-TIME EMBEDDED SOFTWARE SIMULATION TEST ENVIRONMENT DESIGN

6.4.1 RT-ESSTE Architecture Design

Based on the real-time embedded software simulation and testing virtual machine specification, this book gives the design and implementation technology of real-time embedded software simulation and testing environment RT-ESSTE, which adopts a distributed and hierarchical architecture design as shown in Figure 6.3.

RT-ESSTE is an automated simulation test platform for real-time embedded systems and is an integrated software/hardware system, as described in Section 6.1, divided into two parts: the test development system (upper computer) and the test execution system (lower computer). The test development system and the test execution system are connected to each other via Ethernet, and this architecture helps decompose the RT-ESSTE functions while reducing the This architecture not only helps the decomposition of RT-ESSTE functions but also reduces the coupling between the non-directly connected layers of RT-ESSTE, minimizing the impact due to changes in each layer.

6.4.2 Test Development System Design

RT-ESSTE test development system, running on a GUI workstation (upper computer), and the operating system can be a general-purpose operating system. The function of the test development system is to complete the test development work, i.e., the testers complete the test preparation work according to the RT-ESSTVMS specification and finally form the test description file conforming to the RT-ESSTVMS specification. After test initialization, the test description file is pre-processed by the lower

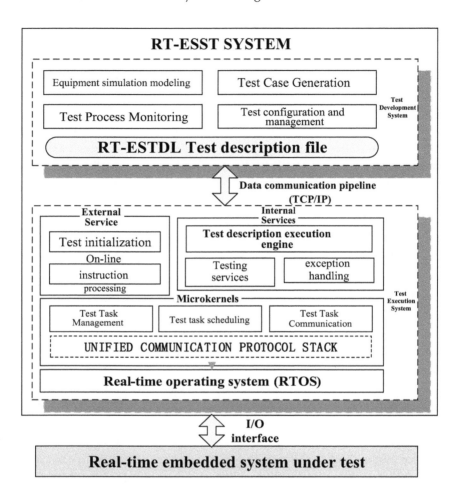

FIGURE 6.3   RT-ESSTE architecture design.

computer to form test instruction sequences conforming to RT-ESSTVMS specification, which can be run on any platform equipped with RT-ESSTE execution system, thus ensuring versatility and portability.

The main functions of the test development system include:

- Device Simulation Model Development. To improve the test efficiency and enhance the reusability of the test description (program), the tester needs to build the simulation model of the real-time embedded system under test and its surrounding cross-linked devices. The simulation model information of RT-ESSTE mainly includes the simulation model identification, the connection method between the simulation model and the system under test, and the variable information of the simulation model. The device simulation model is finally described by RT-ESTDL. Please refer to the related contents of this book for the specific device modeling process and contents, which will not be repeated here.

- Test case generation. RT-ESSTE uses a test case generation method based on a combination of real-time extended UML and RT-EFSM, which is finally described by RT-ESTDL. The specific generation process is described in the relevant part of Chapter 3 of this book and will not be repeated here.

- Test process monitoring. The RT-ESSTE test process is based on the real-time execution of RT-ESTDL, which can realize unattended automated testing through the test description driver. The test initialization, test start and test end commands, as well as the online generation of test cases and downloading and execution during the test process are also handled by the test monitoring.

- Test configuration and management. Allows testers to configure the test environment with information such as system scheduling clock cycle settings, bus type and number settings, and test execution system maximum memory settings. In addition, it allows users to manage the resources involved in testing, such as test result data files and test description files.

6.4.3 Test Execution System Design

RT-ESSTE test execution system, running on a real-time processor node (lower computer) with an operating system using a real-time operating system, such as VxWorks, UC/OS-II, and RT-Linux. Its main function is to receive the test description file generated by the test development system and complete the file pre-processing, and under the real-time scheduling of the test task, complete the sequence of test description instructions The main function is to receive the test description file generated by the test development system, and complete the file pre-processing, and complete the execution of the test description instruction sequence under the real-time scheduling of the test task to drive the test process.

RT-ESSTE test execution system is based on real-time operating system (RTOS), and also adopts the design idea of layering, by decomposing the test execution system functions into external services, internal services, microkernel and unified communication protocol stack, this design reduces the coupling degree between the non-directly connected layers of RT-ESTDES and minimizes the impact caused by the changes of each layer. This design reduces the coupling between the non-directly connected layers of RT-ESTDES, minimizes the impact of changes to each layer, and achieves good real-time, versatility, portability and maintainability. The following is a concrete analysis.

1. **External Services**

   RT-ESSTE external service provides an external interface between the test execution system and the test development system to complete the download/upload communication of test data, with the following main functions:

   - Test initialization process to complete the necessary initialization settings of the test execution system, such as system clock granularity (minimum scheduling period), buffer memory allocation (including allocation of memory space for device simulation models), registration and creation of various tasks in the test, and configuration of hardware I/O drivers. Each simulation model is allocated physical space to determine the I/O information between the simulation model and the system under test, such as I/O type and electrical characteristics configuration information, to facilitate data transfer and task scheduling during the test.

   - Online instruction processing. RT-ESSTE allows testers to download and execute test instructions (test descriptions) online according to test needs during the test process. Online instructions will complete the pre-processing of test instructions and invoke the corresponding test description execution process to ensure that online instructions are executed. See Section 6.5.5 for online instruction processing.

2. **Internal Services**

   RT-ESSTE internal services are built on top of the microkernel of the test execution system, which completes the implementation of the application layer functions of the test execution system by calling the API interface provided by the kernel, with the following main functions:

- The test description execution engine, which is under test scheduling, completes the test description pre-processing order and test execution functions, see Section 6.5 of this chapter for the specific process.

- The function of the test data service program is to complete the real-time collection, upload and display of test data according to the test configuration. The test data collection service saves and backs up all the data in the test (including the historical data of each device simulation model) and meets the data requirements of other programs of the test execution system.

- The exception handler is responsible for handling exceptions thrown by the test process and attempts to fix the current exception. When the system cannot fix the exception, the exception message is output. Exception handling methods can be dynamic using try-catch statements or static table lookup methods. For the consideration of real-time embedded system, RT-ESSTE adopts the static table lookup method, that is, in the implementation of RT-ESSTE, the exception handling table is designed in advance, and when an exception occurs, the error is handled by querying the exception handling table in real time and notifying the tester whether to terminate the test according to the exception level.

3. **Microkernel**

The RT-ESSTE microkernel is built on top of the RTOS and completes the basic core functions in the test execution system by calling the API interface provided by the unified communication stack, as described below:

- The test task management program manages and controls all test tasks in strict accordance with the RT-ESSTVMS requirements for memory management. The implementation of this program is based on the test task chain table, which records the information of all test tasks, such as task name, task type (period type or event type), task priority, task registration, start, and delete and task run period. External service programs can call the API interface to complete the corresponding functions.

- The function of the test task scheduler is to complete the real-time scheduling of various test tasks during the test run, and the scheduling algorithm adopts the improved scheduling algorithm based on RMS.

- The test task communication program provides data communication between the test tasks and the system under test. The design of task synchronization and mutual exclusion must meet the requirements of the ESSTVM specification.

4. **Unified Communications Protocol Stack**

The unified communications protocol stack (UCPS), based on the RT-ESSTVMS specification, encapsulates a series of API interface functions related to communication protocols for real-time embedded software emulation tests for the needs of test tasks and is an important support for the microkernel to provide functional implementation to external service programs.

UCPS also adopts a layered design idea, divided into interface protocol layer, routing protocol layer, bus protocol layer, and driver layer, as shown in Figure 6.4:

- The interface protocol layer is the only interface between the protocol stack and the specific application. This layer is the encapsulation of all the services provided by the protocol stack and is divided into test data interface and test command interface, which correspond to two different types of data respectively.

- The routing protocol layer is a classification process for data communication and uses a static routing mechanism to store data information in the form of routing tables to reduce the dynamic routing overhead during test execution and improve real-time data communication.

- The bus protocol layer is where the test data and test commands parsed by the routing layer are organized according to the bus type in accordance with the respective protocol. According to the bus type, it can be divided into two categories: simulation bus and hardware interface. The simulation bus mainly completes the data and message communication between simulation models, while the data interaction between the test execution system and the system under test is completed through the real IO bus.

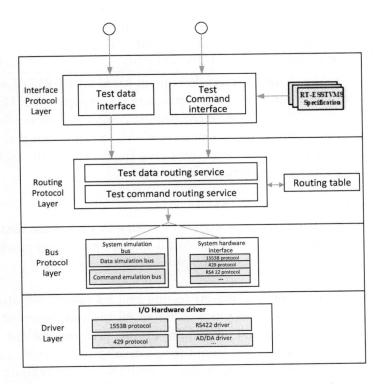

FIGURE 6.4   Design of the unified communications protocol stack.

- The driver layer consists of drivers for various types of buses and IO interfaces, which complete the underlying operations of sending and receiving communication data. Corresponding to the bus protocol layer, each data transmission medium has its own driver.

  As can be seen from the above design, the use of layered UCPS limits interface changes between the protocol stack layer and layer is limited only by the impact of the layer being changed, with good portability and scalability. Especially for real-time embedded software testing, the hardware I/O interfaces required by different systems under test are often very different, using this design, it is easy to quickly complete the adaptation of new hardware I/O interfaces, to complete the interchange of different real-time embedded system hardware devices, with good scalability and versatility.

6.5 DESIGN AND IMPLEMENTATION OF A REAL-TIME EMBEDDED SOFTWARE TEST DESCRIPTION EXECUTION ENGINE

In the RT-ESSTE design, the test description based on RT-ESTDL is the core of the whole test environment execution system operation. On the basis of the completed RT-ESSTE architecture design, this section details the design and implementation process of RT-ESTDEE, the real-time embedded software test description execution engine, and finally analyzes and evaluates the system execution efficiency.

6.5.1 Overall Design of RT-ESTDEE

RT-ESTDEE is designed using a phased model, with each phase completing a different function, consisting mainly of a pre-processing process, a scheduling process and an execution process:

1. The test describes the pre-processing process (which can also be called the compilation process). Based on the completion of test initialization, the test execution engine preprocesses the test description file received from the test development system (upper computer), mainly through lexical analysis, syntax analysis and semantic analysis, to generate test instruction sequences conforming to RT-ESSTVMS specifications. In the pre-processing process, symbol table management and exception handling always run through the whole process.

2. Scheduling process. By the test task scheduler, the test tasks are scheduled according to the test task attributes, and for the test tasks that meet the trigger conditions, they are handed over to the test description execution process for processing.

3. Test description process. The main function of the execution process is to execute the pre-processing generated test instruction sequence in real time when the scheduler meets the trigger conditions and to complete the real-time driving of the test process.

The overall design of the RT-ESTDEE is shown in Figure 6.5.

6.5.2 Test Description Pre-processing Process

The RT-ESSTE pre-processing process based on object-oriented analysis is shown in Figure 6.6.

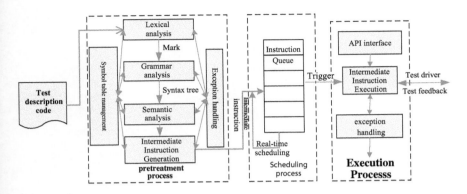

FIGURE 6.5   Overall design of the RT-ESTDEE.

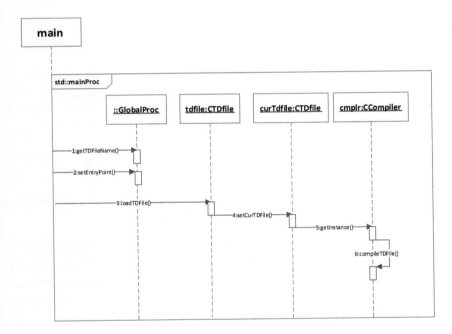

FIGURE 6.6   Test description execution engine pre-processing process.

The pre-processing process involves two main classes, the CTDfile class responsible for test description file management, and the compiler class for the compilation process, as described below:

- The file management class CTDfile completes the management function of the test description file, which mainly contains built-in symbolic information related to the test description, pre-included path

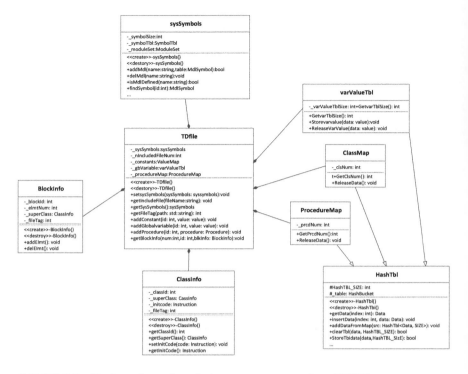

FIGURE 6.7   Design of test description management class CTDfile.

information and global procedure, class, constant and value letters, and the design of CTDfile is given in Figure 6.7.

- The compilation process class CCompiler is mainly responsible for handling the tasks related to compiling the current test description file, which contains the lexical parser CLexer class and the syntax parser CParser class. The design of the CCompiler class is given in Figure 6.8.

   Based on the above design, then the pre-processing process of the test description is as follows:

- The main function calls the test description file loaded by the global method, and sets the file entry procedure name to "main".

- Instantiate an object of CTDfile class and set it as the current test description file curTdfile to be compiled, instantiate an object of compiler class, which calls its own compileFile method to compile curTdfile test description file, and the compilation process needs to

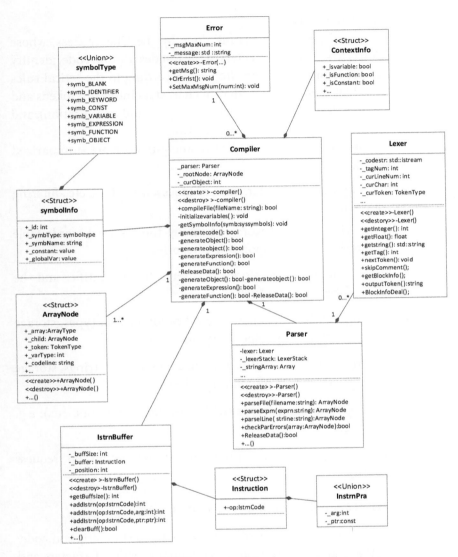

FIGURE 6.8 Design of the test description compiler class CCompiler.

call lexical, syntactic and semantic analysis procedures, and finally form the annotated syntax The compilation process needs to call lexical, syntactic and semantic analysis procedures, and finally form the annotated syntax tree, which is used as the basis for intermediate instruction generation.

1. **Lexical analysis process**

The lexical analysis is mainly done by the CLexer class, whose function is to scan the characters of the test description code, identify various types of word tokens (tokens) according to the lexical rules of RT-ESTDL, combine the relevant characters into word tokens and output them (see Section 4.3.1 for token types and classification), and perform lexical checking at the same time.

The main functions of the lexical analysis work are summarized as follows:

- Filtering white characters such as spaces, tabs, lines, etc., filtering comments, etc.

- Identifying reserved words: checking the reserved words table and storing the corresponding categories.

- Identifying identifier: stores the user-defined identifier and the value of the identifier itself.

- Spelling number: automatic identification of data types, storage of categories and corresponding values.

- Spelling character: identification of characters or strings, storage of categories and corresponding values.

- Spelling compound words (with operators, operators, etc.): e.g. >=, <=, etc.

- Test description source program can be output on request (screen).

The lexical analysis workflow is as follows:

1. Starting from the first character of the test description code, the characters are read in sequentially, white characters and comments are filtered, and various types of word marks (e.g., keywords, identifiers) are identified based on the characters read in, sometimes with a pre-reading ahead to complete the identification of word marks (e.g., numeric constants, string constants, compound operators/operators).

2. Once the word marks are identified and their types determined, the characters are combined into words according to lexical rules and output.

3. During the word combination process, a lexical check is performed at the same time, and a compile-time lexical error message is output if an error is found in the word composition.

2. Grammatical analysis process

The task of syntactic analysis is to identify whether the sequence of word symbols given by lexical analysis structurally conforms to the given grammatical rules. The body of the test description code consists of a series of statements, then the syntax analysis first deals with the function declaration, and then with the function body composed of statements, from the syntax to analyze each statement sentence by sentence: when the syntax is correct, the intermediate instruction code of the corresponding statement function is generated; when the reference of the identifier is encountered, the symbol table is checked to see if there is a correct definition, and if so, the corresponding relevant information is taken from the table for The intermediate instruction code is generated by the Parser class generateCode() and other operations.

The grammar analysis is done by the CParser class, the core of which is the process of generating a grammar tree, as shown in Figure 6.9.

Since RT-ESTDL is structured with context-independent grammars, i.e., type 2 grammars, the syntax is analyzed using a top-down analysis method, recursive descent analysis, as follows:

A subroutine is written for each non-terminal symbol e in the grammar, which accomplishes the task of analyzing and identifying the grammatical components corresponding to that non-terminal symbol. The function of the grammar analysis subroutine for a particular non-terminating symbol is to match the input string with the right symbol string of the rule for that non-terminating symbol. The analysis process is done by assigning tasks top-down by grammar rules, i.e. by calling the relevant subroutine. When the compiler program predicts that the next grammatical component is e based on the grammar and the current input symbols, i.e., when it predicts that the input symbol string to be matched can be matched by the symbol string derived from e, it determines e as the target and calls the subroutine for analyzing and identifying e. In the process of analyzing and identifying e, it is possible that other sub-targets are established and the corresponding subroutines are called. Only when the

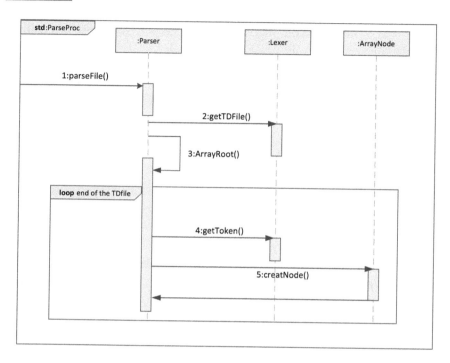

FIGURE 6.9   Test description syntax analysis process.

called subroutine for analyzing and identifying a grammatical component matches the input string successfully and returns correctly, the grammatical component is truly identified and the input string is determined to be free of grammatical errors.

For the sake of space, this book only gives a flow chart of the parseFile() process, as shown in Figure 6.10.

Once the Parser class obtains the lexical analysis results, it starts the grammar analysis, recursively descending to generate the grammar tree, during which it recursively obtains word marks and analyzes them to add them as nodes to the grammar tree. To facilitate searching and traversal, the grammar tree in the execution engine is managed as a binary tree.

Figure 6.11 gives an example of a test describing the grammar tree generated by the grammar analysis.

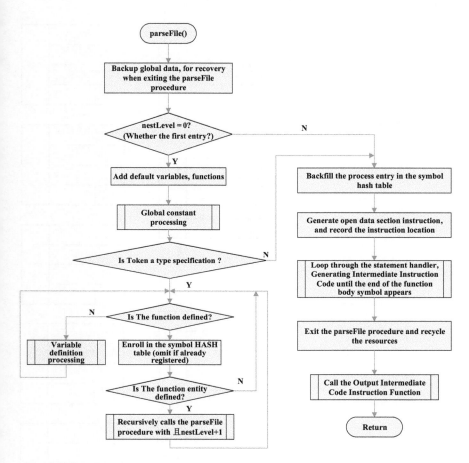

FIGURE 6.10   parseFile() processing.

3. **Semantic Analysis**

The semantic analysis process is used to analyze the static semantics of the test description, including declarations and type checking,
and the results are represented in the form of an annotated syntax
tree. In semantic analysis, the correctness of the test description code
structure is related to the context of that structure. The two issues
that semantic analysis focuses on during the design of the RT-ESTDL
test description execution engine are the identification of nested
scopes and the dynamic binding of data types, as described below:

1. The solution to the problem of identifying nested scopes is to
   record the context-related information in a symbol table, and

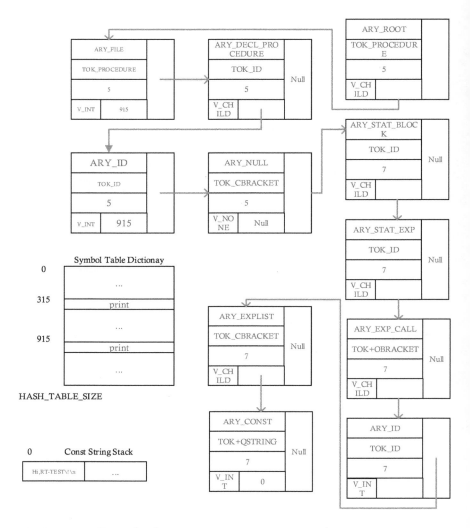

FIGURE 6.11   Example of a syntax tree.

whenever a variable declaration is analyzed, the variable is populated into the symbol table, which ensures that the variable remains in the symbol table if the block in which it is declared is visible during compilation. When a variable reference is encountered in that block, the symbol table can be consulted to determine if the variable conforms to the context of the RT-ESTDL.

2. The lack of explicit declaration of data types is an important feature of RT-ESTDL, which greatly improves the ease of use of

RT-ESTDL and makes it easier for testers to write test descriptions. The execution engine uses dynamic binding to accomplish consistent conversion of data types for operands in assignment statements.

4. **Intermediate instruction generation**

   In virtual machine-based real-time embedded software testing, the technique of separating the front-end and back-end of the test description execution engine is used in order to achieve portability of the test description on different running platforms, as described below.

   1. The pre-processing process of the test description execution engine (including test description loading, lexical analysis, syntax analysis, semantic analysis and intermediate instruction generation) can be called the front-end of the engine, while the execution process that relies on real-time OS instruction set processing can be called the back-end. Theoretically, this means that porting the intermediate instruction sequences generated by the approved test descriptions to a new platform requires only the development of a new back-end.

   2. Suppose that m different languages need to be implemented on n platforms, and that $m*n$ different execution engines need to be written if the intermediate code instruction form is not used. If the front-end and back-end separation approach is used, only m front-ends and n back-ends are needed. By choosing the appropriate front-ends and back-ends, so that intermediate instructions can be executed on the back-end, it can be transformed from $m*n$ different execution engines to a combination of $m+n$ parts by using the above approach.

   From the above analysis, it can be seen that as the interface between the front-end and back-end of the test description execution engine, the description of intermediate instructions must have sufficient expressive ability. Common methods for describing intermediate instructions include Reverse Polish notation, three address statements, abstract syntax trees, directed acyclic graphs, and abstract stack machine code. To improve the execution efficiency of the test description execution engine, an abstract stack machine code is adopted as the intermediate instruction representation, with the structure as follows:

```
struct Instruction{
    IstrnCode _op;        // Instruction Type
    union { int _arg;         // Command parameters
        const void* _ptr; // Citation Data
    }; };
```

where _op represents the type of instruction represented in that middle, and the value _arg or _ptr in the union, depending on the instruction type, is used as additional information to complement the specific meaning of that instruction. The set of test description execution engine instructions is shown in Table 6.4.

In terms of portability, the use of intermediate instructions avoids direct data transfer between the test description generation system and the execution system, allowing user-written test descriptions to be executed on all platforms that can correctly load the test description execution engine, thus greatly improving portability.

5. **Symbol table management**

The role of the symbol table in the compilation process is to check the semantic correctness and to assist in the correct generation of intermediate instructions. These two roles are achieved by inserting and retrieving test description variable attributes in the symbol table. These attributes, such as name, scope, and dimension, are found directly in the declaration or can be obtained indirectly depending on the context in which the name appears in the test description code.

For efficiency and implementation solution reasons, the test description execution engine chooses the form of a hash table to organize the symbol table. Also, since the test description size is generally small, the pathological behavior of constant conflict in hashing does not often occur, thus ensuring a theoretical $O(1)$ average access cost.

The two core issues in hash table implementation are analyzed as follows:

1. Hash function produces uniformly distributed integers

Since the hash table technology has been practically applied in the practice of compiler construction for many years, a large amount of data has been accumulated, and there are numerous theoretical and practical studies. The hash functions selected in

TABLE 6.4   Test Description Execution Engine Instruction Set

Directives	Explanation	Remark
ISTRN_RETURN	Return Instruction	Procedure Return
ISTRN_END	End instruction	Test description execution termination
ISTRN_PUSH_CONST	Constant on the stack	Constant value is the value of _ptr
ISTRN_PUSH_GVAR	Global variable on stack	Hash index of global variable id in symbol table stored in _arg
ISTRN_PUSH_LVAR	Local variable on the stack	Hash index of the local variable id in the symbol table is stored in _arg
ISTRN_PUSH_ARG	parameter on stack	hash index of parameter name in symbol table in _arg
ISTRN_ASSIGN	Assignment operation	The value is stored at the top of the data stack
ISTRN_ASSIGN_INPLACE	Declare and assign	the value to _ptr
ISTRN_LINE	Current number of lines processed	
ISTRN_REF_GVAR	Reference global variable	Hash index of global variable id in symbol table is stored in _arg
ISTRN_REF_LVAR	Reference to local variable	Hash index value of local variable id in symbol table stored in _arg
ISTRN_REF_MEMBER	Reference object member	The hash index of the object member id in the symbol table is stored in _arg
ISTRN_REF_ELEMENT	Reference to an element of an array	The index value of the element is stored in _arg
ISTRN_REF_COMPONENT	Reference to a component of a composite	value The index value of the component is stored in _arg
ISTRN_POP	Top of the data stack is unstacked	
ISTRN_GET_MEMBER	Get object member	The index value of the hash of the object member id in the symbol table is stored in _arg
ISTRN_GET_ELEMENT	Get the element of an array	The index value of the element is stored in _arg
ISTRN_GET_COMPONENT	Get the component of a compound value	The index value of the component is stored in _arg
ISTRN_NEW_OBJECT	Assign a new object	The hash index of the object id in the symbol table is stored in _arg
ISTRN_NEW_ARRAY	Allocate a new array	The hash index value of the array id in the symbol table is stored in _arg
ISTRN_MAKE_COMPOUND	Declare a new compound data	The hash index value of the composite id in the symbol table is stored in _arg

(Continued)

TABLE 6.4 (Continued) Test Description Execution Engine Instruction Set

Directives	Explanation	Remark
ISTRN_MAKE_FUNCTION	Declare a new function	The hash index value of the function id in the symbol table is stored in _arg
ISTRN_INIT_ARRAY	Initializing arrays	The number of elements of the array is stored in _arg
ISTRN_INIT_OBJECT	Initializing objects	Object construction parameters are stored in _arg
ISTRN_INIT_MEMBER	Initialize members	The hash index value of the member id in the symbol table is stored in _arg
ISTRN_PRE_INCDEC	Front self-increasing and self-decreasing	The hash index value of the variable id in the symbol table is stored in _arg
ISTRN_POST_INCDEC	Self-increasing and decreasing posterior	The hash index value of the variable id in the symbol table is stored in _arg
ISTRN_CALL_FUNC	Calling functions	The hash index value of the function id in the symbol table is stored in _arg
ISTRN_CALL_PROC	Calling process	The hash index value of the procedure id in the symbol table is stored in _arg
ISTRN_OP_0	Zero Element Operators	The operator pointer is stored in _ptr
ISTRN_OP_1	Unary Operators	
ISTRN_OP_2	Binary Operators	Operand pointers are stored in _ptr
ISTRN_OP_3	Ternary Operators	Operands are removed from the data stack in reverse order using INSTR_POP
ISTRN_OP_4	Quadratic Operators	
ISTRN_OP_5	Quintuplet Operators	
ISTRN_JMP	Unconditional jumping	
ISTRN_JMP_TRUE	Jump when condition is true	The jump address is stored in _arg
ISTRN_JMP_FALSE	Jump when condition is false	Judgment conditions are stored at the top of the data stack
ISTRN_JMP_CASE	Jump when case condition is met	
ISTRN_JMP_AND	Jump when all conditions are met at the same time	
ISTRN_JMP_OR	Jump when any of the conditions are met	
ISTRN_FORCE_BOOL	Force arbitrary values to Boolean values for logical operations	The value is stored at the top of the stack

the design process of the RT-ESTDL test description execution engine are shown below.

```
static long calStrHash(const CString string){
      unsigned long lhash = 5381;
      int ilen = string.GetLength();
      for (int i=0; i<ilen; i++){
        lhash = (lhash << 5) + lhash + string[i];
      }
      return hash % HASH_SIZE;   }
```

Validation of the test data shows that multiplication factors 31 and 37 are the two better choices. However, the multiplication factor 32 is used in this test description execution engine because using 32 as a multiplication shifts the binary by 5 bits implementation, so that the time saved in computing the hash function can be used to compensate for the resulting slight disturbance to the uniformly distributed function.

2. Conflict resolution

There are two methods for resolving hash table conflicts, namely the split-link method and the open-address method: the split-link method stores a linked table at each index and uses the linked table to hold all conflicting data; this method maximizes execution efficiency in the case of fewer conflicts; the open-address method is a method for resolving conflicts without using a linked table and has a more complex algorithm. In the open-addressing hash algorithm system, if a conflict occurs, both try to select another unit until the empty unit is found. Depending on the choice of conflict resolution function, it can be further divided into linear detection, square detection and double hashing methods. Due to the limited size of the RT-ESTDL test description, the possibility of conflict is small, and considering the execution efficiency and simplicity of the scheme, the split-link method is selected as the conflict solution.

6.5.3 Test Scheduling Process

According to the discussion on scheduling policy selection in Section 6.3.3, the segment-based single rate scheduling policy SBRMS (Segment-Based Rate Monotonic Scheduling) algorithm is used in this book to test the scheduling process for describing task execution, which is an improved RMS scheduling policy, i.e., based on RMS, introducing the (sub)segment concept, the SBRMS scheduling timing is determined by the following algorithm.

```
if ((Base Segment Counter%Task Period ==
              Task Segment Offset) &&(Subsegment
              Counter
        == Subsegment Offset))
    Schedule(Task);
```

From the above equation, it can be seen that a task is scheduled if its segment offset and subsegment offset are met at the current moment, otherwise it is not scheduled. The experimental validation shows that SBRMS is not only able to describe and implement the data dependencies in the execution of each task, but also has good stability and predictability.

Figure 6.12 gives a schematic diagram of the test task scheduling process based on the SBRMS scheduling policy.

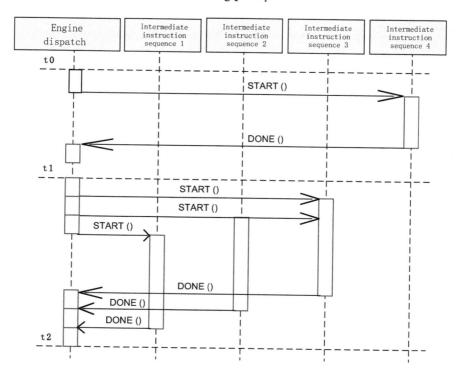

FIGURE 6.12   SBRMS-based test task scheduling execution schematic.

6.5.4 Test Description Execution Process

The test description execution process is the core component of the test description execution engine. Its important function is to cooperate with the scheduling process to complete the real-time parsing of test intermediate instructions and drive the test process.

After the test description code is compiled, the execution process of intermediate instructions is implemented by the test description execution class CExecuter (as shown in Figure 6.13). The execution process of the test description is in the form of an abstract stacker that executes the sequence of intermediate instructions already generated by the compilation process. Its main function is to dynamically maintain the stack (registers) of the abstract stacker because the execution engine must promptly reclaim the stack occupied by the test tasks that have finished running and maintain a complete address operation space for each running and soon-to-be running test task. It then loads the intermediate instruction code of the test task that is about to run, calls the intermediate instruction code handler (by operations such as executeInstrn() of the Executer class) to complete its function, and also catches and handles errors during the execution of intermediate instructions in real time.

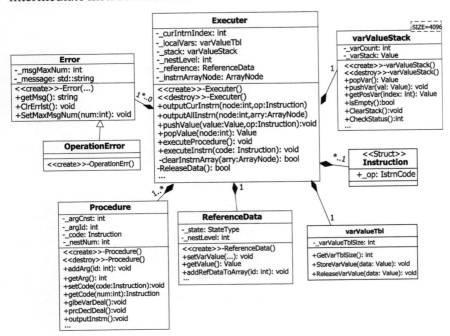

FIGURE 6.13 Design of the test description execution class CExecuter.

6.5.5 Execution of Online Test Descriptions

During the initialization of the RT-ESSTE test execution system, the creation of onlineTDExeTask, an online test description execution task, is completed first, and the task is put in a pending state.

When testers download test instructions (test descriptions) online according to test needs in the testing process, the external service of the test execution system obtains the online task and activates *onlineTDExeTask,* which calls the corresponding lexical analysis program, syntax analysis program and semantic analysis program to complete the pre-processing of test descriptions and generate the online task named *onlineTDExeTask,* which calls the corresponding lexical analysis program, syntax analysis program and semantic analysis program to complete the pre-processing of the test description and generate the sequence of intermediate instructions for the online task, which is finally executed by the scheduler. Figure 6.14 shows the execution process of the online test task.

6.5.6 Test Execution Engine Efficiency Analysis

To verify whether the test description execution engine can meet the real-time requirements of embedded software testing, this book analyzes the

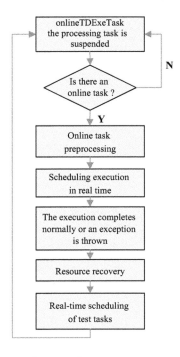

FIGURE 6.14   Online test task execution process.

execution efficiency of RT-ESTDEE with the help of the performance testing tool CodeTEST. The efficiency analysis analyzes the execution efficiency of the engine from two aspects:

- Examine the execution time of individual test description files of different sizes.

- Examine the time for concurrent execution of multiple test descriptions given a medium-sized test description code (30 lines, nested loop statements).

The test describes the environment configuration used to perform the engine efficiency analysis as follows:

- IPC (lower computer): CPU Pentium4/2.8GHz Memory 1G, hard disk: 320G;

- Hardware interface: MIL-STD1553B, ARINC429, RS422, AD/DA;

- Real-time operating system: vxWorks 5.4 (X86).

After analyzing the above test execution efficiency analysis experiments, Figure 6.15 gives the test description execution time for different sizes, and

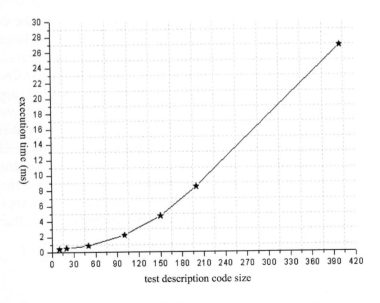

FIGURE 6.15   Execution time for different sizes of test descriptions.

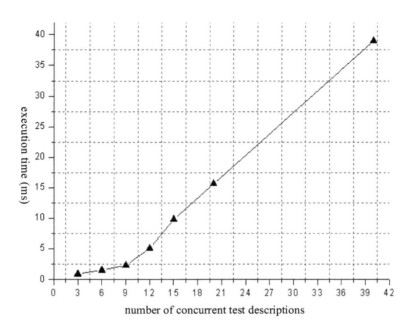

FIGURE 6.16   Medium-scale multiple tests depicting concurrent execution times.

Figure 6.16 gives the concurrent execution time for multiple test descriptions of medium size.

Through the analysis of the execution efficiency of the test description execution engine, it can be seen that the execution time of the execution engine for medium-sized (as a special test description language, RT-ESTDL statements have been highly abstracted and integrated, and the size of test descriptions is generally less than 50 lines) test descriptions is less than 1 millisecond, and since the execution engine supports the sequential and concurrent execution mechanism of multiple test descriptions, it can fully meet the requirements of real-time embedded software (real-time requirements are generally of millisecond level) for real-time and concurrent testing. Therefore, by reasonably controlling the scale of test descriptions and the number of concurrent executions, it can fully meet the requirements of real-time embedded software (real-time requirements are generally milliseconds) testing for real-time and concurrent characteristics.

6.6 SUMMARY

In this chapter, the design of a real-time embedded simulation test environment based on a virtual machine is proposed, the definition and design of a real-time embedded software simulation test virtual machine specification is given, and a real-time embedded software simulation test environment based on this specification is designed and implemented. Then the detailed design of real-time embedded software test description execution engine RT-ESTEE is presented, specifically including the overall structure design, pre-processing process, scheduling process and execution process (Including online test task execution), and the execution efficiency of the test description execution system is evaluated.

CHAPTER 7

Case Study of Real-Time Embedded Software System Testing

T̲O BETTER ENABLE READERS to understand and master the embedded software system testing techniques proposed in this book, this chapter selects a combined inertial/satellite navigation system software as the application object and completes the whole process from system model construction, static/dynamic modeling based on UML real-time extension, to test sequence/use case, test description generation, until test execution and test result analysis.

7.1 INTRODUCTION TO THE SYSTEM UNDER TEST

7.1.1 I/GNS System Overview

Inertial/GPS Navigation System (I/GNS) is a special real-time control software developed for autonomous full-attitude inertial/satellite combined navigation system used in civil airliners, which can provide acceleration, velocity, position, heading, attitude, and time information after aligning to navigation, and has the functions of combined inertial/satellite navigation, pure GPS navigation, position/altitude correction, NAV backup, APR working mode, end-of-flight mode and parameter calibration, etc. Its navigation accuracy will affect the accuracy of the integrated avionics system.

DOI: 10.1201/9781003390923-8

As an important part of a typical real-time embedded system, the software running in a combined inertial/satellite navigation system (Inertial/GPS Navigation System Software (I/GNSS)) is typical of real-time embedded software, which is solidified in the static memory of the system, and the correctness of program operation is related to both logical correctness and real-time. The correctness of program operation is related to both logical correctness and real time.

Typical features of I/GNS systems are as follows:

a. With high real-time requirements, the time period required is 25 ms.

b. Multiple operating state modes and operational processes exist, and the state migration conditions are complex.

c. Data exchange with a variety of avionics systems (see Figure 7.1): e.g., radar, flight control, visual control, mission computer, and data transmission equipment.

d. With a variety of data transmission protocols: such as ARINC429 bus, 1553B bus, and RS422.

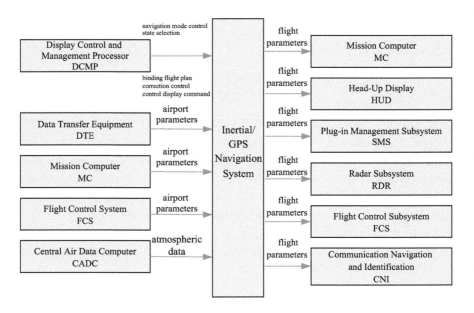

FIGURE 7.1   I/GNS system equipment cross-connection schematic.

7.1.2 Main Functions and Performance

1. The main functions of the I/GNS system software are:

- System self-test, including power-on start-up self-test PBIT, cycle self-test BIT, and start-up self-test IBIT.

- Alignment status, including normal compass alignment, stored heading alignment, and input heading alignment.

- Calibration status, including calibration of acceleration parameters and gyro parameters.

- Attitude status, providing attitude information.

- Navigation status, including external data transmission, combined inertial/satellite navigation, pure inertial navigation, pure GPS navigation; navigation mode control, including backup status, approach status, and end-of-flight status.

- System maintenance status, including ground maintenance, air maintenance, and maintenance work display.

- Other functions, including process control, status request, PFL request, alignment data display request, position correction, and data modification.

2. The main features of the I/GNS system software are:

- The system software timing accuracy is 5 ms.

- Send navigation parameters externally 60 times per second with no loss of accuracy in data transmission.

- CPU margin greater than 30% at peak system load.

- Storage margin of 30%.

7.2 I/GNS SYSTEM STATIC MODELING

7.2.1 Cross-Linked Device Model Construction

According to Figure 7.1, the I/GNS system is a subsystem of the avionics system, and there are more devices cross-linked with it. According to the software requirement specification and the ICD document, the

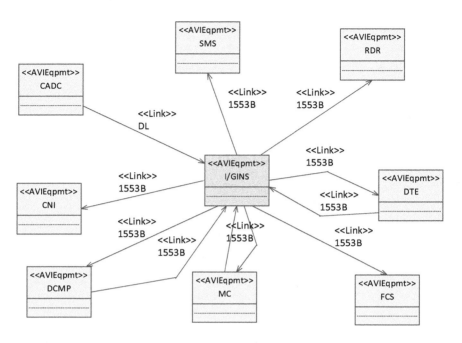

FIGURE 7.2   I/GNS system cross-linking relationship.

interface data information of the I/GNS system that should be interfaced with other avionics subsystems/devices is analyzed, as shown in Appendix 3. According to the data interface information specified in the ICD document, the equipment cross-linking relationship diagram of the I/GNS system can be established as shown in Figure 7.2. The equipment object cross-linking relationship diagram after static modeling based on extended UML class diagram is used for each equipment as shown in Figure 7.3.

7.2.2 Test Description of the Static Model

Based on the above analysis, combined with the RT-ESTDL support for real-time embedded device modeling (see Section 4.4.1 of this book), a test description of the static model of the I/GNS system software can be completed, as shown in Table 7.1.

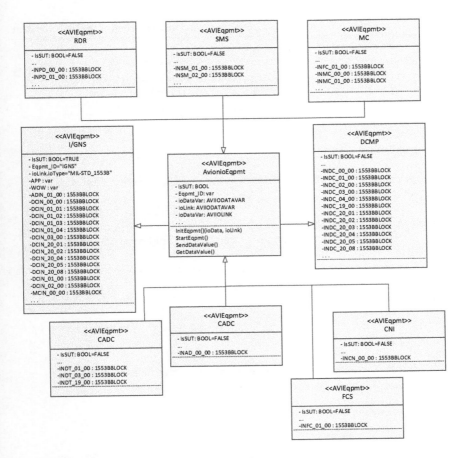

FIGURE 7.3   I/GNS and its cross-linking device static model.

TABLE 7.1   RT-ESTDL Description for Static Modeling of the I/GNS System

```
// avioniceqpmt.mdl
using "RT-ESTDL.mdl"
using "aviiodatavar.mdl"
using "aviiolink.mdl"
using "1553bBlock.mdl"
```

(Continued)

TABLE 7.1 (*Continued*)   RT-ESTDL Description for Static Modeling of the I/GNS System

```
CAVIEqpmt AvionicEqpmt::CEQUIPMENT {
    BOOL IsSUT;       // Is the system under test
    var Eqpmt_ID;     // Equipment identification
    CAVIIODATAVAR ioDataVar; // IO interface data
    CAVIIOLINK ioLink;   // Bus connection type

    procedure InitEqpmt(ioData, ioLink);
    procedure StartEqpmt();
    ...
    procedure SendDataValue (srcEqpmtID, srcVar,dstEqpmtID,
dstVar, iolink);
                                                            //
Sending variable data
    procedure SendDataValue (varValue,dstEqpmtID, dstVar,
iolink);// Send value data
    procedure GetDataValue (rcvEqpmtID, rcvVar, iolink);
// Receiving data /
    ...
}
/******** The following is the I/GNS model **************/
// IGNS.module
IGNSMDL :: AvionicEqpmt{
    IsSUT = TRUE;   // is the system under test
    Eqpmt_ID = "IGNS";
    ioLink.ioType = "MIL-STD-1553B";
    var APP;     // Power-on signal
    var WOW;     // Wheeled signals
    1553BBLOCK  A_ADIN_01_00;
    1553BBLOCK  A_DCIN_00_00;
    1553BBLOCK  A_DCIN_01_01;
    . . .
}
/******** Here is the SMS model **************/
// SMS .module
SMSMDL :: AvionicEqpmt
{
    IsSUT = FALSE;
    Eqpmt_ID = "SMS";
    ioLink.ioType = "MIL-STD-1553B";
    1553BBLOCK  B_INSM_01_00;
    1553BBLOCK  B_INSM_02_00;
    1553BBLOCK  B_INSM_03_00;
    . . .
}
(The following is omitted)
```

7.3 I/GNS SYSTEM DYNAMIC MODELING

7.3.1 Dynamic Modeling Based on UML State Diagrams

According to the requirement specification of the combined inertial/satellite navigation system software, the I/GNS system software state migration diagram based on real-time extended UML can be completed (OCL constraint descriptions are omitted due to space limitations; some UML state diagram modeling examples can be found in the relevant sections of Chapter 3 of this book), as shown in Figure 7.4.

According to Figure 7.4, the typical states of I/GNS system software mainly include BIT self-detection state, process control state, attitude state, calibration state, alignment state, and navigation state, where alignment state, navigation state, maintenance state, and calibration state are composite states (which can be further decomposed into sub-state diagrams):

1. After the BIT self-test is completed, you can choose to perform receive data operation, or enter the process control, and then enter other air corresponding state migration.

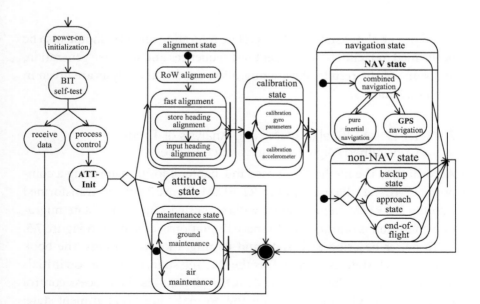

FIGURE 7.4   I/GNS system software state migration.

2. After ATT-Init, the migration of the corresponding air state can be completed according to the DCMP manifest control, such as entering the alignment state, or attitude state, or maintenance state, while the maintenance state can be divided into two sub-states of air maintenance state and ground maintenance according to the wheeled signal.

3. The sub-states of the alignment state are the RoW alignment state and the fast alignment state, and the RoW alignment state and the fast alignment state are sequential.

4. The sub-states of the calibration state are calibration gyro parameters, calibration accelerometer, and they are concurrently related.

5. The sub-states of the navigation state are inertial/satellite combined navigation, pure inertial navigation, GPS navigation, backup state, approach state, and end-of-flight state. Among them, the NAV state (including inertial/satellite combined navigation, pure inertial navigation, and GPS navigation) and the non-NAV state (including backup state, approach state, and end-of-flight state) are concurrent relationship, i.e. AND relationship, while the backup state, approach state, and end-of-flight state in the non-NAV state are OR relationship.

Based on the above state modeling, state migration analysis should also be performed to facilitate subsequent test sequences and test case generation, and some of the results of state migration condition analysis are given in Tables 7.2 and 7.3.

7.3.2 RT-EFSM Model of I/GNS and Analysis of Time-Constrained Migration Equivalence Classes

According to the method proposed in Chapter 4 for transforming a composite UML state diagram into an RT-EFSM, Figure 7.4 can be transformed into the RT-EFSM model shown without nested states (each state migration condition is omitted due to space limitations), as shown in Figure 7.5.

To better describe each state and its migration conditions, the book re-labels each state as follows: S_0 is the starting state, i.e. power-on initialization state; S_1 is the (BIT) self-detection state; S_2 is the process control state; S_3 is the ATT-Init state; S_4 is the normal compass alignment state; S_5 is the stored heading alignment; S_6 is the input heading alignment; S_7

TABLE 7.2   I/GNS Partial State Migration Condition Analysis

Status	Migration Direction	Migration Conditions
Navigation Status(NAV) S1	Transfer out	End of navigation status, end-of-flight turn
		from(NAV)to(GC), and WOW is not activated (up to $S2$)[a]
		from(NAV)to($FAST$), and WOW is not activated (up to $S3$)[a]
		from(NAV)to(GC) or from(NAV)to($FAST$), and WOW has been activated (up to $S1$)[a]
	Transfer in	I/GNSAlready completed the normal compass alignment state (from $S2$), automatic transfer, time <= 100 ms
		I/GNSAlready finished fast alignment state (from $S3$), automatic transfer, time <= 100 ms
Normal Loop Alignment (GC) StatusS_2	Transfer out	I/GNSAlready completed normal compass alignment state (auto to $S1$), time <= 100 ms
		from(GC)to(FAST), Already completed normal compass alignment state (auto to $S1$), time <= 100 ms
		from(GC)to(CAL), and I/GNS for completion of GC coarse alignment (to $S4$), time <= 100 ms
		from(GC)to(ATT) (to $S5$), complete alignment, automatic turn-out, time <= 100 ms[a]
	Transfer in	from(NAV)to(GC), and WOW is not activated (from $S1$)[a]
		from(CAL)to(GC) and coarse alignment is not completed (or) CAL ends after coarse alignment is completed and automatically goes to (from $S4$)
		from(ATT)to(GC) (from $S5$), complete ATT-Init, receive DCMP command, time <= 100 ms
Fast Alignment (FAST) StatusS_3	Transfer out	from($FAST$)to(GC) (to $S2$), time <= 100 ms
		from($FAST$)to(CAL) (to $S4$), time <= 100 ms
		from($FAST$)to(ATT) (up to $S5$), WOW is not activated[a]
	Transfer in	from(NAV)to($FAST$), and WOW is not activated (from $S1$)[a]
		from(GC)to($FAST$), and I/GNS has not completed GC coarse alignment (from $S2$)
		from(CAL)to($FAST$) and coarse alignment is not completed (or) CAL ends after coarse alignment is completed and automatically goes to (from $S4$)[a]
		from(ATT)to(FAST) (from $S5$)
Calibration Status(CAL) S_4	Transfer out	from(CAL)to(GC) and coarse alignment is not completed (or) CAL ends after coarse alignment is completed and automatically goes to (to $S2$)[a]
		from(CAL)to($FAST$) and coarse alignment is not completed (or) CAL ends after coarse alignment is completed and automatically moves to (to $S3$)[a]
		from(CAL)to(NAV), After I/GNS completes coarse alignment, turn CAL ends and automatic turn-in (to $S5$), time <=120 ms

(Continued)

TABLE 7.2 (*Continued*)   I/GNS Partial State Migration Condition Analysis

Status	Migration Direction	Migration Conditions
	Transfer in	from(*NAV*)to(*CAL*) (from *S1*), *WOW* is not activated[a]
		from(*GC*)to(*CAL*), and I/GNS has not completed *GC* coarse alignment (from *S2*), time <= 120 ms
		from(*FAST*)to(*CAL*) (from *S3*), time <= 120 ms
		from(*ATT*)to(*CAL*), and I/GNS=ATT-INIT (from *S5*), *WOW* is not activated[a]
Posture Status(ATT) S_5	Transfer out	from(*ATT*)to(*GC*) (to *S2*), *WOW* is not activated[a]
		from(*ATT*)to(*FAST*) (up to *S3*), *WOW* is not activated[a]
		from(*ATT*)to(*CAL*), and I/GNS completes *ATT-INIT* (to *S4*), *WOW* is not activated[a]
	Transfer in	(Usual cause of failure) turn attitude state, followed by DCMP command, turn end of flight, time <=120 ms
		from(*NAV*)to(*ATT*) (from *S1*), *WOW* is not activated[a]
		from(*GC*)to(*ATT*) (from *S2*), *WOW* is not activated[a]
		from(*FAST*)to(*ATT*) (from *S3*), *WOW* is not activated[a]
		from(*CAL*)to(*ATT*) and coarse alignment is not completed (or) *CAL* ends after coarse alignment is completed, automatic transfer (from *S4*), *WOW* is not activated[a]

[a] This state conversion is a ground debugging process (because WOW has been activated) and is not handled in this book.

TABLE 7.3   I/GNS Partial Sub-state Migration Condition Analysis

Top State	Sub-state	Migration Direction	Migration Conditions
Navigation status *S1*	Combined Navigation *S11*	Transfer out	Missing or invalid satellite data (up to *S12*)
			Inertial guidance gyro failure (to *S13*)
		Transfer in	Satellite data back to normal (from *S12*)
			Inertial guidance returns to normal (from *S13*)
	Pure inertial navigation S_{12}	Transfer out	Satellite data back to normal (to *S11*)
			Inertial guidance gyro failure (to *S13*)
		Transfer in	Missing or invalid satellite data (from *S11*)
			Inertial gyro back to normal (from *S13*)
	GPS Navigation S_{13}	Transfer out	Satellite data back to normal (to *S12*)
			Inertial gyro back to normal (to *S11*)
		Transfer in	Inertial gyro failure (from *S11*)
			Inertial gyro failure (from *S12*)

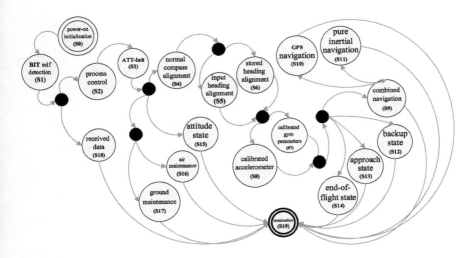

FIGURE 7.5   RT-EFSM model for I/GNS system software.

is the calibrated gyro parameters; S_8 is the calibrated accelerometer; S_9 is the combined navigation state; S_{10} is the GPS navigation; S_{11} is the pure inertial navigation; S_{12} is the backup state; S_{13} is the approach state; S_{14} is the end-of-flight state; S_{15} is the attitude state; S_{16} is the air maintenance; S_{17} is the ground maintenance; S_{18} is the received data; and S_{19} is the termination state.

Based on the above analysis, the analysis of each state migration condition can be completed by combining the software requirement document and ICD file, i.e., the list of time-constrained migration equivalence classes, as shown in Table 7.4 (only the main time-constrained migration equivalence classes are listed here due to the limitation of space), which lays the foundation for the generation of subsequent test sequences, test cases, and test descriptions.

7.4 TEST SEQUENCE, TEST CASE AND TEST DESCRIPTION GENERATION

After constructing the time-constrained migration equivalence classes listed in Table 7.4, the test scenario tree can be constructed according to the method in Chapter 3 of this book (see Appendix 4), and only a few typical state migration test scenario trees are analyzed and test sequence generation work is completed in this part due to the limitation of space.

TABLE 7.4 List of Equivalence Classes for Time-Bounded Migration of I/GNS (partial)

Source Status	Objectives Status	BindingC		Input Information (?I)		Output Information (!O)	
		Variable Constraints	Time Constraints	Input Variables	Input Action	Output Variables	Output Action
S_0	S_1	IGNS.WOW==1	gt<=5 ms	IGNS.APP	NONE	DCMP. INDC_00_00	SendDataValue (IGNS, DCIN_00_00, DCMP, INDC_00_00, 1553B)
S_1	S_2	IGNS. WOW==1;					
INDT_01_00. IN_052>=8.0	gt<=40 ms;	GetDataValue (DTE, INDT_01_00, 1553B);					
lt<=20 ms	IGNS.DCIN_01_00	SendDataValue (IGNS, DCIN_01_00, DCMP, INDC_01_00, 1553B)					
SendDataValue (0x4310, IGNS, DCIN_01_00)	DCMP. INDC_01_00						
S_1	S_{18}	IGNS. WOW==1;					

(Continued)

TABLE 7.4 (Continued) List of Equivalence Classes for Time-Bounded Migration of I/GNS (partial)

Source Status	Objectives Status	BindingC		Input Information (?I)		Output Information (!O)	
		Variable Constraints	Time Constraints	Input Variables	Input Action	Output Variables	Output Action
DCMP.INDC_00_00. VALID==1	gt>40 ms	IGNS. DTIN_01_00	SendDataValue (0x3310, IGNS, DTIN_01_00)	IGNS. DTIN_01_00. VALID=1	NONE		
S_2	S_3	IGNS. WOW==0;					
DCMP.INDC_00_00. VALID==1	gt>40 ms	IGNS. DCIN_01_00	SendDataValue (0x4010, IGNS, DCIN_01_00)	DCMP. INDC_01_00	SendDataValue (IGNS, DCIN_01_00, DCMP, INDC_01_00, 1553B)		
S_3	S_4	IGNS. WOW==0;					
INDT_01_00. IN_052>=7.0	gt>70 ms	IGNS. DCIN_00_00	GetDataValue (DTE, INDT_01_00, 1553B);				
SendDataValue (0x21D0, IGNS, DCIN_00_00) DCMP. INDC_00_00;	DTE.INDT_01_00. IN_052==7.0;						

(Continued)

TABLE 7.4 (Continued) List of Equivalence Classes for Time-Bounded Migration of I/GNS (partial)

Source Status	Objectives Status	BindingC		Input Information (?I)		Output Information (IO)	
		Variable Constraints	Time Constraints	Input Variables	Input Action	Output Variables	Output Action
CADC_INAD_00_00	SendDataValue (IGNS, DCIN_00_00, DCMP, INDC_00_00, 1553B)						
SendDataValue (IGNS, ADIN_00_00, CADC, INAD_00_00, DI)							
S_3	S_{15}	IGNS. WOW==0;	gt>70 ms	IGNS. DCIN_00_00	SendDataValue (0x23D0, IGNS, DCIN_00_00)	DCMP. INDC_19_00 =0x3500	SendDataValue (IGNS, DCIN_00_00, DCMP, INDC_09_00, 1553B)
S_3	S_{17}	IGNS. WOW==1;	gt>25 ms	IGNS. DCIN_00_00	SendDataValue (0x6122, IGNS, DCIN_00_00)	DCMP. INDC_00_00	SendDataValue (IGNS, DCIN_00_00, DCMP, INDC_00_00, 1553B)
S_4	S_5	IGNS. WOW==0;					
INDT_01_00. IN_052<=7.0	gt>150 ms;						

(Continued)

TABLE 7.4 (Continued)   List of Equivalence Classes for Time-Bounded Migration of I/GNS (partial)

Source Status	Objectives Status	BindingC		Input Information (?I)		Output Information (!O)	
		Variable Constraints	Time Constraints	Input Variables	Input Action	Output Variables	Output Action
lt<=100 ms	IGNS.DCIN_00_00						
IGNS.DCIN_01_04	GetDataValue(DTE, INDT_01_00,1553B);						
SendDataValue (0x25D0, IGNS, DCIN_00_00); DCMP. INDC_00_00;	DTE.INDT_01_00. IN_052==6.0; SendDataValue (IGNS, DCIN_00_00, DCMP, INDC_00_00,1553B)						
S_4	S_6	IGNS. WOW==0;					
INDT_01_00. IN_052<=7.0	gt>150 ms;						
lt<=100 ms	IGNS.DCIN_00_00	GetDataValue (DTE, INDT_01_00, 1553B);					
SendDataValue (0x25D0, IGNS, DCIN_00_00); IGNS. INLP_01_00	DTE.INDT_01_00. IN_052==6.0; SendDataValue (IGNS, DCIN_00_00, DCMP, INDC_00_00, 1553B);						

(Continued)

TABLE 7.4 (Continued)   List of Equivalence Classes for Time-Bounded Migration of I/GNS (partial)

Source Status	Objectives Status	BindingC		Input Information (?I)		Output Information (!O)	
		Variable Constraints	Time Constraints	Input Variables	Input Action	Output Variables	Output Action
SendDataValue (IGNS, DCIN_00_00, DCMP, INDC_00_00, 1553B); S_{10}	S_9	IGNS. WOW==0;					
INDT_01_00. IN_052<=4.0 lt<=100 ms	gt>150 ms; IGNS.DCIN_00_00	GetDataValue (DTE, INDT_01_00, 1553B);					
SendDataValue(0x2305, IGNS, DCIN_00_00); IGNS. INLP_01_00	DCMP: INDC_00_00; SendDataValue (IGNS, DCIN_00_00, DCMP, INDC_00_00, 1553B);	NONE	NONE				
S_{14}	S_{19}	NONE	NONE	IGNS. DCIN_00_00	SendDataValue (0x9910, IGNS, DCIN_00_00);	DTE. INDT_03_00	SendDataValue (IGNS, DTIN_03_00, DTE, INDT_03_00, 1553B)

Examples of selected typical (after spreading) test scene trees are as follows:

TST01: $s_0 \rightarrow s_1 \rightarrow s_{18} \rightarrow s_{19}$

TST02: $s_0 \rightarrow s_1 \rightarrow s_2 \rightarrow s_3 \rightarrow s_{17} \rightarrow s_{19}$

TST03: $s_0 \rightarrow s_1 \rightarrow s_2 \rightarrow s_3 \rightarrow s_4 \rightarrow s_5 \rightarrow s_7 \rightarrow s_9 \rightarrow s_{11} \rightarrow s_{19}$

TST04: $s_0 \rightarrow s_1 \rightarrow s_2 \rightarrow s_3 \rightarrow s_4 \rightarrow s_5 \rightarrow s_7 \rightarrow s_9 \rightarrow s_{10} \rightarrow s_9 \rightarrow s_{11} \rightarrow s_{19}$

From the test sequence generation method, each state migration in RT-EFSM corresponds to a number of time-constrained migration equivalence classes. We can use extended test sequences US_{ex} to represent the set of, Definition of by US_{ex}, Then the corresponding test sequences can be generated based on the above test scenario tree as follows:

$$US_{ex}\,01:$$

$$\{(S_0 \rightarrow S_1)\_ < tCnd_{0\rightarrow1}, vCnd_{0\rightarrow1} > \_? < ivVle_{0\rightarrow1}, iAct_{0\rightarrow1} >$$

$$\_! < ovVle_{0\rightarrow1}, oAct >_{0\rightarrow1}\} \cup$$

$$\{(S_1 \rightarrow S_{18})\_ < tCnd_{1\rightarrow18}, vCnd_{1\rightarrow18} > \_? < ivVle_{1\rightarrow18}, iAct_{1\rightarrow18} >$$

$$\_! < ovVle_{1\rightarrow18}, oAct >_{1\rightarrow18}\} \cup$$

$$\{(S_{18} \rightarrow S_{19})\_ < tCnd_{18\rightarrow19}, vCnd_{18\rightarrow19} > \_? < ivVle_{18\rightarrow19}, iAct_{18\rightarrow19} >$$

$$\_! < ovVle_{18\rightarrow19}, oAct >_{18\rightarrow19}\}$$

$$US_{ex}\,02:$$

$$\{(S_0 \rightarrow S_1)\_ < tCnd_{0\rightarrow1}, vCnd_{0\rightarrow1} > \_? < ivVle_{0\rightarrow1}, iAct_{0\rightarrow1} >$$

$$\_! < ovVle_{0\rightarrow1}, oAct >_{0\rightarrow1}\} \cup$$

$$\{(S_3 \to S_{17})\_ < tCnd_{3\to17}, vCnd_{3\to17} > \_? < ivVle_{3\to17}, iAct_{3\to17} >$$
$$\_! < ovVle_{3\to17}, oAct >_{3\to17}\} \cup$$

$$\{(S_{17} \to S_{19})\_ < tCnd_{17\to19}, vCnd_{17\to19} > \_? < ivVle_{17\to19}, iAct_{17\to19} >$$
$$\_! < ovVle_{17\to19}, oAct >_{18\to19}\}$$

$$US_{ex}\,03:$$

$$\{(S_0 \to S_1)\_ < tCnd_{0\to1}, vCnd_{0\to1} > \_? < ivVle_{0\to1}, iAct_{0\to1} >$$
$$\_! < ovVle_{0\to1}, oAct >_{0\to1}\} \cup$$

$$\{(S_1 \to S_2)\_ < tCnd_{1\to2}, vCnd_{1\to2} > \_? < ivVle_{1\to2}, iAct_{1\to2} >$$
$$\_! < ovVle_{1\to2}, oAct >_{1\to2}\} \cup$$

$$\{(S_2 \to S_3)\_ < tCnd_{2\to3}, vCnd_{2\to3} > \_? < ivVle_{2\to3}, iAct_{2\to3} >$$
$$\_! < ovVle_{2\to3}, oAct >_{2\to3}\} \cup$$

$$\{(S_3 \to S_4)\_ < tCnd_{3\to4}, vCnd_{3\to4} > \_? < ivVle_{3\to4}, iAct_{3\to4} >$$
$$\_! < ovVle_{3\to4}, oAct >_{3\to4}\} \cup$$

$$\{(S_4 \to S_5)\_ < tCnd_{4\to5}, vCnd_{4\to5} > \_? < ivVle_{4\to5}, iAct_{4\to5} >$$
$$\_! < ovVle_{4\to5}, oAct >_{4\to5}\} \cup$$

$$\{(S_5 \to S_7)\_ < tCnd_{5\to7}, vCnd_{5\to7} > \_? < ivVle_{5\to7}, iAct_{5\to7} >$$
$$\_! < ovVle_{5\to7}, oAct >_{5\to7}\} \cup$$

$$\{(S_7 \to S_9)\_ < tCnd_{7\to9}, vCnd_{7\to9} > \_? < ivVle_{7\to9}, iAct_{7\to9} >$$
$$\_! < ovVle_{7\to9}, oAct >_{7\to9}\} \cup$$

$\{(S_9 \rightarrow S_{11})\_ < tCnd_{9\rightarrow11}, vCnd_{9\rightarrow11} > \_? < ivVle_{9\rightarrow11}, iAct_{9\rightarrow11} >$

$\_! < ovVle_{9\rightarrow11}, oAct >_{9\rightarrow11}\} \cup$

$\{(S_{11} \rightarrow S_{19})\_ < tCnd_{11\rightarrow19}, vCnd_{11\rightarrow19} > \_? < ivVle_{11\rightarrow19}, iAct_{11\rightarrow19} >$

$\_! < ovVle_{11\rightarrow19}, oAct >_{11\rightarrow19}\}$

$$US_{ex}\,04:$$

$\{(S_0 \rightarrow S_1)\_ < tCnd_{0\rightarrow1}, vCnd_{0\rightarrow1} > \_? < ivVle_{0\rightarrow1}, iAct_{0\rightarrow1} >$

$\_! < ovVle_{0\rightarrow1}, oAct >_{0\rightarrow1}\} \cup$

$\{(S_1 \rightarrow S_2)\_ < tCnd_{1\rightarrow2}, vCnd_{1\rightarrow2} > \_? < ivVle_{1\rightarrow2}, iAct_{1\rightarrow2} >$

$\_! < ovVle_{1\rightarrow2}, oAct >_{1\rightarrow2}\} \cup$

$\{(S_2 \rightarrow S_3)\_ < tCnd_{2\rightarrow3}, vCnd_{2\rightarrow3} > \_? < ivVle_{2\rightarrow3}, iAct_{2\rightarrow3} >$

$\_! < ovVle_{2\rightarrow3}, oAct >_{2\rightarrow3}\} \cup$

$\{(S_3 \rightarrow S_4)\_ < tCnd_{3\rightarrow4}, vCnd_{3\rightarrow4} > \_? < ivVle_{3\rightarrow4}, iAct_{3\rightarrow4} >$

$\_! < ovVle_{3\rightarrow4}, oAct >_{3\rightarrow4}\} \cup$

$\{(S_4 \rightarrow S_5)\_ < tCnd_{4\rightarrow5}, vCnd_{4\rightarrow5} > \_? < ivVle_{4\rightarrow5}, iAct_{4\rightarrow5} >$

$\_! < ovVle_{4\rightarrow5}, oAct >_{4\rightarrow5}\} \cup$

$\{(S_5 \rightarrow S_7)\_ < tCnd_{5\rightarrow7}, vCnd_{5\rightarrow7} > \_? < ivVle_{5\rightarrow7}, iAct_{5\rightarrow7} >$

$\_! < ovVle_{5\rightarrow7}, oAct >_{5\rightarrow7}\} \cup$

$\{(S_7 \rightarrow S_9)\_ < tCnd_{7\rightarrow9}, vCnd_{7\rightarrow9} > \_? < ivVle_{7\rightarrow9}, iAct_{7\rightarrow9} >$

$\_! < ovVle_{7\rightarrow9}, oAct >_{7\rightarrow9}\} \cup$

$\{(S_9 \rightarrow S_{10})\_ < tCnd_{9\rightarrow10}, vCnd_{9\rightarrow10} > \_? < ivVle_{9\rightarrow10}, iAct_{9\rightarrow10} >$

$\_! < ovVle_{9\rightarrow10}, oAct >_{9\rightarrow10}\} \cup$

$$\{(S_{10} \rightarrow S_9)\_ < tCnd_{10 \rightarrow 9}, vCnd_{10 \rightarrow 9} > \_? < ivVle_{10 \rightarrow 9}, iAct_{10 \rightarrow 9} >$$

$$\_! < ovVle_{10 \rightarrow 9}, oAct >_{10 \rightarrow 9}\} \cup$$

$$\{(S_9 \rightarrow S_{11})\_ < tCnd_{9 \rightarrow 11}, vCnd_{9 \rightarrow 11} > \_? < ivVle_{9 \rightarrow 11}, iAct_{9 \rightarrow 11} >$$

$$\_! < ovVle_{9 \rightarrow 11}, oAct >_{9 \rightarrow 11}\} \cup$$

$$\{(S_{11} \rightarrow S_{19})\_ < tCnd_{11 \rightarrow 19}, vCnd_{11 \rightarrow 19} > \_? < ivVle_{11 \rightarrow 19}, iAct_{11 \rightarrow 19} >$$

$$\_! < ovVle_{11 \rightarrow 19}, oAct >_{11 \rightarrow 19}\}$$

On the basis of generating test sequences, test cases based on state, migration coverage criterion, full predicate coverage criterion, transformation pair coverage criterion, and time condition coverage criterion can be generated according to the test case generation methods given in Chapter 4. In addition, according to different methods of black-box testing, test types such as normal function test cases, exception test cases, boundary test cases, performance test cases, interface test cases, resilience test cases, and strength test cases can also be generated (see Chapter 3 of this book for details of the methods). Due to the limitation of space, only two test cases corresponding to the above test sequences are given in this book, as follows:

TestCase01:

$$\{(S_0 \rightarrow S_1)\_ < (IGN.WOW == 1) \& \&(gt <= 5) > \_? < IGNS.APP = 1 >$$

$$\_! < SendDataValue(IGNS, DCIN\_00\_00, DCMP, INDC\_00\_00, 1553B >\} \cup$$

$$\{(S_1 \rightarrow S_{18})\_ < (IGNS.WOW == 1) \& \&(DCMP.INDC\_00\_00.VALID == 1)$$

$$\& \&(gt >= 40) >$$

$$\_? < IGNS.DTIN\_01\_00, SendDataValue(0x3310, IGNS, DTIN\_01\_00) >$$

$$\_! < (IGNS.DTIN\_01\_00.VALID = 1), (NONE) >\} \cup$$

$$\{(S_{18} \rightarrow S_{19})\_[NONE]\_? < IGNS.DCIN\_00\_00),$$

$$SendDataValue(0x9910, IGNS, DCIN\_00\_00) >$$

$$\_! < (DTE.INDT\_03\_00), (SendDataValue(IGNS, DTIN\_03\_00,$$

$$DTE, INDT\_03\_00, 1553B)) >\}$$

TestCase02:

$\{(S_0 \rightarrow S_1)\_ < (IGN.WOW == 1) \& \&(gt <= 5) > \_? < IGNS.APP = 1 >$

$\_! < SendDataValue(IGNS, DCIN\_00\_00, DCMP, INDC\_00\_00, 1553B >\} \cup$

$\{(S_1 \rightarrow S_2)\_ < (IGNS.WOW == 1) \& \&(INDT\_01\_00.IN\_052 >= 8.0),$

$\quad (gt <= 40\,ms) \& \&(lt <= 20\,ms) >$

$\_? < IGNS.DCIN\_01\_00, (GetDataValue(DTE, INDT\_01\_00, 1553B);$

$SendDataValue(0x4310, IGNS, DCIN\_01\_00)) >$

$\_! < DCMP.INDC\_01\_00, SendDataValue(IGNS, DCIN\_01\_00,$

$\quad DCMP, INDC\_01\_00, 1553B) >\} \cup$

$\{(S_3 \rightarrow S_{17})\_ < IGNS.DCIN\_00\_00,$

$\quad SendDataValue(0x6122, IGNS, DCIN\_00\_00) >$

$\_! < DCMP.INDC\_00\_00, SendDataValue(IGNS,$

$\quad DCIN\_00\_00, DCMP, INDC\_00\_00, 1553B >\} \cup$

$\{(S_{17} \rightarrow S_{19})\_ < NONE > \_? < IGNS.DCIN\_00\_00,$

$\quad SendDataValue(0x9010, IGNS, DCIN\_00\_00) >$

$\_! < DTE.INDT\_03\_00, SendDataValue(IGNS, DTIN\_03\_00, DTE,$

$\quad INDT\_03\_00, 1553B) >\}$

After the test cases based on the test scenario tree are generated, the generated test cases can be stored in XML files according to the method in Chapter 3 of this book, and then the contents of the XML files can be parsed and converted into corresponding test descriptions according to the grammar rules of RT-ESTDL, which gives the RT-ESTDL file contents of typical test cases (Table 7.5).

TABLE 7.5   RT-ESTDL **Description** of Typical Test Cases for I/GNS

```
#include "testConfig.tdf"
using "RT-ESTDL.mdl"
using "aviiodatavar.mdl"
using "aviiolink.mdl"
using "1553bBlock.mdl"
using "igns.mdl"
using "sms.mdl"
using "dcmp.mdl"
...
procedure  IGNSTestCase03 ()

{

    var gt;    // Used to record the global clock
    var lt;    // For recording local clocks
    // Device Generation
    IGNSMDL IGNS;
    DCMPMDL DCMP;
    ...


    //S0->S1, Enter BIT self-test
       IGNS.APP =1; //IGNS Add electricity
    gt= GetCurTestTime();
    if((IGNS.WOW==1)&&(gt<=5))  // Time constraint of 5 ms
and a wheel load signal of 1 (on the ground)
        SendDataValue(IGNS,DCIN_00_00,DCMP,INDC_00_00,1553B);
// Perform BIT self-test
    GetDataValue(DTE, INDT_01_00,1553B);   // Obtain DTE
navigation accuracy data
    //S1->S2, Enter process control, aircraft take off
    if(INDT_01_00.IN_052>=8.0){
        IGNS.DCIN_01_00=0x2010;
        SendDataValue(0x4310,IGNS,DCIN_01_00);  // Enter
process control, aircraft take off
        lt= GetCurTestTime()-gt;  // Calculating the local
clock for state migration
        if(lt<=20)
          print("\r\n---≫>IGNS enter process control!---≪\
r\n");  // Screen Printing
      }
      else
        print("\r\n---≫>NAV accuracy failure!---≪\r\n");  //
Navigation accuracy not met
    //S2->S3, Enter ATT-Init
    while(gt>40){  // Get the system clock until it meets 40
ms
```

(*Continued*)

TABLE 7.5 (*Continued*)   RT-ESTDL **Description** of Typical Test Cases for I/GNS

```
 gt= GetCurTestTime();
    if (IGNS.WOW==0)&&DCMP.INDC_00_00.VALID==1)){ // The
aircraft is in the air and the attitude dispersion signal is
valid
        IGNS.DCIN_01_00= 0x4010; // Sending display control
commands
        break;
 }
    wait(20);
    SendDataValue(IGNS,DCIN_01_00,DCMP,INDC_01_00,1553B);
//60 ms ATT-InitDone, refresh the display control
 // Normal Roentgen alignment
 while(gt>70){  // Get the system clock, until it meets 70
ms, ATT-Init and display control refresh is completed.
   gt= GetCurTestTime();
   GetDataValue(DTE, INDT_01_00,1553B);  // Get navigation
accuracy
   if(INDT_01_00.IN_052>=8.0){
       IGNS.DCIN_00_00=0x21D0; // Sending of the rosette
alignment command
       DTE.INDT_01_00.IN_052==7.0; // Set navigation accuracy
       SendDataValue(IGNS,DCIN_00_00,DCMP,INDC_00_00,1553B);
// Display Control Refresh
       SendDataValue(IGNS,ADIN_00_00,CADC,INAD_00_00,DI); //
Set the atmospheric data computer heading parameters valid
   }
 break;
 // Perform input heading alignment
 while(gt>150){  // Get the system clock until it meets
150 ms
     gt= GetCurTestTime();
   GetDataValue(DTE, INDT_01_00,1553B);  // Get navigation
accuracy
   if(INDT_01_00.IN_052<=7.0){
       IGNS.DCIN_00_00=0x25D0; // Send input heading
alignment command
       DTE.INDT_01_00.IN_052==6.0;
       SendDataValue(IGNS,DCIN_00_00,DCMP,INDC_00_00,1553B);
       SendDataValue(DET,INDT_01_00,IGNS,DIIN_00_00,1553B);
// Display heading value
   }
 break;
 }
 ...
```

(*Continued*)

TABLE 7.5 (*Continued*)   RT-ESTDL **Description** of Typical Test Cases for I/GNS

```
// Portfolio Navigation
   IGNS.DCIN_01_00=0x2305; // Enter Portfolio Navigation
   GetDataValue(DCMP, INDC_01_00,1553B);
...
// Enter end-of-flight status
   while((IGNS.DTIN_00_00.STATUS_IN &&0x0800 != 1)){
      DTE.INDT_03_00=0x8120; // Enter EOF operating mode
      print("\r\n---≫>IGNS enter EOF mode!---≪\r\n");
      return;// End of flight
   }
}
```

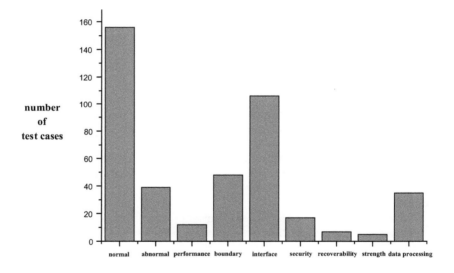

FIGURE 7.6   I/GNS system software test case statistics.

7.5 TEST EXECUTION AND RESULT ANALYSIS

Based on the above analysis, this instance verification tested all functions and performance of the I/GNS system in terms of normal functions, exceptions, performance, boundaries, interfaces, strength, security, recoverability, and data processing, and generated a total of 412 test cases (test descriptions) (see Figure 7.6 for the distribution of cases).

Based on the test cases (test descriptions), the generated test descriptions were imposed on the RT-ESSTE test environment, and the system anomalies during the test were recorded through the real-time operation of the test execution system, and a total of 46 software defects were identified after analysis, including various defects such as missing functions, functional implementation errors, timing errors, and logic errors. Finally, combined with the analysis of software defects (see Table 7.6), the I/GNS software system testing report was formed.

TABLE 7.6   I/GNS Typical Software Defect Analysis

No.	Software Defect Description	Related Status	Potential Impact Analysis
1	Attitude state, I/GNS sub-mode ATT early report 10 seconds	Attitude state	Timing error, if other instructions are triggered within 10 seconds of the early reporting time, it may lead to system timing disorder and affect flight safety.
2	The migration time is <=100 ms for the normal ro-ro alignment state to the stored heading alignment state, and the actual migration time is 120 ms	Normal compass alignment status; stored heading alignment status	Timing errors, which may lead to system timing disruptions and affect flight safety
3	In the combined navigation state, when the constant pressure source failure occurs, the system turns to GPS navigation, and the heading and heading are set as valid (the correct treatment should set the heading and heading as invalid)	Combined navigation status; GPS navigation status	System function implementation error, may affect the pilot's judgment, make wrong instructions, affect flight safety
4	During normal compass alignment, the navigation accuracy does not show 8.0 and no related processing is performed	Normal warp alignment status	Missing features that may cause the alignment process to fail
5	When the normal compass alignment is not completed, the system will automatically switch to the navigation state after receiving the command to switch to navigation several times	Normal compass alignment status; Navigation status	Errors in the logic of the decision maker may lead to confusion in the migration of the system state and enter into an unknown processing process, affecting flight safety

(Continued)

TABLE 7.6 (*Continued*)   I/GNS Typical Software Defect Analysis

No.	Software Defect Description	Related Status	Potential Impact Analysis
6	There is a logical error in the error correction processing of the received data in the received data state	Receiving data status	Wrong logic judgment, resulting in receiving the wrong data, unable to complete the subsequent process
7	During the normal ground compass alignment, the binding altitude is +32,778 m, and the system returns the binding result as −32,768 m	Normal warp alignment status	Lack of protection against abnormal data, resulting in alignment process failure
8	Negative heading cannot be entered in the input heading alignment state	Enter heading alignment status	Missing function, causing the input heading alignment process to fail
9	Ground maintenance state, pitch, roll, and other values exceed the rated range, but still receive the binding	Ground maintenance status	Lack of protection against abnormal data, leading to ground maintenance failures
10	BIT self-test state, the software does not alarm the shell under-temperature fault	BIT Self-Detection Status	The lack of functionality leads to hidden problems in BIT self-detection, affecting flight safety
11	If the ground maintenance status is not completed, the system responds to a new status transition command (e.g., to ATT)	Ground maintenance status	Wrong logic judgment, resulting in confusing system state migration and unknown processing flow
12	The system can accept a binding height of −470 m during normal ground-based compass alignment	Normal warp alignment status	The system lacks security protection for abnormal binding data, which affects flight safety

7.6 SUMMARY

In this chapter, the techniques and methods proposed in the previous chapters of this book are systematically applied in the process of testing the software system of a typical real-time embedded software – inertial/satellite combined navigation system, including: completing the functional and performance analysis of the system under test; completing the static and dynamic modeling using real-time extended UML; completing the design of time-constrained migration equivalence classes; generating test sequences, test cases and test descriptions; applying the obtained test cases to the system testing environment; and finally finding various software defects including timing errors, functional implementation errors and logic errors through test runs. Finally, the obtained test cases are imposed on the system testing environment; through test runs, various software defects including timing errors, functional implementation errors, and logic errors are found. Through engineering examples, the correctness and effectiveness of the techniques and methods proposed in this book are fully verified.

Appendix 1

Mathematical Symbol Index

SCHEDULE 1   Mathematical Symbol Index

Mathematical Symbol	Illustration
$S*$	Set of non-empty finite states in RT-EFSM model
S_0	Initial state of RT-EFSM model
I	RT-EFSM model input event set
O	RT-EFSM model output event set
T	Set of non-empty state transitions in RT-EFSM model
V	RT-EFSM model input variable set
E	Set of connected directed edges in RT-EFSM model
L	Global clock of RT-EFSM model
$Head(t)$	The starting state of migration t
$I(t)$	The input event contained in the input event set I in migration t
$C(t)$	Preconditions for migration t execution
act	Operations during state migration
$O(t)$	Output events contained in output event set O
$Tail(t)$	The arrival state of migration t
t_S	The state migration time is a fixed value
t_F	The state transition time obeys a certain distribution function
t_I	The state transition time is a certain time interval
entry	State entry, prior to any internal actions and migrations
exit	State exit, after all internal actions and migrations
$iact$	State internal action

(Continued)

SCHEDULE 1 (*Continued*)   Mathematical Symbol Index

Mathematical Symbol	Illustration
itran	State internal migration
iTevt	A collection of time-related events within a state
lt	State internal local clock
$RT - SD = (\rho, tp, \theta, gt)$	Real-time extended UML state diagram
$\rho : S^* \mapsto 2^{S^*}$	State refinement function of real-time extended UML state diagram
$tp : S^* \mapsto \{\text{smp}, \text{AND}, \text{OR}, \text{psdo}\}$	State-type function of real-time extension UML state diagram
$tp(s) = \text{smp}$	The state of the real-time extended UML state s diagram is a simple state, and $\rho(s) \neq \varnothing$
$tp(s) = \text{AND}$	The state of real-time extended UML state diagram is AND state
$tp(s) = \text{OR}$	The state of real-time extended UML state diagram is OR state
$tp(s) = \text{psdo}$	The state of real-time extended UML state diagram is pseudo state
$\theta : S^* \mapsto 2^{S^*}$	State default function of real-time extended UML state diagram
gt	Global clock of real-time extended UML state diagram
root	The root node state of real-time extend UML state diagram
$\text{src} : T \mapsto S^*$	Source state of state migration in real-time extended UML state diagram
$\text{evt} : T \mapsto \text{evt}$	Trigger events of state migration in real-time extended UML state diagram
$\text{grd} : T \mapsto \text{grd}$	Monitoring conditions of state migration in real-time extended UML state diagram
$\text{act} : T \mapsto \text{act}$	Actions of state migration in real-time extended UML state diagram
$\text{trgt} : T \mapsto S^*$	Target of state migration in real-time extended UML state diagram
$\pi : S^* \mapsto S^*$	Father state of special state in real-time extended UML state diagram
$S_1 \xrightarrow{\text{evt[grp]/act}} S_2$	State migration of real-time extended UML state diagram
$\text{conf} : S \mapsto 2^{2^{S^*}}$	State pattern function of real-time extended UML state diagram
$\text{actv} : S^* \mapsto \{\text{TRUE}, \text{FALSE}\}$	State active function of real-time extended UML state diagram
$\text{enb} : CT \mapsto \{\text{TRUE}, \text{FALSE}\}$	State enable function of real-time extended UML state diagram

(*Continued*)

SCHEDULE 1 *(Continued)* Mathematical Symbol Index

Mathematical Symbol	Illustration
$\text{conflict}\left(t_i, t_j, c\right)$	State conflict function of real-time extended UML state diagram
$\text{prior}\left(t_i, t_j\right)$	State migration priority of real-time extended UML state diagram
$t_i \leftrightarrow t_j$	State connection of real-time extended UML state diagram
$t = t_i \otimes t_j$	State decomposition of real-time extended UML state diagram
$\{C_1, C_2, \ldots, C_k\}$	Time region division of time constraint ω on system time
$\left\{\left(S_{\text{src}} \rightarrow S_{\text{trgt}}\right)\_[C]\_?I\_!O\right\}$	Time-constrained migration equivalence class
S_{src}	Source state of time-constrained migration equivalence class
S_{trgrt}	Target state of time-constrained migration equivalence class
$C =< tCnd, vCnd >$	Monitoring conditions for the occurrence of time-constrained migration equivalence class migration
$?$	"Input" of time-constrained migration equivalence class
$I =< ivVle, iAct >$	Input variables and operations of time-constrained migration equivalence classes
$!$	"Output" of time-constrained migration equivalence class
$O =< ovVle, oAct >$	Output variables and operations of time-constrained migration equivalence classes
$< \text{time}CTEC_1 \cup \ldots \text{time}CTEC_i \cup \ldots >$	Extended test sequence

Appendix 2

Semantics and Usage of RT-ESTDL

A2.1 LEXICAL RULES

1. **Whitespace and notes**

    In RT-ESTDL, white space is used to separate adjacent identifiers, keywords and constants in the program, mainly including spaces, tabs, line breaks, page breaks and comments.

    In RT-ESTDL, comments can appear between any two tokens, and the following three forms of comment statements can be supported:

    - C language style notes, such as / * @ Hello word! * /, Multi line comments can be supported;

    - C++ style comments, single line comments starting with / /;

2. **Identifier**

    In RT-ESTDL, the identifier consists of letters and numbers, and the requirements are as follows: the first character must be a letter; Underscores are also used as letters; Case sensitive; The identifier can be of any length.

3. **keyword**

The keywords of RT-ESTDL are as follows:

var	*const*	*procedure*	*include*	*using*
equipment	*static*	*string*	*array*	*object*
function	*resource*	*if*	*else*	*switch*
for	*do*	*while*	*break*	*continue*
return	*case*	*default*	*new*	*bool*
int	*float*	*complex*	*vec2*	*vec3*
vec4	*mat2*	*mat3*	*mat4*	

4. **numeric constants**

An integer constant consists of a sequence of numbers. If it starts with 0, it is an octal number, otherwise it is a decimal number, and if it starts with 0x and 0x, it is a hexadecimal number.

Floating-point constants contain integer parts, decimal points and fractional parts, an e or E, and optionally signed integer type exponents. Both integer and decimal parts are composed of a sequence of numbers. There may be no integer part or decimal part (but not both).

for example:

const var $x = 20$;

5. **string constant**

A string constant is a sequence of characters enclosed in double quotes, such as "…".

for example:

For const statements, the string constant string is supported, and only when it is a constant, such as:

const string str = "myString"; // correct

string s = "myString"; // Error, variables of type string are not supported

In addition, string constants can contain all characters except line breaks. How to insert special characters:

\n inserts line break; \t inserts horizontal tab; \" inserts double quotation marks; \\ inserts backslash.

A2.2 VALUE OF EXPRESSION

In RT-ESTDL, a value is the result of an expression, can be stored in a variable, and can be passed to a function or procedure as a parameter, or as the return value of a function or procedure. For example:

var pi;

pi=1+1/1.0+1/2.0+1/3.0+1/4.0+1/5.0+1/6.0+1/7.0;

Refer to relevant sections for operators supported by expressions in RT-ESTDL and their associativity.

1. **Type check**

   Each value has a type, and all type checks are performed at run time. In RT-ESTDL, there is no compile time type declaration and type check, and any variable can refer to any type of value.

2. **Supplementary description of several values**

SCHEDULE 2   Description of RT-ESTDL

Category	Specify
Zero value	The built-in constant null represents a special value. It has no type and is different from all other values. It represents the abnormal state of any value, such as the uninitialized variable.
Simple value	By copy assignment, that is, each variable references a unique independent memory copy.
	There are 11 simple value types: bool, int, float, string, complex, vector container (vec2, vec3, *vec4*), matrix container (mat2, *mat3*, mat4).
	The Boolean value is regarded as an independent type and can only accept two built-in constant values true and false. A string is regarded as an atomic constant value, and a single character in the string cannot be accessed and changed directly. Complex numbers, vector containers and matrix containers are called composite values.
Other values	Assignment by reference, including:
	(1) Variable values include *array* and *object*. An array can store a sequence of values of the same type. Object contains members and methods.
	(2) Immutable values include *function* and *resource*. A function is a value that can be called. When a function is called, parameters are passed to it, and it will return a result. Resources represent resources that can be processed by built-in functions, such as files, display devices, etc.

A2.3 OPERATORS AND OPERATORS

All operators are shown in the following table. The operators are arranged from high to low priority. The priority of the same group is not distinguished before and after, and it is judged according to the direction of the combination law.

SCHEDULE 3   Combination Law of Operator and Operator of RT-ESTDL

Operator	Meaning	Combination Law	Operator	Meaning	Combination Law
::	Name field determination	–	+	Add / string connection	Left
.	Composite member access	Left	-	reduce	Left
[]	Element access	Left	<	less than	–
->	Object member access	Left	<=	Less than or equal to	–
()	function call	Left	>	greater than	–
<>	combination	–	>=	Greater than or equal to	–
new	Object/array construction	–	= =	Identity equality	–
++	Prefix/suffix auto increment	–	!=	Identity is not equal to	–
--	Prefix/suffix self subtraction	–	&	Bitwise AND	Left
^	power	–	|	Bitwise OR	Left
!	Logical non	right	&&	Logic and	Left
~	Bitwise non	right	||	Logical or	Left
+	Positive number	right	? :	Conditional expression	–
-	negative	right	=	assignment	right
*	ride	Left	%	Take mold	Left
/	except	Left	∧	Exponentiation	right

1. **Name field determination**

In RT-ESTDL global procedures, the namespace of symbols allows only global and built-in symbols to be found.

The namespace determination operator ":" can be processed in two ways:

- <*equipment*>::<symbol> indicates that the symbol is processed into the specified device, and the special identifier "super" is used *to* refer to its parent device.

- ::<symbol> indicates that the symbol is processed as a global or built-in namespace.

2. **Operator description**

SCHEDULE 4   Usage Description of RT-ESTDL Operators

Category	Usage	Specify
Composite-type member access	<combined_ *exp*>. < **component**>	Member access operator "." Allows reading and writing of a member of a composite value.
Array element access	<array_ *exp*> [<index_ exp>]	The array element access operator '[]' allows reading and writing to a member of the array.
Object member access	<object_ *exp*> -> <member_ id>	The member access operator '- >' allows you to read and write member variables of an object.
Self-increasing and self-decreasing	*var++; ++ var; var--; -- var*	Complete self-increasing and self-decreasing functions. The same can be applied to array elements or object members.
Arithmetic operator	*var1+var2;* *var1-var2;* *var1*var2;* *var1/var2;* *VAR1% var2 / / mold taking* *VAR1 ^ var2 / / exponentiation*	Note: 1. Vectors and matrices of the same size can be added or subtracted 2. Vectors and matrices can also multiply and divide a floating-point number. 3. If the size between vector and matrix matches, multiplication and division can be performed. 4. The + operator can be used to connect two string values. 5. The operators + and - can also be used as unary operators to represent positive or negative.

(*Continued*)

SCHEDULE 4 (*Continued*)   Usage Description of RT-ESTDL Operators

Category	Usage	Specify
Comparison operator	*var1>var2;* *var1>=var2;* *var1<var2;* *var1<=var2;* *if(var1==var2)* ... *if(var1!=var2)* ...	Note: 1. In addition to being used to compare two integers or floating-point numbers, relational comparison operators can also compare two strings in dictionary order. 2. Identity comparison operator == and= The calculation result is Boolean, true or false.
Bitwise operators	Slightly	Including bit and (&), bit or (|) and bit non (~). The operand must be an integer value and the result is still an integer value.
Logical operator	Slightly	Including logical and (& &), logical or (|) and logical non (!). The operand of a logical operator must be Boolean and the result must be Boolean.
Assignment operator	Slightly	It can assign variables, object members, array elements, or composite values.
Conditional Operator	<condition_ *exp>?*<true_ exp>: <*false_* exp>	The conditional operator solves the Boolean value of the first expression. If the value is true, the second expression will be solved and return its value; otherwise, the third expression will be solved and return its value.
Combination operator	< <component_ *exp>,...;<* component_ *exp>,...;...* >	Finish creating a vector or matrix.
Array construction operation	new <*type*> [<size_exp>]; new <*type*> [[<size_ const>]] { <init_exp>,... }	Creates an array of the given type and size.
Object or device model construction	new <device> ([<arg_exp>,...])	Create an instantiation of the specified device type, initialize the member with the given parameters, and call the constructor.

A2.4 DECLARATION

RT-ESTDL statements can be regarded as composed of constants, global variables, procedures or objects. The statements are compiled to produce intermediate instruction sequences. RT-ESTDL statements contain pre-inclusion and declaration statements. A file can contain other files, and the contents of the included file are processed at *include*. All declared symbols in each file are globally visible in the namespace of the compiled test description statement.

Declarations of constants, variables, procedures, and classes are processed before initializing the procedure body and variables. Allows procedures or initializers to access symbols declared later.

After the test description statement is compiled, the global and static variables are initialized (the initialization order is the same as the declared order).

The usage of pre-inclusion and constants, variables, functions and procedures in RT-ESTDL statements is shown in the following table.

SCHEDULE 5   RT-ESTDL Pre-inclusion and Usage of Constants, Procedures, etc.

Category	Usage	Specify
Pre-inclusion	#include "filename.tdf" #using "modefile.mdl"	Pre-inclusion starts with the keyword *include* or *using* and ends with a semicolon. Can appear anywhere in the file except the declaration body. 1. *include* precompiling enables the compiler to read the contents of another file. Each file is read only once. If repeated inclusion, redundant inclusion will be ignored. 2. *using* precompiling indicates that you need to provide the corresponding model file to compile. If the model is not defined, the compiler throws an error.
Constant	const <id> = <value>,...;	A constant is a symbol that contains a value and can only be a simple type. The constant value can be a number, a string constant, or an expression that can be solved by the compiler. Defined constants and built-in constants can be used to define new constants.
variable	var <id> [= <initializer>],...;	A variable is a symbol that can refer to any value of any type. Initialization can be any expression. If the variable is not initialized, its initial value is zero and null.

(Continued)

SCHEDULE 5 (*Continued*)   RT-ESTDL Pre-inclusion and Usage of Constants, Procedures, etc.

Category	Usage	Specify
Function	function *<id>* ([*<arg>*,...*]*)= *< expression>*;	A function is a constant value that is a function value. A function can accept up to 8 parameters. Calling a function is a process that uses these parameters to solve, and the calling efficiency of a function is higher than that of a process.
Process	procedure *<id>* ([*<arg>*,...]) { <statements> }	A procedure is a block of code that can pass parameters or return values. The local variables in the process do not need to be declared. When they appear as lvalues, they are declared and assigned immediately.
Equipment model	equipment *<id>* [: <virtual *equipment* >] { <declarations> ... }	In RT-ESTDL, the real-time embedded device model is a declaration of a group of members, methods and static symbols. 1. The device model can inherit the symbols of the virtual device model or override these inherited symbols. Each device model creates a separate namespace to hold the symbols declared therein. The device model name should be different from the global symbol and other class names. 2. Member objects are declared with the *var* keyword. Members do not need to display declarations, and new members can be added to an object at any time. However, member initialization is performed automatically when a new instance is created. 3. Member functions are declared with the *function* keyword. 4. Member methods are declared with the *procedure* keyword. Member methods contain an implicit pointer *this*. No matter member variables, member functions or member methods, they cannot be accessed directly like local variables, but must be accessed through *this* pointer. 5. Static symbols should be declared with the *static* keyword.

A2.5 STATEMENT

In RT-ESTDL, the expression followed by a semicolon is the basic form of simple statements. A series of statements can form a statement block by expanding with curly braces {}. The use of curly braces does not change the determination of name field.

SCHEDULE 6   Usage Description of RT-ESTDL Statement

Category	Usage	Specify
Process control	return [<return_exp>];	End the current process and return the return_ exp value
	break;	End innermost loop or switch statement
	continue;	Ends the current interaction of the innermost loop
Conditional statement	if (<condition_exp>) <statement> [else <statement2>];	Complete the condition judgment according to the value of the condition expression.
	switch (< condition_exp>) { case <constvalue1>: <statement1> case < constvalue2>: <statement2> ... [default: <statement>] }	Complete the branch selection according to the value of the conditional expression.
Circular statement	for([<init_exp>];[<condition_ exp>];[<step_exp>])<statement>; while(<condition_exp>) <statement>; do{ <statements> }; while (<condition_exp>);	Three cyclic treatment methods

A2.6 SELF-OWNED LIBRARY FUNCTION

SCHEDULE 7 Self-Owned Library Functions Provided by RT-ESTDL

Function Name	Function Prototype	Function	Return Value	Remarks
print	*void print(…);*	Output to standard display	nothing	Parameters can be any type of variable or constant.
abs	*int abs(int)*	Find the absolute value of an integer	Calculation results	
acos	*double acos(double)*	Calculate arccosine	Calculation results	
asin	*double asin(double)*	Calculate inverse sine	Calculation results	
atan	*double atan(double)*	Calculate arctangent	Calculation results	
atan2	*double atan2(double x, double y)*	Calculate the arctangent of x/y	Calculation results	In radians
cos	*double cos(double)*	Compute cosine	Calculation results	
cosh	*double cosh(double)*	Compute hyperbolic cosine	Calculation results	
exp	*double exp(double x)*	Calculate ex	Calculation results	
fabs	*double fabs(double)*	Find the absolute value of floating-point number	Calculation results	
floor	*double floor(double x)*	Find the largest integer not greater than x	Calculation results	
fmod	*double fmod(double, double)*	Find the remainder of an integer divided by X/y	Calculation results	
log	*double log(double)*	Find LNX	Calculation results	
log10	*double log10(double)*	Find log10x	Calculation results	
pow	*double pow(double, double)*	Find XY	Calculation results	

(Continued)

SCHEDULE 7 (Continued) Self-Owned Library Functions Provided by RT-ESTDL

Function Name	Function Prototype	Function	Return Value	Remarks
rand	int rand(void)	Generate -90 to 32767 random integers	Calculation results	For sampling calculation
sin	double sin(double)	sin	Calculation results	In radians
sinh	double sinh(double)	Find hyperbolic sine calculation	Calculation results	X shall be ≥0
sqrt	double sqrt(double x)		Calculation results	
tan	double tan(double)	tan	Calculation results	In radians
tanh	double tanh(double)	Find hyperbolic tangent	Calculation results	
srand	void srand(int)	Random number seed	Calculation results	
wait	void(int)	Time waiting	nothing	Used for waiting time during testing
GetCurTestTime	long GetCurTestTime()	Get the current system global clock	Current system global clock	Since the test starts timing, you can get the global clock by calling this function
InitEqpmt	BOOL InitEqpmt(CIODATAVAR ioData, CIOLINK ioLink)	Device initialization	Is it true	Used for initialization of equipment simulation model
StartEqpmt()	BOOL StartEqpmt (this-> Eqpmt_ID)	Device startup	Is it true	Used for startup and operation of equipment simulation model
SuspendEqpmt()	BOOL SuspendEqpmt (this-> Eqpmt_ID)	Device pending	Is it true	Make the device simulation model pending
RestartEqpmt()	BOOL RestartEqpmt (this-> Eqpmt_ID)	Device restart	Is it true	Restart operation for equipment simulation model
StopEqpmt()	BOOL StopEqpmt (this-> Eqpmt_ID)	Equipment stop	Is it true	Shutdown for equipment simulation model

(Continued)

SCHEDULE 7 (Continued) Self-Owned Library Functions Provided by RT-ESTDL

Function Name	Function Prototype	Function	Return Value	Remarks
AddVar()	*void AddVar (CIODATAVAR ioDataVar)*	Add interface I/O variables to the device	nothing	
DeleteVar()	*void DeleteVar (CIODATAVAR ioDataVar)*	Add interface I/O variables to the device	nothing	
SendDataValue()	*void SendDataValue (srcEqpmt. Eqpmt_ID, srcEqpmt.srcVar, dstcEqpmtID. Eqpmt_ID, dstcEqpmtID.dstVar CIOLINK iolink)*	Change the target device model variables by sending interface variables	nothing	See data communication for equipment model
SendDataValue()	*void SendDataValue (var value, dstcEqpmtID. Eqpmt_ID, dstcEqpmtID.dstVar CIOLINK iolink)*	Change the target device model variables by sending data values	nothing	
GetDataValue ()	*void GetDataValue (rcvEqpmtID, rcvVar, CIOLink ioLinkr)*	Get target device model variable data	nothing	See data communication for equipment model

Appendix 3

Software Interface Data Definition of I/GNS System

SCHEDULE 8   I/GNS System Receiving Data List

Serial Number	Data and Content		Size[a]	Refresh Cycle (ms)	Transmission Type
1	A/ADIN/01-00	Atmospheric data	8	100	PRD
2	B/DCIN/00-00	System control	3	–	UPE
3	A/DCIN/01-01	Latitude modification	4	200	PRD
4	A/DCIN/01–02	Longitude modification	4	–	UPE
5	B/DCIN/01–03	Height modification	6	–	UPE
6	B/DCIN/01–04	Course modification	6	50	PRD
7	A/DCIN/03-00	Runway binding	4	–	UPE
8	A/DCIN/20–01	MFL request	2	–	UPE
9	B/DCIN/20–02	Mbit command	2	100	PRD
10	A/DCIN/20–04	Memory check	2	–	UPE
11	B/DCIN/20–05	Other parameter requests	3	50	PRD
12	B/DCIN/20–08	Drift data request	2	–	UPE
13	A/DTIN/01-00	Airport data	28	50	COND
14	A/DTIN/02-00	System data modification	4	–	PRD
15	B/MCIN/00-00	PUU data	8	–	UPE
16	B/MCIN/02-00	Aircraft sideslip angle	2	50	PRD

[a] *Note:*   The data size unit is WORD (16-bit binary number).

SCHEDULE 9   I/GNS System Sending Data List

Serial Number	Data and Content		Size[a]	Refresh Cycle (ms)	Transmission Type
1	A/INLP/01-00	IN data	8	50	PRD
2	B/INPD/00-00	IN data	8	100	PRD
3	B/INPD/01-00	IN data	26	50	PRD
4	B/INSM/01-00	IN data	8	100	PRD
5	A/INSM/02-00	Base alignment data	20	100	PRD
6	A/INSM/03-00	Navigation data	16	100	UPE
7	B/INCN/00-00	Magnetic heading	3	50	PRD
8	A/INDC/00-00	System state	6	–	UPE
9	A/INDC/01-00	Alignment display data	16	200	COND
10	B/INDC/02-00	Backup navigation data	10	50	PRD
11	B/INDC/03-00	Display data	30	50	UPE
12	B/INDC/04-00	Attitude data	12	50	PRD
13	A/INDC/19-00	PFL list	31	–	UPE
14	A/INDC/20-01	MFL status	32	–	UPE
15	B/INDC/20-02	Mbit status	32	50	PRD
16	B/INDC/20-03	MFL list	31	–	UPE
17	A/INDC/20-04	Store data	32	50	PRD
18	B/INDC/20-05	Other parameters	30	–	UPE
19	B/INDC/20-08	Drift data	30	–	UPE
20	A/INDC/27-00	Flight test data	30	100	PRD
21	A/INDT/01-00	Alignment data	18	–	UPE
22	A/INDT/03-00	Maximum acceleration	6	50	PRD
23	B/INDT/19-00	Fault data	32	–	UPE
24	B/INFC/01-00	Backup data	4	100	PRD
100	B/INMC/00-00	Backup data	2	100	PRD
26	B/INMC/01-00	Backup data	30	50	PRD
27	A/INMC/02-00	Backup data	10	200	PRD

[a] *Note:*   the data size unit is WORD (16-bit binary number).

Appendix 4

Software Testing Scenario Tree List of I/GNS

SCHEDULE 10   Software Testing Scenario Tree List of I/GNSS

$s_0 \to s_1 \to s_{18} \to s_{19}$

$s_0 \to s_1 \to s_2 \to s_3 \to s_{15} \to s_{19}$

$s_0 \to s_1 \to s_2 \to s_3 \to s_{16} \to s_{19}$

$s_0 \to s_1 \to s_2 \to s_3 \to s_{17} \to s_{19}$

$s_0 \to s_1 \to s_2 \to s_3 \to s_4 \to s_5 \to s_7 \to s_9 \to s_{19}$

$s_0 \to s_1 \to s_2 \to s_3 \to s_4 \to s_5 \to s_7 \to s_9 \to s_{10} \to s_{19}$

$s_0 \to s_1 \to s_2 \to s_3 \to s_4 \to s_5 \to s_7 \to s_9 \to s_{10} \to s_9 \to s_{19}$

$s_0 \to s_1 \to s_2 \to s_3 \to s_4 \to s_5 \to s_7 \to s_9 \to s_{11} \to s_{19}$

$s_0 \to s_1 \to s_2 \to s_3 \to s_4 \to s_5 \to s_7 \to s_9 \to s_{11} \to s_{19}$

$s_0 \to s_1 \to s_2 \to s_3 \to s_4 \to s_5 \to s_7 \to s_9 \to s_{10} \to s_9 \to s_{11} \to s_{19}$

$s_0 \to s_1 \to s_2 \to s_3 \to s_4 \to s_5 \to s_7 \to s_9 \to s_{11} \to s_9 \to s_{19}$

$s_0 \to s_1 \to s_2 \to s_3 \to s_4 \to s_5 \to s_7 \to s_9 \to s_{11} \to s_9 \to s_{10} \to s_{19}$

$s_0 \to s_1 \to s_2 \to s_3 \to s_4 \to s_5 \to s_7 \to s_{12} \to s_{19}$

$s_0 \to s_1 \to s_2 \to s_3 \to s_4 \to s_5 \to s_7 \to s_{13} \to s_{19}$

$s_0 \to s_1 \to s_2 \to s_3 \to s_4 \to s_5 \to s_7 \to s_{14} \to s_{19}$

$s_0 \to s_1 \to s_2 \to s_3 \to s_4 \to s_6 \to s_7 \to s_9 \to s_{19}$

$s_0 \to s_1 \to s_2 \to s_3 \to s_4 \to s_6 \to s_7 \to s_9 \to s_{10} \to s_{19}$

$s_0 \to s_1 \to s_2 \to s_3 \to s_4 \to s_6 \to s_7 \to s_9 \to s_{10} \to s_9 \to s_{19}$

$s_0 \to s_1 \to s_2 \to s_3 \to s_4 \to s_6 \to s_7 \to s_9 \to s_{11} \to s_{19}$

$s_0 \to s_1 \to s_2 \to s_3 \to s_4 \to s_6 \to s_7 \to s_9 \to s_{11} \to s_{19}$

$s_0 \to s_1 \to s_2 \to s_3 \to s_4 \to s_6 \to s_7 \to s_9 \to s_{10} \to s_9 \to s_{11} \to s_{19}$

$s_0 \to s_1 \to s_2 \to s_3 \to s_4 \to s_6 \to s_7 \to s_9 \to s_{11} \to s_9 \to s_{19}$

$s_0 \to s_1 \to s_2 \to s_3 \to s_4 \to s_6 \to s_7 \to s_9 \to s_{11} \to s_9 \to s_{10} \to s_{19}$

$s_0 \to s_1 \to s_2 \to s_3 \to s_4 \to s_6 \to s_7 \to s_{12} \to s_{19}$

$s_0 \to s_1 \to s_2 \to s_3 \to s_4 \to s_6 \to s_7 \to s_{13} \to s_{19}$

(Continued)

SCHEDULE 10 (*Continued*) Software Testing Scenario Tree
List of I/GNSS

$s_0 \rightarrow s_1 \rightarrow s_2 \rightarrow s_3 \rightarrow s_4 \rightarrow s_6 \rightarrow s_7 \rightarrow s_{14} \rightarrow s_{19}$

$s_0 \rightarrow s_1 \rightarrow s_2 \rightarrow s_3 \rightarrow s_4 \rightarrow s_5 \rightarrow s_8 \rightarrow s_9 \rightarrow s_{19}$

$s_0 \rightarrow s_1 \rightarrow s_2 \rightarrow s_3 \rightarrow s_4 \rightarrow s_5 \rightarrow s_8 \rightarrow s_9 \rightarrow s_{10} \rightarrow s_{19}$

$s_0 \rightarrow s_1 \rightarrow s_2 \rightarrow s_3 \rightarrow s_4 \rightarrow s_5 \rightarrow s_8 \rightarrow s_9 \rightarrow s_{10} \rightarrow s_9 \rightarrow s_{19}$

$s_0 \rightarrow s_1 \rightarrow s_2 \rightarrow s_3 \rightarrow s_4 \rightarrow s_5 \rightarrow s_8 \rightarrow s_9 \rightarrow s_{11} \rightarrow s_{19}$

$s_0 \rightarrow s_1 \rightarrow s_2 \rightarrow s_3 \rightarrow s_4 \rightarrow s_5 \rightarrow s_8 \rightarrow s_9 \rightarrow s_{11} \rightarrow s_{19}$

$s_0 \rightarrow s_1 \rightarrow s_2 \rightarrow s_3 \rightarrow s_4 \rightarrow s_5 \rightarrow s_8 \rightarrow s_9 \rightarrow s_{10} \rightarrow s_9 \rightarrow s_{11} \rightarrow s_{19}$

$s_0 \rightarrow s_1 \rightarrow s_2 \rightarrow s_3 \rightarrow s_4 \rightarrow s_5 \rightarrow s_8 \rightarrow s_9 \rightarrow s_{11} \rightarrow s_9 \rightarrow s_{19}$

$s_0 \rightarrow s_1 \rightarrow s_2 \rightarrow s_3 \rightarrow s_4 \rightarrow s_5 \rightarrow s_8 \rightarrow s_9 \rightarrow s_{11} \rightarrow s_9 \rightarrow s_{10} \rightarrow s_{19}$

$s_0 \rightarrow s_1 \rightarrow s_2 \rightarrow s_3 \rightarrow s_4 \rightarrow s_5 \rightarrow s_8 \rightarrow s_{12} \rightarrow s_{19}$

$s_0 \rightarrow s_1 \rightarrow s_2 \rightarrow s_3 \rightarrow s_4 \rightarrow s_5 \rightarrow s_8 \rightarrow s_{13} \rightarrow s_{19}$

$s_0 \rightarrow s_1 \rightarrow s_2 \rightarrow s_3 \rightarrow s_4 \rightarrow s_5 \rightarrow s_8 \rightarrow s_{14} \rightarrow s_{19}$

$s_0 \rightarrow s_1 \rightarrow s_2 \rightarrow s_3 \rightarrow s_4 \rightarrow s_6 \rightarrow s_8 \rightarrow s_9 \rightarrow s_{19}$

$s_0 \rightarrow s_1 \rightarrow s_2 \rightarrow s_3 \rightarrow s_4 \rightarrow s_6 \rightarrow s_8 \rightarrow s_9 \rightarrow s_{10} \rightarrow s_{19}$

$s_0 \rightarrow s_1 \rightarrow s_2 \rightarrow s_3 \rightarrow s_4 \rightarrow s_6 \rightarrow s_8 \rightarrow s_9 \rightarrow s_{10} \rightarrow s_9 \rightarrow s_{19}$

$s_0 \rightarrow s_1 \rightarrow s_2 \rightarrow s_3 \rightarrow s_4 \rightarrow s_6 \rightarrow s_8 \rightarrow s_9 \rightarrow s_{11} \rightarrow s_{19}$

$s_0 \rightarrow s_1 \rightarrow s_2 \rightarrow s_3 \rightarrow s_4 \rightarrow s_6 \rightarrow s_8 \rightarrow s_9 \rightarrow s_{11} \rightarrow s_{19}$

$s_0 \rightarrow s_1 \rightarrow s_2 \rightarrow s_3 \rightarrow s_4 \rightarrow s_6 \rightarrow s_8 \rightarrow s_9 \rightarrow s_{10} \rightarrow s_9 \rightarrow s_{11} \rightarrow s_{19}$

$s_0 \rightarrow s_1 \rightarrow s_2 \rightarrow s_3 \rightarrow s_4 \rightarrow s_6 \rightarrow s_8 \rightarrow s_9 \rightarrow s_{11} \rightarrow s_9 \rightarrow s_{19}$

$s_0 \rightarrow s_1 \rightarrow s_2 \rightarrow s_3 \rightarrow s_4 \rightarrow s_6 \rightarrow s_8 \rightarrow s_9 \rightarrow s_{11} \rightarrow s_9 \rightarrow s_{10} \rightarrow s_{19}$

$s_0 \rightarrow s_1 \rightarrow s_2 \rightarrow s_3 \rightarrow s_4 \rightarrow s_6 \rightarrow s_8 \rightarrow s_{12} \rightarrow s_{19}$

$s_0 \rightarrow s_1 \rightarrow s_2 \rightarrow s_3 \rightarrow s_4 \rightarrow s_6 \rightarrow s_8 \rightarrow s_{13} \rightarrow s_{19}$

$s_0 \rightarrow s_1 \rightarrow s_2 \rightarrow s_3 \rightarrow s_4 \rightarrow s_6 \rightarrow s_8 \rightarrow s_{14} \rightarrow s_{19}$

Bibliography

ADS2: Avionics Development System 2nd Generation.www.techsat.com.

Amalfitano D., Fasolino A. R., Tramontana P., Ta B.D., Memon A.M., MobiGUITAR - A tool for automated model-based testing of mobile apps. *IEEE Software,* 2014, 32(5):53–59.

Amnell T., David A., Fersman E., Moller M.O., Pettersson P., Yi W. Tools for Real-Time UML: Formal Verification and Code Synthesis. In Proceedings of the SIVOES Workshop, part of the ECOOP 2001, Budapest, Hungary, June 18-22, 2001. Springer.

Anand S., Naik M., Harrold M.J., Yang H. Automated concolic testing of smartphone apps, In *Proceedings of the ACM SIGSOFT 20th International Symposium on the Foundations of Software Engineering (FSE2012)*, New York: ACM, 2012, pp. 59:1-59:11.

Android Instrumentation. https://developer.android.google.cn/reference/android/app/Instrumentation.html.

Android operating system. https://www.android.com.

Android uiautomator. https://developer.android.com/tools/help/uiautomator/index.html.

Apostolidis D., Tepelmann D., Rennoch A., Vouffo A., Use of TTCN-3 for the development of SIGTRAN test, In *18th International Conference Software & System Engineering and Their Application-ICSSEA*, Paris, 2005.

Arzt S., Rasthofer S., Fritz C., et al. FlowDroid: Precise context, flow, field, object-sensitive and lifecycle-aware taint analysis for Android apps. *ACM Sigplan Notices*, 2014, 49(6):259–269.

AsyncTask. https://developer.android.com/reference/android/os/AsyncTask.html.

Azim T., Neamtiu I. Targeted and depth-first exploration for systematic testing of android apps, In *Proceedings of the 2013 ACM SIGPLAN International Conference on Object Oriented Programming Systems Languages & Applications (OOPSLA2013)*, New York: ACM, 2013, pp. 641–660.

Bourhfir C., Aboulhamid E., Dssouli R., Rico N. A test case generation approach for conformance testing of SDL systems. *Computer Communications*, 2001, 24:319–333.

Cavarra A., Crichton C., Davies J. A method for the automatic generation of test suites from object models. *Information and Software Technology*, 2004, 46:309–314.

Chen W., Xue Y., Zhao C., Li M. A real-time system test method based on time automata. *Journal of Software*, 2007, 18(1):62–73.

Chen W.H., Lu C. Executable test sequence for the protocol control and data flow property with overlapping, In *Proceedings of the Seventh International Symposium on Computers and Communications*, Taormina-Giardini Naxos, Italy, 2002, pp. 251–257.

Choi W., Necula G., Sen K. Guided GUI testing of android apps with minimal restart and approximate learning, In *Proceedings of the 2013 ACM SIGPLAN International Conference on Object Oriented Programming Systems Languages & Applications (OOPSLA2013)*, New York: ACM, 2013, pp. 623–640.

Chu W., Zhang F., Fan X. A review of software architecture of integrated modular avionics system. *Journal of Aeronautics*, 2009, 30(10):1912–1917.

Clover. https://www.unlimax.com/clover.html.

Cui Y. Research on Test Generation Based on UML State Diagram[D]. Central China Normal University, 2009.

Diaz E., Tuya J., Blanco R. Automated software testing using a metaheuristic technique based on tabu search, In *Proceedings of the 18th IEEE International Conference on Automated Software Engineering (ASE'03)*, Montreal, QC, 2003.

Duale A.Y., Uyar M.U. A method enabling feasible conformance test sequence generation for EFSM models. *IEEE, Transactions on Computers*, 2004, 53(5):614–627.

Ella. https://github.com/saswatanand/ella.

Emma. https://emma.sourceforge.net/.

ETSI ES 201 87301 V2.2.1(2003-02) Methods for Testing and Specification (MTS) [R]; The Testing and Test Control Notation Version 3; Part1: TTCN-3 Core Language.

Flake S. Real-time constrains with the OCL, In *5th IEEE International Symposium on Object-Oriented Real-Time Distributed Computing*, Washington, DC, 2002.

Gu B., Dong Y.-W., Wang Z. Formal modeling approach for aerospace embedded software. *Journal of Software (in Chinese)*, 2015, 26(2):321–331.

Hao S., Liu B., Nath S., et al., PUMA: Programmable UI-automation for large-scale dynamic analysis of mobile apps, In *Proceedings of the 12th Annual International Conference on Mobile Systems, Applications, and Services (MobiSys2014)*, New York: ACM, 2014, pp. 204–217.

Hessel A., Larsen K.G., Nielsen B. Time-optimal test cases for real-time systems, In *Proceedings of the 1st International Workshop on Formal Modeling and Analysis of Timed Systems (FORMATS'03)*, 2003.

Hirayama M., Yamamoto T., Okayasu J., Mizuno O., Kikuno T. A selective software testing method based on priorities assigned to functional modules, In *Proceedings of Second Asia-Pacific Conference on Quality Software*, Hong Kong, China, 2001, pp. 259–267.

Hou G., Zhou K., et al. Formal modeling and verification method of software based on time STM. *Journal of Software*, 2015, 26(2):223–238.

Hu Z., Shatz S.M. Explicit modeling of semantics associated with composite states in UML state charts. *Journal of Automated Software Engineering*, 2006, 13(4):423–467.

Huai J., Li Q., Hu C. Research and design of virtual computing environment based on virtual machine. *Journal of Software*, 2007, 18(8):2016–2026.

Jacoco. https://www.eclemma.org/jacoco/.

Jie P., Watanabe M., Kuanjiu Z., Haoran L., Kai C. Formal modeling methods for embedded software. *Computer Engineering and Applications*, 2018, 54(8):61–71.

Jurjens J. Model-based security testing using UMLsec a case study. *Electronic Notes in Theoretical Computer Science*, 2008, 220:93–104.

Kaynar D.K., Lynch N., Segala R. et al. Timed I/O automata: A mathematical framework for modeling and analyzing real-time systems, In *Proceedings of the 24th IEEE Int'l Real-Time Systems Symposium*, Cancun, Mexico. IEEE Computer Society, 2003. pp. 166–177.

Konrad S., Cheng B.H.C. Real-time specification patterns. Technical Report MSU - CSE-04-37, Computer Science and Engineering. Michigan State University, East Lansing, Michigan, September 2004, pp. 372–381.

Lai M., You J. Formalization of UML state diagrams with time extension using time automation. *Computer*, 2003, 8(23):4–6.

Lee D., Chen D., Hao R., Miller R.E., Wu J., Yin X. A formal approach for passive testing of protocol data portions, In *10th IEEE International Conference on Network Protocols (ICNP 2002)*, Paris, France, IEEE Computer Society, 2002, pp. 122–131.

Lin C. *Stochastic Petri and System Performance Evaluation*. Beijing: Tsinghua University Press, 2000.

Liu B., Nath S., Govindan R., Liu J. DECAF: Detecting and characterizing ad fraud in mobile apps, In *Proceedings of the National Spatial Data Infrastructure (NSDI2014)*, Seattle, WA, 2014, pp. 57–70.

Liu X., Liang B., Liu L., et al. *Theory, Method and Technique of Complex System Modeling*. Beijing: Science Press, 2008.

Machiry A., Tahiliani R., Naik M. Dynodroid: An input generation system for android apps, In *Proceedings of the 2013 9th Joint Meeting on Foundations of Software Engineering (ESEC/FSE 2013)*, New York: ACM, 2013, pp. 224–234.

Memon A., Banerjee I., Nagarajan A., GUI ripping: Reverse engineering of graphical user interfaces for testing, In *Proceedings of the 10th Working Conference on Reverse Engineering (WCRE2003)*, Washington, DC: IEEE Computer Society, 2003.

MessageMagic. https://www.messagemagic.elvior.ee/index.html.

Mu K., Gu M. Research on automatic generation method of test cases based on UML activity diagram. *Computer Application*, 2006, 26(4):844–847.

NASA Software Safety Guidebook[R], NASA-GB-8719.13, NASA, 2004.

Nilsson R., Offutt J., Mellin J. Test case generation for mutation-based testing of timeliness. *Electronic Notes in Theoretical Computer Science*, 2006, 164:97–114.

Ning H., Hong Y. Formal verification methods for embedded operating systems. *Aeronautical Computing Technology*, 2015, 45(2):96–100.

Paradkar A., Klinger T. Automated consistency and completeness checking of testing models for interactive systems, In *Computer Software and Applications Conference (COMPSAC)*, Hong Kong, China, 2004, pp. 342–348.

Rethy G. Application of TTCN-3 for 2.5 and 3G Testing, The TTCN-3 User Conference 2004, Sophia, Antipolis, France, 2004, pp. 1–24.

Rothermel G., Harrold M. J. Empirical studies of a safe regression test selection technique[J]. *IEEE Transactions on Software Engineering*, 1998, 24(6):401–419.

RT-LAB/ATB:RT-LAB Distributed Real-Time Power.www.opal-rt.com.

Sadjadi S.M., Kalayci S. A self-configuring communication virtual machine, In *IEEE International Conference on Networking, Sensing and Control*, Sanya, China, 2008, pp. 739–744.

Shan J., Jiang Y., Sun P. Research progress on software testing. *Journal of Peking University (Natural Science Edition)*, 2005, 41(1):134–145.

Shan J., Zhang L., Zhang T. Extension of real-time embedded software time abstract state machine. *Journal of Peking University (Natural Science Edition)*, 2019,55(2):197–208.

Shu G., Formal methods and tools for testing communication protocol system security[D], PhD thesis, The Ohio University, 2008.

Sinha A., Paradkar A., Williams C. On generating EFSM models from use cases, In *International Conference on Software Engineering archive (ICSE 2007)*, Minneapolis, MN, 2007.

Tang B., Liao W. Test case generation method for unified modeling language state diagram. *Computer Emulation*, 2007, 24(8): 90–92.

TestQuest, Inc. TestQuest Pro(tm). https://www.testquest.com.

The Monkey UI android testing tool. https://developer.android.com/tools/help/monkey.html.

Tip F. Infeasible paths in object-oriented programs. *Science of Computer Programming*, 2015, 97:91–97.

Ural H. Test generation based on control and data dependencies within system specification in SDL. *Computer Communications*, 2000, 23(7):609–627.

Verified's RT-Tester. https://www.verified.de/rtt.html.

Wang X., Xuan L., Zhang W. Modeling and implementation of UMLbased embedded real-time control system. *Computer Technology and Development*, 2006, 17(7):239–241.

Watkins J., Translated by He Hongwei et al., *Practical Software Testing Process*. Beijing: China Machine Press.

Xiao J., Zhang D., Chen H., Dong H. Combining model detection and theorem proof to develop and validate highly trusted embedded software. *Journal of Jilin University (Engineering Edition)*, 2005, 35(5):531–536.

Xiao P., Yin Y., Jiang B., Malaiya Y.K. Adaptive testing based on moment estimation. *IEEE Transactions on Systems, Man, and Cybernetics: Systems*, 2020, 50(3):911–922

Yang X. Research on Automatic Generation of Test Cases Based on Z Language and State Diagram. Master's Thesis of Central China Normal University, 2006.

Yin Y., Bin L., Deming Z., Tongmin J. On modeling approach for embedded real-time software simulation testing. *Journal of Systems Engineering and Electronics*, 2009, 20(2):420–426.

Yin Y., Liu B., Li G., Wang Z. Embedded software simulation testing virtual machine: Design and application. *Applied Mechanics and Materials*, 2010, 26-28:405–410.

Yin Y., Liu B., Lu M., Li Z. Test cases generation for embedded real-time software based on extended UML, In *International Conference on Information Technology and Computer Science*, Kiev, Ukraine, 2009, vol. 1, pp. 69–74.

Yin Y., Liu B., Ni H. Real-time embedded software testing method based on extend finite state machine. *Journal of Systems Engineering and Electronics*, 2012, 23(2):276–285.

Yin Y., Su Q., Liu L. Software smell detection based on machine learning and its empirical study, In *The Second Target Recognition and Artificial Intelligence Summit Forum (TRAI 2019)*, Changchun, China, Aug. 28-30 2019.

Yuan Y. *Reliability Technology in Real-Time Systems*. Nanning: Guangxi Science and Technology Press, 1995.

Zeng J. An improved sparse representation face recognition algorithm for variations of illumination and pose. *Journal of Information & Computational Science*, 2015, 12(16):5987–5994.

Zhan X., Miao H. An approach to formalizing the semantics of UML statecharts, in *Conceptual Modeling - ER2004*, Springer, LNCS 3288, 2004. doi: 10.1007/978-3-540-30464-7_56.

Zhao W., Bai X., Wang W., et al. A novel alarm processing and fault diagnosis expert system based on BNF rules, In *Transmission and Distribution Conference and Exhibition*, Asia and Pacific, 2005.

Zheng M., Alagar V., Ormandjieva O. Automated generation of test suites from formal specifications of real-time reactive systems. *The Journal of Systems and Software*, 2008, 81:286–304.

Zhou X., Qu Y., Zhao B. Shortening the length of test sequences of EFSM using reverse determinism. *Journal of Communications*, 2000, 21(11):48–55.

For Product Safety Concerns and Information please contact our EU
representative GPSR@taylorandfrancis.com
Taylor & Francis Verlag GmbH, Kaufingerstraße 24, 80331 München, Germany

www.ingramcontent.com/pod-product-compliance
Ingram Content Group UK Ltd.
Pitfield, Milton Keynes, MK11 3LW, UK
UKHW021116180425
457613UK00005B/114